$40 A DAY

RACHAEL RAY
BEST EATS IN TOWN ON
$40 A DAY

by rachael ray

lake isle press   new york, ny

Published by:
Lake Isle Press, Inc.
16 West 32nd Street, Suite 10-B
New York, NY 10001
(212) 273-0796
E-mail: lakeisle@earthlink.net

Distributed to the trade by:
National Book Network (NBN), Inc.
4501 Forbes Boulevard, Suite 200
Lanham, MD 20706
1(800) 462-6420
www.nbnbooks.com

Library of Congress Control Number: 2004110160

ISBN: 1-891105-17-5

Food photography and recipes: Courtesy of the Food Network

Book and cover design: Ellen Swandiak

This book is available at special sales discounts for bulk purchases as premiums or special editions, including personalized covers. For more information, contact the publisher at (212) 273-0796 or by e-mail, lakeisle@earthlink.net

10 9 8 7 6 5 4 3 2 1

A WORD OF THANKS to all establishments who responded to our call for information and materials. Thanks, too, to the Food Network for their help and cooperation in making this project possible.

Dedication

To fans of $40 a Day everywhere.

See you on the road!

special thanks

● To my mom, Elsa, thank you for encouraging me to be an adventurer. Thank you for showing us by example that a rich life is not only for the wealthy. Thank you for the personal sacrifices you've made to include us (we three kids) in your travels, rather than hiring a sitter. Thank you for all the wonderful memories of exploring parts of this world that we've found together, even on days when we had much less than $40 to spare or to spend. Thank you, in your own words, for always being "in constant pursuit of beauty." Thank you for getting me a passport when I was three and for making sure I used it!

● To my dad, Jim, thank you for having a great nose for food and wine and a wonderful ear for music. You teach me still.... Kids may seem as if they're not paying attention, but they hear 'ya ! From caviar to Chet Baker, opera to grappa, gumbo to zydeco, your tastes are a part of me and my heart. I am better at my job and better at living life because of your appreciation of its finer points.

● To the Food Network and Scripps Howard networks, like so many of our viewers, I too thank you for improving my life and the lives of my family. Thank you for having such confidence in me; I am proud to be on your team. Special thanks to Judy Girard for always green-lighting my ideas and for letting me remain me. Thanks to Kathleen for letting go of the "The Rich Man," in favor of the poor girl! To Allison, thanks for sharing food, drink, and so many ideas, at any price! To Brooke, new lady on the block, thanks for supporting this book, for your vision, and for plain, straight talk. You walk-the-walk!

● Thanks to Hiroko, my publisher, and Ellen, Pimpila, and The A Team in publishing for taking a pile of scrapbook entries and making them into a real book. Thanks for helping me, yet again, deliver a product that we can all feel proud of, while keeping prices low for our readers. Thank you for all the hours, for your creativity, and for the respect you have shown me over the years. My respect for each of you is in part what drives me after seven books and even more years of working together.

● I work with the greatest road crew in cable. Many thanks to creators and owners of Pie Town Productions, the company that shoots and delivers every episode of $40 a Day. To Tara and Jennifer, you two have great taste in coworkers! Working with your top-notch staff and crew is more than rewarding, it's fun!

● Wade, with you, I've danced on a bar in Miami, gotten up on long board in Hawaii, and finally learned to drive a stick shift in Italy! Thank you for inspiring and encouraging me to conquer so many of the firsts in my life. You are special. I've learned a lot from you about making great TV and overcoming our fears. (You know, you'll always

be Mom's favorite, too.) A big shout-out to Soul-sista Karen as well. Thanks for letting us take Wade out to play for prolonged periods of time and for your terrific company when you joined in the fun and cocktails!

● Thank you, Lesley, for putting so much heart (and giggle) into the show. Your instincts for shopping really raised the bar! I have purchased many of my favorite things and taped many of my favorite moments with you. You are like fine wine, you get more wonderful as time goes on. Kevin, you are a very lucky man!

● Mark Daniels, you are one of the greatest cameramen on the planet! Mark, you make the lens romance barbecued beef, green eggs and ham, spirulina health shakes, and a host who does her own hair and make up! Thanks for making life brighter, richer, and even more colorful than it really is. To Mrs. Mark, Nancy Daniels, I want to say that you two add up to one great couple! Thanks for turning Mark loose and back out on the road so soon after Sam-the-Man's arrival. From the road we've all watched videos of your life together and we are reminded that, in the end, no matter how terrific the travels, there's no place like home!

● A big shout-out to Nate Beta-Man Hamlin, you wild and crazy guy! Thanks for all your great cameos! Nate, I miss all ten of your faces! You are a talented cameraman, but, more importantly, you are one heck of an IMI: International Man of Intrigue. I hope I spot you in your latest disguise as a big, important Hollywood TV producer someday soon. I miss you!

● Susan and Toulani, you two are better than all three of The Supremes! You are both beautiful, smart, hard-working, and funny. You rock—behind the scenes or on the road. Thanks for the hundreds of tough phone calls you've had to make and for trying to plan ahead for six other people. Susan, that spanking incident in New Orleans, you know what I mean. I always think of that when I think of you! Also, congrats to you on becoming a "Little Mrs." Yup, Jake makes total sense! Toulani, GIRL! How can you chow down so much BBQ and still look as you do? You are incredible! An icon!

● To Ilana Urbach, my thanks for sharing your very unique mind and style: your humor, your writing skills, your tee-shirt art, your attention to detail, and taste in music are all inspiring. Lastly, I'm glad you're female, thus evening up the teams in the field!

● Hey, hey to Mr. Sanli Atelier! I hope your back is better and I'm so sorry if the sound gear contributed to your aches and pains. I thank you for your smile, for sharing your HUGE heart, for making Mark's candid shots look like New Yorker cartoons, and for all the laughs you gave to our crew on long, hard shoots in many far off places.

● Gary, sorry about your knees! Thanks for enduring great pains on the road, from sore joints to a cold and grumpy host. You raise our cool factor wherever we go. Thanks for sharing interesting asides with me and for being a true professional on set.

● Merci, Fred! Fries are debatably Belgian, but you are certainly one French creation who makes work more appetizing and seem more like play.

● To Forrest, you had some great shots out there and a nice mic technique, too (very warm hands). Plus, without you, "it's grrr-eat!" in a cheap Irish brogue would not be a Rachael-ism today!

● Courtney, how's it goin, eh? You are a Canadian Princess and I thank you for all the many hours of work behind the scenes and on the road. I'm only sorry that we never enjoyed karaoke night together. I'm sure you can belt it out!

● To Jeff, Mr. New Guy: Thanks for walking down the mountain with me! You are a pleasure to work with. You are very considerate to your crew and I'm proud to be working with you.

● Don, another new guy. You are the strong, silent type. Thanks for your work in the field and for leaving even more room in the car for my luggage. You are the tallest man we've ever had on crew, yet you pack the smallest bag—ever! Cool.

● To the writers, thanks for understanding my limited acting skills and for letting me be me. Thanks for watching me mangle your thoughtful lines into goofy asides, as I place my foot firmly in my mouth. Oh, and thank you for creating the one and only Rachael Ray "Wall of Shame."

television show.

● To those in the editing bay, no thanks at all! You guys could have made me look cool. You could have cut kindly. Instead, you all chose to share my most embarrassing moments with a few million Americans. Thanks? I think not. I'm looking for you all! Let's dance! Bring it on!

● Thank you to my loving dog, Boo, who is always waiting for me to come home. This world is too cold to our warm, furry, loved ones. Boo, I should be able to buy you a seat next to mine, anywhere. I wish I could bring you with me everywhere. Big, wet dog kisses for still loving me even when I'm not around.

● Thanks and love to John for his support, encouragement, and understanding. John, no matter the budget, my travels are richer when you can join me and you make coming home even sweeter when you cannot.

● None of the above, including yours truly, would have any thanks to give or a job to do without the loyal viewers who keep tuning in and talking back! So, the biggest thank you goes to Food Network viewers, everywhere. We listen to you. We read your mail and e-mail. Keep it coming! We value being able to talk to you in the field, as well. We hope you see in our shows your own ideas and suggestions looking back at you! You're all terrific associate producers and you've provided me many of my most valuable memories. You all make my life richer, even on just $40 a Day!

Rachael

$40 A DAY

Catfish and Okra

Recipe Page 81

Pumpkin Tortellini

Recipe Page 53

Bratwurst & Knockwurst

Recipe Page 122

west

Venison Enchilada

Recipe Page 132

hawaii

Macadamia Bread Pudding

Recipe Page 210

europe

Tiramisu

Recipe Page 241

travel + tips

Tried and true ways to save money while getting the most out of your trip.

Ask the locals.

Whether you travel with a master plan or you're more spontaneous in nature, remember that local residents—just people in the neighborhoods—are wonderful sources of information. The hotel concierge may be tri-lingual, good looking, and a sharp dresser, but often he or she will steer you to very fine restaurants, where you will be surrounded by other very fine tourists. Whether you can afford four- or five-star dining, for an even richer travel experience, mix it up with the locals! Choose places with a comfortable ambiance; the better your mood, the better your food will taste. Neighborhood restaurants offer regional foods at affordable prices, but they can also provide something more—the unexpected—new "interesting" foods, new friends, new travel tips. Think back on your most colorful travel stories. They're often set in less-than-perfect surroundings with people you wouldn't necessarily seek out at home. Go have fun exploring!

Many beautiful places are free.

Many of the world's finest properties are open to you, whether you spend money there or not. Two of my favorite views to behold on planet earth, the dancing fountains in front of The Bellagio on the Vegas strip as they spray up a kick line to

Hey, Big Spender, and the amber-red glow of fall foliage in the Adirondacks (my home!), viewed from the back lawn of the five-star Sagamore resort on Lake George, NY, can be experienced for free. Go have a look around wherever you find yourselves.

Get off the beaten path and stay there!

Some of my best meals and certainly my biggest belly laughs have been found when and where I've been lost! The best meal I've had in the UK was a pepper steak at a neighborhood pub in Scotland, which I found after falling asleep on a bus and missing my stop! And I've come upon small trattorias in Italy, quite by accident, that I now return to on each trip. The best Vietnamese food I've had in the States was at a restaurant called Jennifer's in the Hawaiian islands. Located in a small, totally residential neighborhood, it has no sign, and the only marker you're to look for is a satellite dish! So, the next time you get lost, look around. Sometimes the best food and experiences are found in unexpected places.

Picnics.

Take-away is a tasty idea for meals when you are traveling. Cities with famous ethnic districts, such as San Francisco's Chinatown or Boston's North End offer great take-out possibilities, and signature foods, a po'boy or muffaletta sandwich in New Orleans, for example, are perfect to-go, as well. They become even more delicious when you enjoy them with a great view! From Aspen mountain tops to the Trevi Fountain, the restaurants with the best views are the ones you create by finding a seat and eating something delicious out of a sack. The price is right, too.

Take a tour of breweries and wineries.

From Oregon to Italy, I have sipped myself silly, for free! Many specialty brew houses and great wineries offer free tours to tourists. Some charge small fees for entrance, but all offer a tasting of their products. Cheers!

Keep a record.

Once you make a great find, record it! Pick up a small address book and use it just for travel. Make entries of all the restaurants you enjoy, and index them either by city name, food type or restaurant name, depending on what works best for you.

Can I show you my clippings?

I have spent hundreds of dollars over the years on travel books, many of which I've never opened. In the past, each time I planned a trip, I would run out and buy a travel guide for that destination. Then, I'd get where I was going and become so excited, I'd just run off in ten directions and go with the flow. Today, I still run off in ten directions, but I am usually running towards something specific that I've read about in a current publication rather than some thick, too-much-information-to-be-useful book. I'm always on the lookout for a new clipping of interest. I keep files on places I've loved visiting and another on destinations I hope one day to visit, my wish list. If I were more computer literate, I suppose the information could be scanned into my laptop, but for now, it remains in dog-eared folders, a technique with tradition that I picked it up from my travel-bug mother. Now, when I get ready to go anywhere, I've got these articles of special interest to me right in hand!

my personal favorite resources for cool clippings:

Saveur This glossy, rich-looking magazine is actually my favorite resource on food and travel here in the US and abroad. It provides the real scoop on real people, and the foods they love to prepare and eat. In each issue, the articles begin with story-telling about the people, then they explore the sights, and finally, they punctuate the vividly painted scenes with a discussion of the regional foods. *Saveur* can make eating loose-meat sandwiches in middle America sound every bit as appealing as nibbling caviar in Kiev. From date milkshakes in California to frozen champagne cocktails in Venice, I've savored many tasty moments, thanks to *Saveur*. At the end of all feature articles, the magazine provides a short, easily-clipped listing of places to stay and dine, for every budget.

The New York Times I am a New Yorker (albeit an Upstater...) so perhaps I am biased, but *The Times* really does deliver the world. I have found great tips in every section of this paper. The Travel section and Sunday Magazine are obvious treasure troves, but I found the most delicious and least expensive ice cream in NYC in a City section (Sunday) that my friend Hiroko saved for me. In it, an article about Mark Thompson, a young entrepreneur who turned an old ferry-boat ticket house into The Brooklyn Ice Cream Factory. I'll tell you more about this amazing guy in the New York section of this book, but what I read in *The Times* really got my interest going. *The Times* named Mark an "ice cream sommelier" and boy, is he ever! He limits production of his carefully chosen flavors to just five-gallon batches, and he lets the sweetness of the cream "shine through" by adding just three tablespoons of sugar to each batch. At half the price of a Ben & Jerry's bar from any Central Park vendor, this ice cream will truly make you cry—it's that good!

In-Flight Magazines Yup. The magazines in the seat backs on airplanes that often get buried under snack wrappers and used plastic cups are good for more than checking the in-flight movie—they actually can and often do contain smart, current, and concise travel advice, just when you need it. I always check the smaller columns, those blurbs on what's hot and what's not and the trends in restaurants, bars, hotels worldwide. They're fun to read like *The Post*'s Page Six. I especially enjoy the in-flight column that's become a series of spin-off books, Three Perfect Days in… (a feature city).

Free Local Papers On the streets in cities across America you will find dispensers for free local guides. These are great resources for your return trip! They have the most current and specific local information on new restaurants and markets. Thumb through a copy the next time one catches your eye.

Go online I am a total geek-loser on the internet, I can't find my way around. Still, with all my ineptitude, the internet allows me to wander around any city on earth long before I arrive. From the hottest, hippest, and coolest restaurant to the teeny-tiniest café, you will be amazed at the amount of current information you can download about a place. These days, when I travel for $40 a Day, I've already read some of the restaurant menus online, and I have my order planned before I've even left my desk!

Call ahead.

A little phone work can save weary travelers a lot of leg work. Call ahead and ask to see menus via fax. Ask if restaurants offer any of the following: weekday/weekend specials, live entertainment, discounts, happy hour, half portions or tapas menus. What are the hours of operation? What are the specialties of the house? If you don't surf the net or if you want to supplement information you've already gathered, just pick up the phone!

Hmm… a line…

If you're walking past a line, take the time to ask why. A long line at breakfast time means you may be strolling past the best pancakes in town. Lines at lunch say great burgers, sandwiches, soups. Lines at dinner time can indicate anything from great food to live music to very reasonable prices. Check them out!

Use mass transit.

New York and London are perfect examples, but many cities today have easy, affordable, accessible mass transit of one form or another. Aside from the obvious convenience, when you use mass transit you get a chance to visit with a captive audience of natives! I've gotten great tips from chatting with locals-in-the-know between stops. Plus, mass transit puts you out there into the mix, and you can hop on and off a train or bus on a whim whenever you pass something that looks really interesting.

Be a blabbermouth.

Not only does it pay to be friendly when you travel, I say tell your friends and associates about your travel plans when you're still at home, too! Some may know more about your destinations than you realize. Share your travel plans with your personal network; the odds are that someone will know about a fabulous place off the beaten track!

Go with your gut.

Don't be so commanded by your research that you ignore your gut. If you see a restaurant or neighborhood that really catches your eye and speaks to you, go for it! By that same token, if you show up at a restaurant that sounded great on paper, but, in person, just feels wrong (or worse, smells wrong) chances are your sixth sense is trying to help you out—it's okay to say no thanks!

Neighborhoods.

Are you into museums? Do you love antiques? Do you love shopping for regional crafts? Are you a biker or a banker? Many travel destinations are organized around cities. Cities have districts, neighborhoods with unique characteristics and activities. Match your likes to the right district and chances are the restaurants in that section will appeal to you as well. I love modern art, funky crafts, and inexpensive, but interesting boutiques. So, when I travel, I seek out neighborhoods that attract students and artists. The restaurants in these neighborhoods, because of their customer base, often have creative and affordable menus that suit my taste best.

Off season, off peak, off price.

I grew up in resort towns on Cape Cod and then in The Adirondacks on Lake George, NY. I've always enjoyed off-season more than peak because I can enjoy the true beauty of our region without having to fight the crowds. If you want to ski Telluride, go in the late spring rather than January. Mountain lakes and seaside resorts are fabulous in the fall and spring. And in Europe, my favorite vacation to date was to Sicily—in December! Everything was half the price of summer rates and the villages were quiet, calm, and beautifully decorated for the Christmas holiday. I felt lucky at each shop and restaurant because I was given so much individual attention, even though my purchases were modest.

Think outside the entrée.

When I do find myself traveling peak season or when I really want to experience a four- or five-star resort or restaurant, I do not deny myself, I just think outside the entrée. I enjoy the same level of service and lovely surroundings at lunch, or go for an appetizer and cocktail, or simply for dessert. Lunch menus are often half the price of dinner. Appetizers and desserts, even at the swankiest of locations, usually fall within most everyone's travel budget.

Don't settle.

I've traveled on a budget for many years and I've rarely felt forced to eat junk or fast food. (Although, I have had many great dishes that I could buy and eat within minutes.) Enjoying flavorful, diverse food on a budget is not really as challenging as many people think.

Consider this:

Every far-off place, no matter how exotic or elaborate it appears, is inhabited by people who have been there for generations. We all want to eat well, drink, be merry, and enjoy the quality of our lives. So, talk to the locals wherever you go, and listen carefully. They will reward you with tips on where they and their families love to eat. By being open-minded and friendly, you'll dine well on $40 a day and have great stories to tell when you get home!

Happy traveling!

inside gossip

QUESTIONS I SHOULDN'T ANSWER... BUT, I WILL

"Who eats all that food?" and "You eat too much in one day! Are you getting fat?"

Thanks. I guess I needed that...I'll try to get to the gym more often. Truth is, I can eat like ten men. Sometimes, the crew helps me out. On most shoots, we record many "beauty shots" of dishes that I order, so by the time I dig in, the food, while still tasty, is usually quite cold. I always comment on the flavor, never the temperature. Then, after we wrap for the day, I get a hot order of the same dish or something very similar, which I gobble up, too!

What's the deal with the tips and gratuities?

I was a waitress for many years. I agree, 15% should not be the standard, but while it is, we need to use that percentage. We count every penny! When that standard gets raised, we'll have to rethink the budget! (In our personal lives, the crew and I grossly over-tip).

Do you ever not like the food?

Very rarely have I been disappointed; maybe two or three times in over 200 locations. I wish my baseball team had that average! I will not "name names" because I've never had an inedible dish and sometimes a dish may simply not jazz dance on my taste buds. It happens to all of us. Tastes in food are so subjective.

How do you find your locations?

In cities I'm familiar with, I tape at my favorite restaurants. In others, we do research and take recommendations from locals! I live in the same manner I work: I prefer affordable, casual, neighborhood restaurants or hang-outs or joints to fine dining rooms. I like to put my elbows on the table. I like to make new friends. I live loudly. I laugh, tell jokes, and my voice carries. I love restaurants in which this sort of behavior does not turn heads. I also like to immerse myself in my surroundings when I travel, to really be among the people who live there. They keep my memories of places alive. There are hard, long days of shooting. Some cities appeal to me more than others, but I sincerely appreciate the differences in every place we've traveled.

Do I need an assistant to join me on my travels?

I have many, but I can't physically take anyone with me on the road. In a way, the many viewers of $40 a Day I meet while dining at past locations are assistants, too. I have to thank many of you for mentioning our show when you try out our picks.

What can $40 get you these days?

Picture this: a Parisian picnic of burgundy wine, herb-coated discs of fresh chevre, sliced farmhouse bread, olives in herb and lemon brine, and crisp fresh pears, all spread out before you. You sit on the velvety, manicured grass at the base of the Eiffel Tower. Ah, April in Paris! This was my lunch in our Paris episode of the Food Network's $40 a Day. My picnic cost less than $12.00.

So, how do you get a job where you are paid to travel, eat, and spend money (albeit 40 bucks)?

Some years ago, I had a fun sideline to my "real" job as gourmet foods buyer and manager of the production kitchen of Cowan & Lobel, a specialty marketplace in Albany, NY. After hours, I was also an on-air lifestyles reporter. Each week, on Thursday nights, if you were watching WRGB (CBS, Channel 6), you would see me teaching a viewer how to make a tasty, simple gourmet dinner, in his or her own kitchen, in 30 minutes or less. One day, when I was feeling especially brave (or stupid) I said to the news director that if he enjoyed my talent for gourmet cooking on a budget, he should be equally impressed with the way I enjoyed a rich social life on a near-poverty income. So launched my what-to-do-when-you're-not-at-work segments. The news director did his part in keeping me quite poor, indeed. And I did my part, too. I had lots of fun! At the same time, I like to think I was actually sharing important quality-of-life information with my friends, neighbors, and community. My guidelines were simple: anything and everything goes, as long as it costs less than $100.00 and lies within 100 miles of "point A," our viewing area.

We called the segment R&R, Rest and Relaxation (also, my initials). It wasn't all food-related reporting and some segments were hardly relaxing: I jumped out of airplanes (where I discovered you cannot take in quite enough air to scream when you are three miles up), I covered the return of disco roller-skating, I got my American history straight at West Point, I chased llamas across fields in Cherry Valley, and I shared the proper techniques for apple-picking and scarecrow-stuffing in the orchards of Vermont. After all this, the most viewer mail always came in response to the segments on how to find great food at reasonable prices when you're on the road. As much as WRGB viewers wanted to learn how to cook gourmet-for-everyday, they were equally hungry to learn where to eat gourmet on an everyday budget. Sound familiar?

Flash-forward a year later. My publisher and I are in a meeting at the Food Network to discuss my 30 Minute Meal program and how the idea might become seed for a national show. I also describe my R&R segments that shared the same concept as my cooking show, namely, you don't have to be rich to live a rich life. They have a related idea in mind, focusing on the rich man vs. poor man premise; one guy gets $5,000 to spend, another just $50. Both set out to spend a day in some fabulous city where they must find the best breakfast, lunch, and dinner possible within their respective budgets. My point, why bother with the rich guy? While the whole Prince and The Pauper/Roman Holiday/Freaky Friday juxtaposition interests me, I feel the rich are already well served. Most of these "What's Hot Now" shows leave me cold. I also believe that a television show shouldn't have the power to make one feel left off the first-string team in life.

We left the meeting with the promise to make two pilots: 30 Minute Meals and $40 a Day. The rest, as you know, is history!

To me, the poor guy is the whole story.
He wants to know where he can afford to go and everyone, rich or poor, wants to know where the good deals are to be found.

north

ADIRONDACKS
SARATOGA
COOPERSTOWN
VERMONT
MONTREAL
PORTLAND
BOSTON
CAPE COD
NEW YORK CITY
PHILADELPHIA
WASHINGTON, DC

You know the saying, "You can't see the forest through the trees?" Well, they were right! I grew up on Lake George, New York, in the Adirondacks, known for its wonderful woods. My mom worked hundred-hour weeks to be able to afford to keep her three kids on beautiful Lake George while we were growing up. Prime real estate, indeed. But, we three punks (especially in our teens) complained about how far away we were from the outside world. To hear us whine about the Adirondacks (six million pristine acres of mountains, lakes, and clean air) one would have thought we were in solitary confinement on Mars. After I did real hard-time, living in Queens in NYC, working 100-hour weeks myself at my job in New York, the city I so longed to be a part of all those years, I found myself dreaming about the Adirondacks: the blackness of the night skies, the scent of pine, the peace. Then, I would wake abruptly to the sound of my hideous alarm clock. I would face the reality of my studio apartment with its choking, defunct air conditioner. I would wipe away a few tears and sleep from my eyes, as I checked for roaches in my slippers. Life in the fast lane! Today, I love New York. I love all of it: Manhattan and the mountains and lakes. But the Adirondacks will always be my first love. I have made my home here, again, because I finally grew up and saw these fine forests through the trees. Today I can say, Mom, you knew what was best for us, once again. And I find, after ten years back, I am just beginning to uncover the true beauty and the many secrets these mountains hold. In fact, I have added a few secrets of my own.

breakfast

Steve Sutton took a small piece of family land and started a small business, selling fresh-picked apples in the Fall. He also had a cider press in the parking lot, out in front of his barn. Inside, was a donut machine behind a glass partition. When I was eight, back in 1976, living just across the street and up the hill, my family would take me over there and I would crawl up on a wooden stool and drool as I peered through the glass at the warm cider donuts. Almost thirty years later, when I go back to those donuts, I am a kid again with every tasty bite. Today, Sutton's is so much more than donuts, thanks to the vision of Steve's wife, Donna. When Sutton's first went into business, Donna Sutton was a teacher. One day at the store, she set up a table and put a few locally-made rag dolls out for sale. She went to work and when she returned, all of the dolls were gone and she discovered that her one table had made more in sales than all the apples and donuts combined! And so, the retail division of Sutton's was born. These days, Sutton's is a cottage industry, or dare I say, a barn empire? There are now two barns and a cottage. The original barn houses: specialty foods, cookbooks, stationary and journals, garden and home accessories, gifts, tabletop, women's apparel, leather goods, jewelry by several local artists, holiday and seasonal decorations, candy and fine chocolates, a full-service restaurant offering breakfast, lunch, and dinners on weekends, a large bakery and, of course, the donut counter. The second barn is home to custom home-furnishings, rugs and textiles, and outdoor furniture. The cottage holds a really cool toy store, free of video-game boxes and play guns. Plan half a day here and don't forget to have that cinnamon cider donut before you leave!

● **Sutton's Market Place, 1066 Route 9, Queensbury, NY, (518) 798-1188**

" Almost thirty years later, when I go back to those donuts, I am a kid again with every tasty bite. **"**

Sutton's
MARKET PLACE

lunch

As you know, I grew up on gorgeous Lake George, which is over 32 miles long. Still, I never learned how to water ski or ice skate. Now that I am in my thirties, I thought I had better get around to learning before I get old enough to risk breaking a hip! For my money, the easiest and best place to rent a boat and learn to water ski is at Chic's Marina. It's been sitting on this small, beautiful bay in Bolton Landing on Lake George for as long as I can remember. There's a lot of traffic in and out: locals launching boats, tourists renting all things aquatic, para-sailing, and more. Chic's shares a bay with the equally popular Algonquin Restaurant, home of my most favorite fish sandwich. So, I made a deal with myself that if I could get up on skis, I would treat myself to one of my favorite meals, dockside. To sum up the waterskiing lesson, let me say that I took on lake water into places I didn't know existed on my body. I also quickly made the observation that water

moving at 40 mph can hurt your face, and the water was cold. I coughed, sneezed, and fought with my swim wear after each fall. Then, I rose like a phoenix, popped up like a cork, briefly. I stood up on the skis three times. Then, shaking, teeth chattering, and water-logged, I scratched "learning to water ski" off the life-list and headed over in my scuffs to settle down, lakeside, for my true favorite activity, eating. The Gonq, as we locals call it, is great because you can drive in by car or by boat. By day, you are welcome in flip-flops and cover-ups. By night, the restaurant becomes a fine-dining establishment with a fantastic bar and stunning views to enjoy during leisurely dinners on white-clothed tables. Some of the same menu items are offered at lunch and dinner, just in different presentations. My flounder sandwich is the same flounder served at dinner. At night, it comes with vegetables and pasta, rice or potatoes. At lunch, the flounder is dipped in egg, grilled, then set on a bun and served with a lunch side dish; I get fries. The fish sandwich is very affordable, so if dinner is a bit pricey or if you just want to enjoy a great lakeside lunch, head on over to The Gonq!

" The Gonq, as we locals call it, is great because you can drive in by car or by boat. "

● **The Algonquin on Lake George, 4770 Lake Shore Drive, Bolton Landing, NY, (518) 644-9442**

snack

This five-star hotel sits on a tiny island in Lake George and it is grand! The main building is a huge columned structure with a large veranda and a sprawling backyard that rolls downhill to the water. From the lawn behind the veranda, you have the best view of Lake George, the islands, and the surrounding mountains. You feel as if you have really arrived in life. I worked at this resort years ago managing the bars and restaurant and never tired of the beauty of this place. The view is free, even if you're not a guest, so you are welcome to come and enjoy a drink or a cup of tea and take in the sights. I especially enjoy high tea at the

Veranda bar. My favorite tea is cinnamon and I love their selection of savory finger sandwiches, each piece a small work of art. In the episode we shot with my friend, the elegant Mary Demarsh, Queen of the Sagamore Veranda, I had several sandwiches with smoked chicken salad, salmon and herb chevre, and cucumber-cress. When you go to the Veranda, kiss Mary for me. P.S. If you go for sunset cocktails rather than tea, you might hear my friend Ray playing great jazz out on Mary's Veranda. What he does to an old standard on his piano is far beyond standard! Enjoy!

● **The Sagamore, 110 Sagamore Road, Bolton Landing, NY, (518) 644-9400**

dinner

Ye-ha! I live near the oldest weekly rodeo in America, The Painted Pony. I love horses. I love barbecue. I love cowboys and cowboy hats, cold beer, and (some) country music, too. For all of these reasons, I love to go over to the Painted Pony any Wednesday, Friday, or Saturday from Memorial Day through Labor Day. My niece Jessica comes to visit me every summer and she loves all that stuff, too (except for the cold beer). The rodeo starts at 8:00 in the evening, but we go early to get in on the barbecue they've been cooking up all day long. At 6:30, you can find us cowgirls on line, loadin' up on huge plates of barbecue chicken with ziti, beans, and salad on the side. We belly up to a table and work our way through all that food, onto the strawberry shortcakes that come with dinner, too. After that, we head over to the bleachers to stake our claim on some seats. Jessie still manages to have room left for candy, amazingly enough. We both love barrel-racing the best. Our next favorite event is bull-riding. Go cowboys!

● **Painted Pony Rodeo, 703 Howe Road, Lake Luzerne, NY, (518) 696-2421**

❝ At 6:30, you can find us cowgirls on line, loadin' up on huge plates of barbecue chicken with ziti, beans, and salad on the side. ❞

SARATOGA

The slogan "Saratoga, the august place to be" says it all. Though it refers to the world-class thoroughbred racing session that meets here in late summer, it speaks, too, to all the other wonderful attractions Saratoga has to offer. I have lived near Saratoga Springs most of my life, my father lives there now, and I can tell you, this is a great place to be anytime of the year. Saratoga is home to SPAC, The Saratoga Performing Arts Center, which, in turn, is the summer home of the New York Philharmonic, the New York City Ballet, the Metropolitan Opera, and every big-name rock and pop star on tour. They perform in the partially enclosed amphitheater that spills out onto a great lawn that can hold tens of thousands of people, under the cool trees and dark starry night skies. Also, there are the mineral springs, bath houses, and spas, and a rich fine arts community, strengthened by Skidmore college. There are numerous jazz clubs and rocking juke joints, all with live music, too. Then there are the night clubs, like Luna, started by a very creative Italian, David Zecchini and his gorgeous wife and business partner, Maria. They also own Chianti, one of my absolute favorite restaurants on US soil. Chianti is out of the $40 a Day budget, but if you want to splurge, going to Chianti is far cheaper than a trip to Tuscany. Fabrizio, the humble and masterful chef, has been blessed by God with his culinary gifts. Check out The Wine Bar, too, which offers more than 100 choices of wine by the glass, from an eclectic, well-conceived selection. The Lyrical Ballad, another local gem not to be missed, is a second-hand book store and rare-book vault owned by a couple who used to read poetry to each other by Saratoga Lake. How romantic is that! They have books valued from two to many thousands of dollars, but browsing is free.

❝ I had a plan: to watch the morning workout of the racehorses at the flat track. Then I stop in for a fruit drink and a race-track picnic pack ❞

breakfast

I have a special place in my heart for a well-run and truly unique specialty-market because I worked in specialty markets as a buyer and retail manager for many years. In today's world, a small marketplace has to remain competitive by reinventing itself, and this one did. Once located on Putnam Street it's now one of the crown jewels on the main strip, Broadway. It's also less precious, more mainstream, offering very fairly priced prepared salads, entrees, sandwiches, and bakery creations for locals and tourists on the go. In addition, the market portion includes a few pantry basics, a "killer" cheese selection and deli and many fantastic packaged specialty foods, everything from a great snack to a locally made edible souvenir to the perfect hostess, shower, or birthday gift. The marketplace also owns a sister wine shop, next door. I usually stop in for lunch—the sandwiches rock! On the day we taped, I had a plan: to watch the morning workout of the racehorses at the flat track. Then I stop in for a fruit drink and a race-track picnic pack of their excellent quiche, made with lots of fresh thyme, bacon and cheese, and some fresh-cut fruit. I love horses, but I'm terrible at betting, so I prefer to hang out at the gorgeous track before the starting bell. Stay and bet a few if you like. But, don't miss stopping by Putnam Market on Broadway.

● **Putnam Market, 435 Broadway, Saratoga Springs, NY, (518) 587-3663**

lunch

This shop, according to both *Food and Wine* magazine and me, may be the best bakery in America. I love the London's and have done my part to spread the word about the place, not that they needed any help. The shop is always packed. Mr. and Mrs. London are both bakers and chefs and they met, fell in love, and married literally while there was a cake in the oven. Today, they are local icons. They are both so wonderful, good looking, and talented that you cheer them on as a couple and a business.

" You simply cannot take your eyes off the pastries. Each one is so perfect, you cannot believe it is handmade. "

Their son is a fantastic prodigy chef who cooked his first meal while in his teens and today, just in his twenties, will become the chef of the family's new venture, a full-service restaurant named after him, Max. The restaurant will occupy part of my favorite store in Saratoga, belonging to two other friends, and another super couple, Mark and Betty. Called Mabou, which I think is a Native American word meaning sparkling waters, the store has everything from jewelry and small gifts to insanely unusual home furnishings akin to ABC Carpet and Home in NYC. Mabou takes up two storefronts which sandwich Mrs. London's, so make a complete sweep of both businesses. At Mrs. London's I took-a-load off with my friend Vicki, who is like family. We had put in some hard work, shoe shopping and cruising Mabou, so we treated ourselves to a girly "lunch" of fabulous pastries. At Mrs. London's the croque monsieur (ham, cheese, and béchamel sauce) and other sandwiches are all fantastic, but you simply cannot take your eyes off the pastries. Each one is so perfect, you cannot believe it is handmade. The pastry and cake displays look like the Sistine Chapel of baking. I had a lime mousse tart with raspberries that was a near religious experience. They also carry grainy, super bitter chocolates from Sicily and excellent imported dry semolina pastas and a few condiments: I buy one of each to take home. Start dieting now, so that you can get on that plane and fly to Mrs. London's to indulge. It's worth the trip.

● **Mrs. London's Bakery and Café, 464 Broadway, Saratoga Springs, NY, (518) 581-1652**

dinner

Leon's (Lee-owns) is a fairly new place owned by a very successful semi-retired jockey, Filiberto Leon, and his gorgeous wife, Roberta, who was pregnant when I met her—congrats on the little Leon! This is a really nice find: a family-run, reasonably-priced restaurant specializing in real Mexican cuisine which has little to do with fast-food type fajitas. I had a delicious chicken dish with a delicately flavored sauce and queso-fresco. The salsas are very good, and the portions generous and surprisingly light.

● **Leon's Mexican Restaurant, 135 Crescent Street, Saratoga Springs, NY, (518) 587-2346**

LEON'S

drink

One Caroline is owned by yet another super couple (must be something extra-romantic in the air in Saratoga), Dianne and David Pedinotti, and their five kids. Look for Sarah, one of their daughters, on the Billboard music charts. Her pipes grace our segment here. She is amazing! One Caroline is my favorite jazz club and it's an excellent bistro, too, thanks to David's cooking and Dianne's everything else. My daddy is a regular here, too. I've known this place from the get-go, when I did a local news story on their opening years ago. Since then, many famous jazz groups coming to play at SPAC, also stop in here to play and jam. The music is always fantastic and the food magical. I came in for our $40 a Day taping to try their new drink and meet up with my daddy. I had to battle him for the check. I had a Trifecta, a drink named for a betting term in horse racing where you pick three (hopefully) winners. This drink paid big! It was a concoction of three vodkas, and it was good!

● **One Caroline Street Bistro,**
1 Caroline Street, Saratoga Springs,
NY, (518) 587-2026

recipe courtesy One Caroline St. **$40ADAY**

APP - SOUP/SAL - ENTREE - VEG/POT - DESSERT - BEV

Trifecta

SERVES 1

1/3 Shot of Stoli Lemon
1/3 Shot of Stoli Orange
1/3 Shot of Stoli Raspberry
1/2 shot of Roses Lime Juice
Splash of sour mix
Splash of cranberry juice
Lemon twist for garnish

● Pour all ingredients over ice and shake vigorously. Strain into a chilled martini glass that has been generously rimmed with sugar. Garnish with a lemon twist. Enjoy with live jazz!

COOPERSTOWN

I love baseball. This dictates that I love Cooperstown, NY, too. After all, this is the home of baseball, of Doubleday Field and, of course, The National Baseball Hall of Fame. If that weren't enough, there is also Glimmerglass Opera, James Fennimore Cooper, the Otis-Saga Hotel, and the Farmer's Museum, to get excited about.

museum

> **❝ No trip to this area can be considered complete without a trip to The National Baseball Hall of Fame. ❞**

No trip to this area can be considered complete without a trip to The National Baseball Hall of Fame. I have an old friend who works here, too. Milo Stewart, Jr., a fantastic photographer, is also the official photographer for The Hall of Fame. I met Milo when I filmed a story about him performing his duties on an induction day. I am a huge Boston Red Sox fan, and while following the story of Milo, I actually got to meet Carlton Fisk. Cool! All these years later, whenever I make it to town, I always stop in to say hi. So should you. Baseball fan or not, Milo's photos are amazing.

● National Baseball Hall of Fame and Museum, 25 Main Street, Cooperstown, NY, 607-547-7200

Corn Cake Breakfast Stacks with Maple Butter

Corn Cakes:

4 large eggs

1 & 1/2 cups buttermilk

3 tablespoons butter, melted

1 cup fresh sweet corn kernels (about 2 medium ears of corn)

1 cup yellow cornmeal

1 cup all-purpose flour

2 tablespoons sugar

1 & 1/2 to 2 teaspoons salt

1 teaspoon baking powder

Maple Butter:

1 cup (2 sticks) butter, softened

1/2 cup dark amber maple syrup

8 strips thick-cut smoked bacon

2 Granny Smith apples, cored and sliced

Ground cinnamon, to taste

Salt

1/4 cup (1/2 stick) butter, for the pan

1/2 cup dark amber maple syrup, warmed, for serving

Fresh mint sprigs, for garnish, optional

Confectioners' sugar, for garnish, optional

Fresh blueberries, for garnish, optional

● Start the corn cakes: Whisk together eggs, buttermilk, and melted butter in a medium mixing bowl. Stir in corn kernels. In a separate bowl, sift together cornmeal, flour, sugar, salt, and baking powder. Add the dry ingredients to the buttermilk-corn mixture and stir until just combined.

Corn Cake Stacks

Let stand for 20 minutes in a cool place.
● Meanwhile, make the maple butter: Blend softened butter with maple syrup in a small bowl and set aside.
● Preheat oven to 250°F. In a 10-inch nonstick skillet on medium heat, brown bacon strips. Drain them on paper towels and transfer to a cookie sheet. Sprinkle apple slices with cinnamon and salt, to taste. Sear them in bacon fat until golden brown, and place them on the sheet pan with the bacon.
● Wipe out the skillet and return it to medium heat. Add just enough butter to coat the bottom of the skillet and ladle 1/4 cup corn batter onto hot skillet. Let cook until the edges of the pancake start to brown and bubbles appear on the surface, about 2 minutes. Flip, cook another 2 minutes, then transfer to the cookie sheet with the apples and the bacon. Repeat until you have a dozen corn cakes. Place the cookie sheet and serving plates in the oven until everything is warm, about 4 minutes.
● On each plate, place 1 corn cake, top that with 2 strips of bacon, another corn cake, 2 slices of apple, and another corn cake. Top with maple butter and drizzle the plate with some of the warmed maple syrup. Garnish with a sprig of mint, a dusting of confectioners' sugar, and a few fresh berries, if desired.

breakfast

My first stop in the show was to see old friends Garth and Doug, owners of the American Hotel in Sharon Springs, NY, a former spa city which today is a tight-knit community; it's about a half hour's drive outside of Cooperstown. Since I live upstate, I rarely need to stay overnight, but if you're traveling to the area, stay here at the America Hotel. When they first owned it, Garth and Doug called the place a terrarium because there were so many plants and animals living inside this nearly condemned historic site. But the guys took on its restoration as a labor of love and the result is this amazingly beautiful hotel and dining room. Lee, Garth's cousin, is the chef. He made me some delicious corn cakes stacked with green apples and bacon (see recipe on previous page). Yumm-o!

● **American Hotel, 192 Main Street, Sharon Springs, NY, (518) 284-2105**

❝ When they first owned it, Garth and Doug called the place a terrarium because there were so many plants and animals living inside this nearly condemned historic site. ❞

drink

Throughout the taping of this show, I've been spending time with dear friends such as Don and Wendy, owners of Ommegang Brewery. To call this place just a brewery is misleading. Ommegang means a festive parade in Flemish and that is what a trip here feels like: a party! Ommegang is housed in a reproduction Belgian farmhouse where the beers are brewed in open vats, a style of brewing done no where else in America. In fact, Don and Wendy were given a special award by the royal family of Belgium for all they have done to promote Belgian culture here in the US. At Ommegang, you can attend the annual festival of waffles and puppets (also, try REAL Belgian fries with flavored, mayonnaise dipping sauces—nothing "French" about them, according to Don, Wendy, and all of Belgium) Yes, kids love it here year round! For them, the retail section has a large selection of Smurf figurines and Tintin books, all imported from Belgium. You can also buy tee shirts, Belgian chocolates, and gold-rimmed beer glasses, specially designed for each style of beer sold. You can enjoy a beer-tasting while sampling local cheeses, and you can take a free tour of the brewery with the brewmaster himself. You may go away wondering why Don and Wendy chose to build this brewery here in Cooperstown—why this place? Well, Cooperstown is not only the hometown of baseball, it is also the hometown of beer. The hops fields in Cooperstown were the first in this country and the hops grown in these fields made America's first mass-produced beers.

● **Ommegang Brewery, 656 County Highway 33, Cooperstown, NY, (800) 544-1809**

> **❝ Ommegang is housed in a reproduction Belgian farmhouse where the beers are brewed in open vats, a style of brewing done no where else in America. ❞**

picnic

On the show, I made a picnic for myself called a ploughman's lunch: cheese, bread, onions, and a beer, buying my foodstuffs at Danny's Main Street Market. And then I enjoyed this lunch by the lakefront. In real life, Danny's also makes killer salads and pizzas, subs and sandwiches. You'll want to come here several times a day when you're in town and put together many a picnic. Check it out, Danny's on Main.

● **Danny's Main Street Market, 92 Main Street, Cooperstown, NY, (607) 547-4053**

recipe courtesy Brooks' House $40ADAY

APPT - SOUP/SAL - ENTREE - VEG/POT - DESSERT - BEV

Barbecued Chicken
SERVES 6 TO 8

6 (22-ounce) chicken halves (fryers are best)
2 (16-ounce) bottles barbecue sauce
5 to 7 pounds charcoal briquettes
Lighter fluid

● Arrange the grill grate 25 to 27 inches from the charcoal. If it is too close, the chicken will cook too fast, burn, and dry out. Pile the charcoal in a pyramid. Sprinkle with lighter fluid and ignite. Once the top portion of the charcoal has turned white, spread the charcoal out evenly using a fireproof tool such as a metal rake or shovel.
● Place the chicken on the grill. About every 5 minutes, turn the chicken with tongs (being careful not to tear the skin) and baste with the sauce each time (for best results, use a clean squeeze bottle). Grill for 60 to 75 minutes. Add more charcoal, if necessary, to finish off (maybe 1/2 to 2/3 way through the cooking process), making sure not to use any more lighter fluid; just sprinkle the new charcoal over the existing. The chicken is done when an instant-read thermometer inserted into the thickest part of the thigh reads 165°F.

66 You can smell it more than a mile before the exit. This is the largest barbecue pit in the Northeast, possibly on the whole seaboard. **99**

recipe courtesy Brooks' House $40ADAY

APPT - SOUP/SAL - ENTREE - VEG/POT - DESSERT - BEV

Barbecued Ribs
SERVES 4 TO 6

5 pounds charcoal briquettes (if using a charcoal grill)
Lighter fluid (if using a charcoal grill)
6 pounds pork ribs (baby back or spareribs)
1 tablespoon barbecue meat dry rub seasoning
1 (16-ounce) bottle barbecue sauce

● If using a charcoal grill, pile the charcoal in a pyramid in the bottom of the grill. Sprinkle with lighter fluid and ignite. Once the top portion of the charcoal has turned white, spread the charcoal out evenly using a fireproof tool such as a metal rake or shovel. Spread the coals over half of the bottom of the grill, leaving the other half empty. If using a gas grill, only ignite one side of the burners.
● Evenly spread the meat seasoning over both sides of the ribs. Let stand in the refrigerator unless using right away. Place the ribs on the side of the grill that is not hot. Cover and turn every 20 minutes for 60 to 75 minutes. For the last 10 minutes of cooking, baste ribs with barbecue sauce and cover again. Turn the ribs over and baste again. Do this every 2 minutes. While ribs are still on grill, cut them up individually and baste once more.

dinner

Brooks' House of Bar-B-Que is located just outside Cooperstown, off I-88 in Oneonta. You can smell it more than a mile before the exit. This is the largest barbecue pit in the Northeast, possibly on the whole seaboard. More than 54 feet in length, the pit is so long that it takes a rack of chickens, which are basted and turned every 5 minutes, a full hour to make its way from one end to the other. Prices are stuck back in the '50s. The food is beyond finger-licking

BBQ Chicken

good and you can even buy the secret sauces to take home, though your chickens and ribs will never taste quite as good as Ryan Brooks'. He's a third generation barbecue master here, and like many family recipes, only a real Brooks family member can do Brooks' chicken and ribs just right! (see recipes on opposite page)

● **Brooks' House of Bar-B-Que, 5560 State Hwy. 7, Oneonta, NY, (607) 432-1782**

snack

To me, one of the most moving, beautiful places on God's green earth is Cooperstown Dreams Park. My dear friend Lou Presutti went to the Hall of Fame years ago with his dad and his young son. His dad commented, while walking through the Hall, how wonderful it would be if all kids could play baseball here, in the home of baseball, just once. The idea never left Lou; it became a passion, a vision to pursue. Though he made a nice living in demographics, one day he asked his beautiful wife Linda if he could take their life savings, their retirement money, and buy an old patch of hops fields in Cooperstown to build a "field of dreams" for kids. Today, Cooperstown Dreams Park has not one but fourteen fields. Kids come here from all over America, and Canada, too.

There are no skills tests and no affiliations with organized leagues, no Little League or Babe Ruth teams. Every kid who comes here stays in a special village where only players and coaches are allowed. They come and play, in any weather, up to four games in a single day. Each Thursday night, there's a mini-World Series game, free and open to the public. There are fireworks, great food, and family fun

and the best youth baseball you'll ever find. Each kid, every week, no matter his or her record, gets inducted into the Youth Baseball Hall of Fame and all get a Hall of Fame ring. Lou has secured corporate sponsors to keep costs down for families, so every boy and girl can afford to come here. Lou's son, Louis, executed the building of the park. His beautiful daughters Leslie and Laurie help mom Linda with food concessions, retail products, and operations. Lou P. is still the visionary and his brother Joe works in the operations end of things, too. I went here on the show to have a snow ball (a snow cone with fresh fruit), but in real life, food has nothing to do with this place. You come here for your soul.

● **Cooperstown Dreams Park, 4550 State Hwy. 28, Milford, NY, 704-630-0050**

VERMONT

Many episodes of $40 a Day have been filmed in the Northeast because this is where I live today and where I have spent all 35 of my years. Because this is my backyard, I have an easy time talking to viewers about the region and sharing my favorite picks. The Vermont border is just half an hour from my home and I travel there often, especially in the fall and winter months.

breakfast

I love shopping in Manchester, Vermont. This is outlet heaven! There's Peruvian Connection, DKNY, J. Crew, Patagonia Sports, Jones, Klein, Lauren, and more. If they were to add a Prada outlet, I would be forced to move here permanently. Anyway, when I'm in Manchester, shopping, I always eat breakfast at the Little Rooster Cafe. It's as tiny as can be, but the food has big, bold, wonderful flavors. The drink menu alone is worth a trip! Their brunch cocktails are every bit as creative as the food. My favorite is a concoction of fresh grapefruit juice, vodka, and a splash of soda. Also, they have one of the best Bloody Mary's I've ever had. Their potato cakes are golden and delicious. Eggs come every which way, including stacked with smoked trout or spinach as alternatives to Eggs Benedict; omelets are light. Pancakes are just slightly sweet. It's all mighty delicious at a fine price. In this episode, I think I had the corned beef hash. (see recipe on opposite page) WOW! So good! The beef is corned on site and is super lean and yummy. Hub Poelmann is your chef and owner, and his lovely wife will greet you. The only thing better than shopping in Manchester, is enjoying a meal at Little Rooster Cafe.

● **Little Rooster Cafe, Route 7A, Manchester, VT, (802) 362-3496**

APPT - SOUP/SAL - **ENTREE** - VEG/POT - DESSERT - BEV

> I always eat breakfast at the Little Rooster Cafe. It's as tiny as can be, but the food has big, bold, wonderful flavors.

Corned Beef Hash

SERVES 2 TO 3

12 ounces chopped corned beef
2 potatoes, peeled, cooked, and grated
1/2 cup chopped mixed peppers
1/2 cup chopped red onions
1/2 cup chopped scallions
1 tablespoon chopped fresh parsley leaves
1 tablespoon chopped fresh rosemary leaves
1/2 teaspoon salt
1/2 teaspoon fresh pepper

● Mix all of the ingredients together in a bowl. Heat a large skillet over medium-high heat. Add corned beef mixture and sauté until golden brown, about 8 minutes. Serve.

Corned Beef Hash

lunch

Sesame Chicken

Here in Quechee, there's a great, deep gorge that attracts people who like to walk, hike, and commune with nature....Me, I come to Quechee to shop and "commune" with fine glass, tabletop, and woven goods at Simon Pearce, a wonderful store where you can watch real artisans at work, hand-blowing glass and hand-throwing pottery. The "seconds" rooms allow you to purchase these one-of-a-kind pieces at deep discounts; the imperfections are often undetectable. Whether you come to watch or purchase, stay for a meal in the dining room at The Mill, where the wall of glass allows you to overlook the rushing waterfalls below. The award-winning menu and equally fine wine list are impressive, One of my menu favorites is a classic here, sesame-seared chicken with spicy dipping sauce. (see recipe on next page)

● **Simon Pearce Restaurant at The Mill, 1760 Main Street, Quechee, VT, (802) 295-1470**

SIMON PEARCE

Original Designs in
Glass and Pottery

recipe | SERVES 5 | courtesy Simon Pearce Restaurant at The Mill | $40ADAY

APPT - SOUP/SAL - **ENTREE** - VEG/POT - DESSERT - BEV

Sesame Chicken with Spicy Dipping Sauce

1 small onion, minced

3 cloves garlic, minced

1 (1/4-inch) piece peeled fresh ginger

6 ounces (3/4 cup) lemon juice

6 ounces (3/4 cup) olive oil

3 ounces (6 tablespoons) soy sauce

3 ounces (6 tablespoons) dark rum

1 tablespoon crushed red pepper

2 tablespoons sugar

2 tablespoon salt

5 chicken breasts

1 cup sesame seeds, toasted

2 cups all-purpose flour

Canola oil, for sautéing

Sesame Noodles (recipe follows)

Soy-Ginger Vinaigrette (recipe follows)

Mesclun Greens

Spicy Apricot Sauce (recipe follows)

Pickled ginger, for garnish

● In a food processor, combine the onion, garlic, and ginger and pulse to mince. Transfer mixture to a container with a lid (or a bowl) and combine with the lemon juice, olive oil, soy sauce, rum, crushed red pepper, sugar, and salt. Shake, or stir well, before using.

● Cut the chicken breasts into 2-inch strips. Place chicken in a resealable plastic bag with the marinade. Marinate in the refrigerator overnight.

● Preheat the oven to 400°F.

● Combine sesame seeds with the flour in a shallow bowl. Remove chicken from marinade and dredge in the flour-sesame mixture. In a skillet, heat enough canola oil to lightly coat the bottom of the skillet until hot, but not smoking. Add chicken and cook on both sides until golden brown. Transfer to a shallow roasting pan and finish in the oven, if necessary.

● To assemble: Toss the Sesame Noodles with some Soy-Ginger Vinaigrette and mesclun greens. Place the noodle salad on a plate and top with the chicken. Drizzle some apricot sauce over the chicken. Garnish with pickled ginger and a side of the apricot dipping sauce.

Sesame Noodles:

1 pound fresh angel hair pasta

1/2 bunch cilantro, leaves chopped

1 bunch chopped scallions

2 tablespoons olive oil

2 tablespoons toasted sesame oil

● Cook angel hair pasta in a large pot of boiling, salted water for 2 minutes or until al dente. Drain and rinse with cold water to stop the cooking. Toss noodles with cilantro, scallions, olive oil, and sesame oil until combined well.

Soy-Ginger Vinaigrette:

1/4 cup soy sauce

1/4 cup lemon juice

1 tablespoon minced ginger

1/2 cup olive oil

1/2 cup canola oil

1 ounce boiling water

● Combine all ingredients, except for the water, in a blender. Blend for 30 seconds. Add the water and blend for another 10 seconds.

Spicy Apricot Sauce:

2 cups apricot glaze

1 cup balsamic vinaigrette

2 tablespoons soy sauce

1 tablespoon red pepper flakes

1 tablespoon grated ginger

1/2 cup mirin

● Put all ingredients in a saucepan and heat over medium heat until the glaze melts. Whisk until smooth. Let cool to room temperature for serving. Add a little water if sauce becomes too thick while cooling.

sweet

Harry Diamond is one of the most enthusiastic humans I have ever met in my life. He owns The Apple Barn and operates it with his wife Leah. What a character! I've never met a grown man who can so fully embrace a child's ability to play, imagine, and be so free spirited. At The Apple Barn, you can run through a cornfield maze, whose shape changes annually. You can visit with the apple dragon—careful, she's 20 feet tall, fire-breathing, with eyes that glow. Or, you can invest your time in my favorite Apple Barn activity: the apple catapult target practice.

Take your family on a pilgrimage to The Apple Barn. Oh yeah, the apples, pie, and cider are all good, too.

● **The Apple Barn & Country Bake Shop, Route 7 South, Bennington, VT, (802) 447-7780**

Apple Pie

recipe	SERVES 8	The Apple Barn & Country Bake Shop	$40ADAY

APPT - SOUP/SAL - ENTREE - VEG/POT - **DESSERT** - BEV

Vermont Apple Pie

3 pounds peeled, cored, and sliced tart baking apples

3/4 cup sugar

3 tablespoons ground cinnamon

4 tablespoons all-purpose flour

Pinch nutmeg

2 (9-inch) prepared piecrusts

2 tablespoons butter, cut into small pieces, optional

1 egg

1 tablespoon water

● Preheat the oven to 350°F.
● Toss apples with sugar, cinnamon, flour, and nutmeg. Place 1 of the piecrusts into a 9-inch pie plate. Pour the apple mixture into the piecrust. Dot with butter, if desired, and cover with the top crust. In a small bowl, beat egg and water with a fork to make an egg wash. Brush the top crust with the egg wash for a glossy appearance. Place pie on a sheet pan to prevent juices from spilling into the oven. Bake for 50 to 55 minutes.
● Test pie with a sharp knife to feel if apples are tender enough for your taste. If necessary, cook pie for 5 more minutes and test again. Cool pie and then serve with ice cream or any of your favorite toppings.

dinner

Huh? What Marina? Which water? Where in Vermont? To be totally fair, we taped at The Marina completely out of season on a cold and windy night. It was mostly unfair to the restaurant. This place was clearly designed to be a campy, warm-weather hot spot. I do remember being relaxed in my surroundings, but very, very cold. I was longing to return to my room and the warmth of my bed covers. The "spicy shrimp" was cold in temperature and really not very spicy at all. The beer was fine, but made me colder still. The servers, diners, and hostesses were all nice and welcoming. If you happen to be in Brattleboro in the summer months, check out The Marina.

Spicy Shrimp

● **The Marina on the Water, 28 Spring Tree La., Brattleboro, VT, (802) 257-7563**

MONTREAL

Montreal is my Paris. I love the idea that in less than two hours from my home, for the cost of a few gallons of gas, I can be in Europe, sort of. Montreal is beautiful and very easy to navigate. I always drive in and out and have no problems getting around or parking.

There are two main streets that I hang out on: St. Laurent and St. Denis. I like to wine, dine, and shop, up and down these funky boulevards and for a change of pace, I love to savor my time, wandering the narrow cobblestone streets in Old Montreal, which date back to the 1500s. That's old, especially for an American. No matter where you dine or shop, because of the current favorable exchange rate, you can deduct about 25 to 30% off the Canadian price to get the US equivalent. I feel so guilty enjoying so much for so little here, but I get over it. Plus, if you spend more than $200.00 per trip on shopping and hotels and if each receipt is over $50.00, you get taxes back at the border! C'est magnifique! There are two food-musts worth mentioning, though time did not allow them to get on the show. There is Toque, a very funky, fancy French restaurant on St. Denis, and Schwartz's World-Famous

Delicatessen, which wins my award for best pastrami on the continent. It's on St. Laurent. One last general tidbit: You cannot get bad food in Montreal, really, you can't. I've been in the most obscure parts of town, gone into small bars for a snack or to use the "ladies," and even at random, whatever I order is usually among the best I've ever had. Because everyone in Montreal likes to eat and hang out at night, bars and cafes are really packed from nine to midnight; prices are kept low and tourist rip-offs rare. Also, standards everywhere are high, thanks to the discriminating tastes of the locals. My favorite places to stay are: L'Auberge Les Passant de San Souci (Inn of the Gentle Passersby) in Old Montreal on Francis Xavier, and Hotel Nelligan, a cool, boutique hotel that's really fun, sleek, and sexy, also in Old Montreal. Uptown, near the shopping and the bustle of St. Denis and St. Laurent, I stay at Hotel Delta Montreal on President Kennedy. Ask for a club room which comes with appetizers at cocktail hour and breakfast in the morning served right outside your room.

coffee

Every trip I make to Montreal includes a trip to see my friend Adamo who owns Capitol Grocery in the Jean-Talon, a huge indoor and outdoor market near the Italian section of Montreal, located off upper St. Laurent. I pack lightly for my trips to Montreal so that I can save room in my trunk for more groceries! Again, because of the current exchange rate, the Italian specialty groceries are a bargain. My shopping bags get stuffed with San
Marzano tomatoes, evoo (extra virgin olive oil), pastas, taralli biscuits, cookies, cheeses, sausages, olives, bottles and tins of anchovies, Italian sodas, on and on. Tell Adamo that you need to cross the border and he will properly wrap your items so they can pass inspection. Go into the open part of the market at Jean-Talon to sample many locally grown fruits and vegetables. Also, look for a large bread shop and bakery here, the smell of which will drive you crazy until you track it
down. After shopping, I wanted a cappuccino, so I went to check out a Faema store, famous for making espresso machines, but at this location, also sells coffees by the cup. My cappuccino was served in a fine china cup, with a design of cocoa powder in the shape of a flower on top of my perfect froth. It went down fast and smooth. After many decades of perfecting coffee-brewing appliances, it is no surprise that these guys at Faema are master baristas, too.

● **Faema, 14 Jean Talon West, Montreal, Quebec, Canada, (514) 276-2671**

❝ Tell Adamo that you need to cross the border and he will properly wrap your items so they can pass inspection. ❞

breakfast

Let's give it up and let these guys own the rights to the breads we know as bagels. Voted Best Bagels in Montreal year after year, I think they are the best ever, anywhere. They are covered in poppy or sesame seeds that get toasted in the wood-burning oven where their flavors and nutty qualities really develop. When these bagels are hot, just out of the oven, well, I could eat a dozen, so I only buy two at a time to limit myself. They are almost crisp outside with a firm, but not overly chewy texture inside. They freeze well, but nothing is the same as that first hot bite! Two bagels will cost you less than a buck. The shop is easy to find. Go up St. Laurent, turn left on St. Viateur, and it will be on your right.

● **St. Viateur Bagels, 263 St. Viateur Street, Montreal, Quebec, Canada, (514) 276-8044**

lunch

❝ The placemats at each table setting are rimmed with a saying: everything is better with 'wodka.' ❞

There are several blocks in Old Montreal that I haunt when I am in town. I go shopping at Ambre boutique for unusual women's wear, dresses and coats, and I always make a stop at my favorite exotic imports shop, Meli Melo, owned by my beautiful friend Elise, to check out jewelry and home accessories from far-off places. Just across the way from these shops is a Polish restaurant called Stash Café. I discovered Stash years ago when I saw one of the ladies from Ambre run-

ning across the street, back into the shop, with a hot, steaming plate of pierogies and stuffed cabbage on a fine plate, silver in hand. I followed the food in and a few minutes later (and a lovely parka that I purchased at Ambre later) I discovered Stash for myself. A lovely woman named Ewa owns this café and the atmosphere has as much to offer as the rich plates of true Polish cuisine. From the low ceilings of this ancient stone structure hang modern posters by talented Polish artists. The lampshades are cloaked in bold, rich fabrics. You sit in old church pews or on wooden chairs in a dining room that is permanently in twilight, even at midday. It is soothing to be here. At night, you might happen upon a violin and piano performance. It will inevitably either move you to tears or to vodka, whichever comes first. The placemats at each table setting are rimmed with a saying: everything is better with "wodka." At lunch, I thought it too early to take the advice literally. I had a meat-stuffed pepper that was slightly salty and sweet at the same time. The food here is comforting, like a hug from the inside out. Ewa should charge extra for that.

● **Stash Café, 200 St. Paul West, Montreal, Quebec, Canada, (514) 845-6611**

dinner

I found this bistro because of it's location. I had to try it, as it is just off the coin de la Rue Rachel (the corner of Rachel Street) on the boulevard St. Denis. My namesake brought me good fortune, bon champs. Le Continental is too cool. The bistro is Casablanca-like in its decor with art-deco lighting and huge antique maps on the walls. The menu is simple bistro fare, featuring duck, lamb, chicken, horse steak (big with the French), and pasta. I've had the pasta carbonara here, a dish I never order in a restaurant because while simple (pancetta, eggs, and pasta), it is often made incorrectly with cream and vegetables, and all sorts of weird stuff going on. At this place, it's right on the money. The egg yolk is served in the shell that sits on top of the steaming hot pasta, cheese, and bacon; you toss it yourself at the table! On the show I had an incredibly tender, ginger and honey chicken that was seasoned with fresh thyme, making it fragrant and delectable. (see recipe on next page) So simple and well prepared, it has become a new favorite. The bistro is always busy so make a reservation. And remember, nothing really gets going here until late, so plan for supper at nine or ten, just like Paris!

● **Continental Bistro, 4169 St. Denis Street, Montreal, Quebec, Canada, (514) 845-6842**

Ginger Honey Chicken

❝ Remember, nothing really gets going here until late, so plan for supper at nine or ten, just like Paris! ❞

recipe | SERVES 6 TO 8 | courtesy Continental Bistro | $40ADAY

APPT - SOUP/SAL - **ENTREE** - VEG/POT - DESSERT - BEV

Ginger and Honey Chicken

6 tablespoons olive oil

5 pounds boneless, skinless chicken breast, cut into strips

Salt and freshly ground black pepper

1 bok choy, julienned

1 small daikon radish, julienned

1/2 Chinese cabbage, julienned

2 carrots, julienned

2 tablespoons peeled and minced fresh ginger

1 teaspoon minced garlic

3 tablespoons honey

1 cup chicken stock

1 teaspoon cornstarch

2 tablespoons cold water

1/2 pound fried vermicelli egg noodles (recipe follows)

1/2 cup minced fresh cilantro leaves, for garnish

6 mint leaves, minced, for garnish

1/3 cup pickled ginger, for garnish

● Heat 2 tablespoons olive oil in a large heavy skillet over medium-high heat. Season chicken with salt and pepper. Work in batches to avoid overcrowding the pan. When oil is hot, add a few chicken strips and sauté until chicken is browned and just cooked through, 4 to 5 minutes, depending on the size of the strips. Remove chicken from the pan and set aside.
● Add 2 more tablespoons olive oil to the skillet and heat over medium-high heat. Add the julienned vegetables and cook until crisp-tender, 2 to 3 minutes.

Season with salt and pepper, to taste. Remove the vegetables from the pan and set aside.
● Add the remaining 2 tablespoons olive oil to the skillet, reduce the heat to medium, and add ginger and garlic. Cook, stirring constantly, until fragrant, 1 to 2 minutes. Add honey and chicken stock and let the sauce reduce slightly. Meanwhile, in a small bowl, whisk cornstarch with 2 tablespoons cold water until cornstarch has dissolved. Add the cornstarch slurry to the sauce and cook until sauce has thickened, 1 to 2 minutes.
● Return the chicken and vegetables to the skillet and cook until just heated through. To serve, arrange the fried noodles as a base on each plate. Spoon the chicken, vegetables, and sauce over the noodles. Garnish with cilantro, mint, and pickled ginger.

Fried Vermicelli Egg Noodles:

Vegetable oil, for frying

1/2 pound vermicelli egg noodles

● Fill a deep pot with 3-inches of the vegetable oil. Heat the oil to 360°F. Carefully place the vermicelli in the oil and fry until they turn golden brown. Be careful as the noodles with brown within a few seconds. Drain on a paper towel lined plate.

sweet

Creme Caramel

Everyone gets a nightcap in Montreal and I like to take one of two routes to scope out a good place. Some nights I'll stroll by Notre Dame (they've got one of those here, too) and duck into a jazz club down in Old Montreal. Other nights, I stay uptown and go over to St. Laurent where the younger set hangs out. Montreal is home to many colleges and McGill University, so the city maintains a youthful presence. There are a few bars that have been around forever. La Cabane is one of them. It has an enormous selection of port wines, an after-dinner favorite. Desserts are very good as well.

● **Bar Terrasse La Cabane, 3872 Boulevard St. Laurent, Montreal, Quebec, Canada, (514) 843-7283**

❝ There are a few bars that have been around forever. La Cabane is one of them. ❞

recipe	SERVES 6	courtesy Bar Terrasse La Cabane	$40ADAY

APPT - SOUP/SAL - ENTREE - VEG/POT - **DESSERT** - BEV

Crème Caramel

1 & 1/4 cups sugar
2 cups water
2 cups milk
1/2 lemon, zest grated
1/2 teaspoon pure vanilla extract
1 & 1/2 drops yellow food coloring
4 eggs

● In a large heavy saucepan, combine 3/4 cup sugar with 2 cups water and bring to a boil over high heat. Reduce the heat to medium and simmer, without stirring, until thick and amber in color. When caramelized, remove from the heat and pour evenly into 6 individual crème caramel cups or ramekins. Let caramel cool to room temperature.
● Preheat oven to 350°F. In a medium bowl, combine the remaining 1/2 cup sugar, the milk, lemon zest, vanilla, food coloring, and eggs, and mix very well. Pour this mixture into the cups or ramekins; fill each until nearly full.
● Place the crème caramel cups into a large baking dish. Make a water bath by pouring water into the dish so that it comes about halfway up the sides of the cups. Bake 45 minutes. Carefully remove from the water bath, let cool to room temperature, and then refrigerate until completely chilled before serving.

PORTLAND

I am a Northeastern girl so I am an easy-sell when it comes to states on this seaboard. I had a great time in Portland, especially because of LL Bean. I didn't buy any clothes or outdoor gear, but I went to their Outdoor Discovery School—Paddling Center at Wolfe's Farm, and had a kayaking lesson, which was a very good (and inexpensive) idea. Give yourself a day at camp and be a kid again. I had such a good time and since I live so close to Lake George, I am going to get myself the tiny red Ferrari-like kayak I sped around in while in Freeport. Go Bean-ers!

breakfast

This is a case of go wherever there's a line and the food will be just fine. The line was out the door at Becky's and the blueberry pancakes were the main attraction! It would un-American to go to Maine and not enjoy some Maine blueberries. You might as well have them surrounded by Becky's tasty cakes!

● Becky's Diner, 390 Commercial Street, Portland, ME 04101, (207) 773-7070

lunch

More long lines of locals was the tip-off that this might be the place to have some Maine lobster. When a food such as lobster is generally too pricey, go to its source, and you'll find prices somewhat lower. Save even more money by having that lobster for lunch, not dinner. Lastly, do not order an expensive lobster, at a place with white table-cloths and candles, but rather go to an elbows-on-the-table shack. This was one-helluva lobster roll at one helluva-price!

● **Harraseeket Lunch and Lobster, End of Main Street, South Freeport, ME, (207) 865-3535**

snack

Wine, olives, and cheese samples were being passed around as I entered this market, making me a customer forever. This place reminded me of the fun I had for many years working and buying for gourmet markets. Foods and raw ingredients here were selective, appealing, fairly priced, and collected from around the globe, carefully. The cheese selection was especially well thought out. Easy recipes and samples were available in every corner of the store and their baked

goods were of high quality; the brownies were not too sweet and crispy at the corners and on top, too.

● **Portland Greengrocer, 211 Commercial Street, Portland, ME, (207) 761-9232**

dinner

For some reason, I often find that organic and vegetarian restaurants have chef-owners who are way too serious and short on fun. Not here. Everyone is friendly, the décor funky,  the menu diverse and not strictly vegetarian nor wholly organic. My healthy, tasty, oven-baked quesadilla with crab, corn, and asparagus was really, really good. I had fun and loved the reasonable prices.

● **Pepperclub, 78 Middle Street, Portland, ME, (207) 772-0531**

When I was in grade school, fourth grade maybe, we took a field trip to Quincy Market in Boston. We also took a walk on the Freedom Trail and went on guided tours through many important buildings and meeting halls, all central to our American history, but, as nine or ten-year-olds, all we kids cared about was going to "the big mall" in Faneuil Hall and Quincy Marketplace. Our parents had given us spending money; some had as much as twenty-five dollars, which, twenty years ago, was a lot of buying power. We shopped and ate and shopped and ate and then, having worked up an appetite, we ate some more. In twenty years, not much has changed. In Boston, I began my day at Faneuil Hall.

breakfast

Carol Ann Bake Shop is in the middle of the food hall, which has everything from Middle Eastern food to pizza, bagels to smoothies—it's all here. At Carol Ann, we

Cranberry Muffin

worked with homemade cranberry muffins (New England being home to cranberry bogs), but they're not on the menu just now. Never mind you won't miss them, because there are so many other delicious options. Everything is really affordable, so if you have kids, plan a meal at this colorful marketplace.

● **Carol Ann Bake Shop, 200 Faneuil Hall Marketplace, Boston, MA, (617) 742-5502**

66 Everything is really affordable, so if you have kids, plan a meal at this colorful marketplace. 99

lunch

Clam Roll

Out in Revere, there's a place called Kelly's, whose beef sandwiches and seafood rolls are really famous. It's a blast-from-the-past, walk-up window, with terrific food. Truth be told, I probably wouldn't drive out of Boston just for a sandwich, but if you are driving by Revere, make the side trip. I have a behind-the-scenes story at Kelly's that is worthy of Hitchcock's film, The Birds. As I sat down by the ocean, with my Kelly's lunch sandwich and a soda, and just as I was about to take my first bite, a seagull as big as a pterodactyl swooped down like a stealth bomber. He punctured my roll and made off with my sandwich before I could blink. I SCREAMED, ran off, top speed—all of it caught on tape—crying for my mommy. Good stuff!

● **Kelly's Roast Beef, 410 Revere Beach Boulevard, Revere, MA, (781) 284-9129**

dinner

I have to say that Boston has one of the best Italian neighborhoods of any major city I've visited. The food is great at most places on Hanover Street, but Giacomo's is special. It is so hip! Physically, it's bright, white, clean, and unpretentious, with the menu on a chalk board on the wall. It's also tiny, which makes for long lines most nights. This is an elbows-on-the-table kind of place and the food is amazing! Have the calamari—so tender—fried with hot peppers. Yum! Pastas are homemade and dead-on authentic. I had a pumpkin tortellini that transported me to northern Italy on the spot. Mangia tutti a Giacomo's!

● **Giacomo's Ristorante, 355 Hanover Street, Boston, MA, (617) 523-9026**

---

recipe courtesy Giacomo's Ristorante $40ADAY

APPT - SOUP/SAL - ENTREE - VEG/POT - DESSERT - BEV

Pumpkin Tortellini
SERVES 4

2 tablespoons butter

Salt and freshly ground black pepper

2 tablespoons chopped fresh sage leaves

6 tablespoons mascarpone

1 cup heavy cream

1 bag pumpkin- or butternut-squash-filled ravioli or tortellini

1/4 cup or less grated Pecorino Romano cheese

● In sauté pan over low heat, melt butter with a pinch of pepper, the sage, and mascarpone. Add cream, reduce to a thick sauce, about 10 minutes.
● Meanwhile, cook pasta according to package directions. Drain and add to the sauce. Toss the pasta in the sauce over low heat until well coated. Add cheese and salt and pepper to taste.

drink

This is the kind of really cool bar that I thought, at age 35, perhaps I was too old to frequent any longer. Wrong! If you hang out in Grendel's Den during happy hour, you'll be mixing it up with plenty of college kids, but you'll also meet electricians, doctors, stock brokers—you might even make friends, as I did, with a Harvard lawyer. I had a nice cold beer. The food all looked great! Had I more money left, I would have tried the vegetable lasagna which looked especially delicious! Incidentally, The Den looked really familiar to me—was it in the movie Good Will Hunting? Regardless, it rocked!

● **Grendel's Den Restaurant & Bar, 89 Winthrop St., Cambridge, MA, (617) 491-1160**

CAPE COD

Ilived here when I was very small. I went to Mashpee Central School for kindergarten and for part of first grade. I remember being very disappointed in school food. My grandfather Emmanuel lived with us at the time, and we ate well. Garlic, olive oil, cheese, bread, meats, seafood, salami, eggplant, bitter greens, anchovies: these were the staples in our home. What the heck were Cheese Doodles and fish sticks? Yuck! We lived in a Yankee Barn. My room was in the hay loft. Only my mom and I could actually stand up straight in it—everyone else was just too tall. I hated wrinkles in my clothes, but otherwise I was very un-girl like. I did not want my mother to dress up my hair. I didn't care for dresses, except for the one with stick figure drawings all over it. I did love my easel, my Casual Observer book, and my erector sets which I kept in three tool boxes—red, blue, and yellow. Today, some 30 years later, I occasionally drive through the Cape with my mom. We go out to Martha's Vineyard and Nantucket as well. We are satisfied to stop along the way for fried fish and crab cakes at just about any place we happen to get "stomach-hungry" as mom calls it. I have yet to have expensive or bad seafood on The Cape. For this episode, we got pretty lucky, overall. I plan on returning to every one of our locations soon.

breakfast

The name of this little, out-of-the-way place is a double entendre. Jack is the owner and he is often "out back" either cooking or helping tend to other aspects of the business. Also, the restaurant itself is "out back," set in, off the main road. Jack is actually rather notorious in the area of Yarmouth Port. He is said to be cantankerous, demanding, and generally inhospitable. After having eaten there and after having been in the way of his regular, paying customers for several hours, I have to "out" Jack as being one helluva guy. He's kind, person-able, and worst of all, accommodating! Suck it up, Jack! You know

Stuffed French Toast

this is the truth: You're a nice guy! What a character Jack is! Edward Gorey, a local and a very famous artist agrees. Edward's art is lousy-over-the-joint, hang-ing everywhere. He happens to be one of my father's all-time favorites, so imme-diately upon spying his work, I'm biased for Jack. Lucky for me and my limited career, this Jack turned out to be legit: the food is better than good. I had the "stufed French toste" misspelled on the menu, on pourpose, for a laugh, I tink...which consisted of two thick-cut, grilled, egg-dipped slices of bread, filled with sweetened ricotta cheese, then topped with sliced peaches, berries, and bananas and served with syrup. A great breakfast spe-cial! For nice, cheap food, go find Jack. He's out back. One last heads-up: at Jack's, you'll take your own order, serve yourself and bus your own table. And yet, you will still be expected to tip, by contribut-ing to a big bucket marked "The Orphan's Fund" and if you try to skip-out, Jack will have no qualms about publicly humiliating you. All in fun.

● **Jack's Outback, 161 Main Street, Yarmouth Port, MA, (508) 362-6690**

❝ At Jack's, you'll take your own order, serve yourself and bus your own table. ❞

---

recipe adapted from Jack's Outback   **$40ADAY**

APPT - SOUP/SAL - ENTREE - VEG/POT - DESSERT - BEV

Stuffed French Toast

SERVES 5

1 (15-ounce) container ricotta cheese
1/4 cup sugar
1 orange, zested
1 lemon, zested
2 eggs
1/2 cup milk
3 tablespoons butter or margarine
10 slices white bread
Maple syrup, for serving

● Blend ricotta cheese, sugar, and orange and lemon zests in a medium mixing bowl. Cover and set aside. Beat eggs and milk in a wide, flat bowl.
● In a large saucepan or griddle, melt 1 tablespoon of the butter on medium heat. Dip each piece of bread into the egg mixture briefly on each side. Place in saucepan, in batches, and cook until browned on each side, adding more butter, as nec-essary. Spoon about 2 to 4 tablespoons of the ricot-ta mixture onto each of 5 pieces of French toast and spread. Place remaining 5 pieces of toast on top of mixture. Serve with maple syrup.

lunch

The name of this place is Captain Parker's Pub, but I like the pirate-like sound of "Capt'n." Actually, this place is very un-Capt'n like. There are no fake pirates, no boats in a bottle. There is, however, a lot of golf-related memorabilia, including a large collection of patches, as I recall. Also conspicuous are many trophies, plaques, and photos of chowder competitions. Captain Parker's chef, Jim Gardnier, makes his award-winning clam chowder with fresh thyme, root veggies, stock, milk, fresh clams, and his own special, New England mojo. A little hot sauce

and a few oyster crackers, and you've got yourself a bowlful of Cape Cod's creamiest claim to fame. (see recipe on opposite page) The restaurant is in West Yarmouth on Route 28. Next time you're driving through the Cape, stop off at the Capt'n P's Pub.

● **Captain Parker's Pub, 668 Route 28, West Yarmouth, MA, (508) 771-4266**

Captain Parker's Chowder

2 ounces salt pork, cut into 2-inch chunks

2 cups (4 sticks) unsalted butter, softened

1 & 1/2 cups all-purpose flour

4 cups chopped onion

1 & 1/2 cups chopped celery

1 pinch dried thyme

1 teaspoon celery seed

1 bay leaf

1 quart water

3 large russet potatoes, peeled and diced

6 ounces clam base, such as Minors

1 quart chopped fresh clams and their juice

1 quart light cream

1 teaspoon salt

1 teaspoon freshly ground black pepper

● Put salt pork on a microwave-safe plate and wrap in plastic. Cook in microwave 2 & 1/2 minutes.

● Meanwhile, make a roux: Melt 1 & 1/2 cups (3 sticks) of the butter in a large skillet over low heat. Once the butter is melted, stir in the flour. Cook until the mixture bubbles and resembles pancake batter. Do not allow the roux to brown at all. Remove from the heat and keep warm.

● In a heavy-bottomed pot over medium heat, place the remaining stick butter and the salt pork. When salt pork is lightly browned, remove from pan; discard. Add onion, celery, thyme, celery seed, and bay leaf and sauté for about 5 minutes. Add water and potatoes and bring it to a boil. Stir in clam base; keep stirring so the base and potatoes don't stick or burn to the bottom of the pot. Add clams and their juice and bring to a gentle simmer. When the potatoes become slightly tender, about 15 minutes, bring everything back to a boil and start adding the hot roux. Turn the flame down a little and let simmer for about 5 minutes. Slowly add cream until you get a creamy chowder, not too thick or thin. Season with salt and pepper, to taste.

Linguini Puttanesca

Linguini Puttanesca

1/4 cup extra-virgin olive oil

1 teaspoon minced shallots

1 teaspoon minced garlic

1/2 teaspoon dried oregano

1/2 teaspoon dried basil

3 anchovy fillets, chopped medium

1/2 cup large capers, rinsed

1 cup pitted gaeta or kalamata olives

1/2 cup dry white wine

1/4 cup fresh clam juice

2 cups diced plum tomatoes

2 cups homemade or store-bought marinara sauce

Salt and freshly ground black pepper

1 & 1/2 pounds fresh linguini

Chopped fresh flat-leaf parsley leaves, for garnish

● In a sauté pan over medium heat, place olive oil, shallots, garlic, oregano, basil, and anchovy fillets. Sauté until anchovies begin to break down and begin to melt, about 30 seconds. Add capers and olives and sauté 1 minute. Add white wine and stir to scrape up browned bits on the bottom of the pan. Add clam juice, bring to a simmer and cook until reduced by 1/3. Add plum tomatoes and thoroughly incorporate. Add marinara sauce and simmer on low heat for 5 minutes. Season, to taste, with salt and pepper.

● In a separate pot, cook linguini in boiling salted water to al dente, 4 to 5 minutes; stir so there is no clumping.

● Add cooked pasta to puttanesca sauce and toss. Garnish with parsley.

❝ I am rocked and blown away by the delicious, truly traditional puttanesca prepared here. ❞

dinner

The name of this restaurant conjured up visions of blues and barbecue, two things I had a hard time picturing on the Cape. Luckily, once again, I had the wrong idea. Phew! I love Hyannis. My family had a restaurant here when I was small. Aside from personal nostalgia, the quality of food and entertainment at The Road House Cafe now rates among my reasons to return to this town. There are a few dishes I rarely order in a restaurant because I like them prepared a certain way, my way. Now "my way" when it comes to the preparation of pasta dishes is not "mine" at all, it's the family way. Carbonara, marinara, and puttanesca are classic Italian sauces made with traditional ingredients, but each family has little rules when it comes to the preparation and execution of a dish, even a classic. I pride myself on not being a food snob in any way, except when it comes to classic Italian cooking. I am a traditionalist. And what happens? I am rocked and blown away by the delicious, truly traditional puttanesca prepared here: evoo, anchovies, black oil-cured olives, capers, tomatoes, and flat-leaf parsley combined with al dente pasta, cooked to hot and starchy perfection. (see recipe on opposite page) After my last bite, I had a moment of complete happiness. The food was way more than enough of a reward, but then the music started. A fantastic jazz band messed up the joint and had this road house swingin'! Bring your dancing shoes and a big appetite 'cause this Road House is outta sight!

The Roadhouse Cafe • Food & Drink

● **The Roadhouse Cafe, 488 South Street, Hyannis, MA, (508) 775-2386**

❝ After my last bite, I had a moment of complete happiness. ❞

drink

When we went to shoot in Provincetown, I realized that I hadn't been there for about 30 years! Though I've traveled back to The Cape throughout my adult life, I really never made a point to go back to P'town. It's very quaint and cute. Off season, when we rolled into town, the streets were eerily quiet. We wandered around and I window shopped. At sunset, we went into Mews for

Cape Codder

a cocktail and their bar proved to be one of the best I've ever been to. Lined with dark wood, brass, and mirrors, the bar boasts a collection of vodkas that spans the globe. They have over 100 different kinds, derived from anything you can think of, including cow's milk. And the bottles come in unusual shapes, from rifles to musical instruments. I had a Cape Codder cocktail made with a Nantucket corn vodka. It was really good.

● **Mews Restaurant & Café, 429 Commercial Street, Provincetown, MA, (508) 487-1500**

Most viewers were skeptical about $40 a Day being able to make budget in The Big Apple. I was confident, but I also knew it would be challenging because there are so many options. New York is a patch-work of many villages, each with its own specialties; ethnic foods from the four corners of the planet are all here. While the choices are limitless, so are the prices. Whether you spend a dollar or several hundred, you can find great food here 24/7, if you know where to look for it. At Thalia, for example, a favorite of mine in the theater district, you can have great oysters, hoisin chicken skewers, excellent frittatas, and a sirloin burger with applewood bacon, cheese, and herb fries, plus a mesculin salad, all at reasonable prices. At Saturday or Sunday brunch, you get a free drink—a mimosa, bloody Mary or other choice. When you go, tell Patrick the chef, Ryan at the bar, and Avi at the door that Rachael sent you and her love.

breakfast

Breakfast Bruschetta

The Noho Star is my go-to place for friends, family, or me and my boyfriend because it is has a great menu of American and Chinese eats, and it's open until midnight most nights. Late night, I have chicken lettuce wraps. For breakfast, everything is good. I let the Chef Bill Rodgers decide which dish to film: breakfast bruschetta won. (see recipe on opposite page) Yeah for me and my stomach, too! This farmhouse-style bread with scrambled eggs, tomato, pesto, and goat cheese crumbles is outrageously delicious!

● The Noho Star, 330 Lafayette Street, New York, NY, (212) 925-0070

recipe SERVES 4 · courtesy The Noho Star · $40ADAY

APPT - SOUP/SAL - **ENTREE** - VEG/POT - DESSERT - BEV

Breakfast Bruschetta

8 slices Tuscan-style bread

12 eggs

1/4 cup water

1/4 tablespoon hot red pepper sauce

1 teaspoon kosher salt

2 tablespoons sweet butter

5 & 1/2 ounces Montrachet goat cheese, softened

1 & 1/2 ounces marinated sun-dried tomatoes, julienned

Basil Pesto (recipe follows)

Fresh basil leaves, for garnish

● Toast the bread and keep warm while preparing the eggs. Combine the eggs, water, hot sauce, and salt in a bowl and whisk until smooth. In a large non-stick omelet pan set over medium heat, melt the butter and add the egg mixture, stirring with a spatula until the eggs are gently scrambled. Spread goat cheese equally over the slices of toast. Top cheese with scrambled eggs. Cut each piece of toast in half. Place 4 halves on each plate and top with sun-dried tomatoes. Drizzle with basil pesto and garnish with fresh basil leaves.

Basil Pesto:

3/4 cup chopped fresh basil leaves

3/4 cup grated Parmigiano-Reggiano

1/4 cup pine nuts

2 cloves garlic, chopped

1/4 teaspoon kosher salt

1 turn fresh black pepper

2 teaspoons lemon juice

1 cup olive oil

● In a blender, combine all of the ingredients, except for the olive oil. Process until smooth. With the blender running, slowly drizzle in the olive oil and process until combined.

> **He used a selection of vegetables from the beautiful Union Square Green Market to prepare a special treat for me: a Bombay-style vegetable Frankie (or wrap).**

lunch

Vegetable Frankie

One of my favorite tips is to try expensive, upscale restaurants for lunch or for appetizers and drinks, rather than for dinner. Tabla is one of New York restauranteur Danny Meyer's places, and considering the New York restaurant scene, Tabla and her sister restaurants are reasonably priced. However, with just $40 a day to spend, the Meyer Group seemed at first well out of the ball park. Then I heard about a new lunch menu at Tabla, featuring more than 10 items for under $10 each. I tripped over myself racing to check it out! Chef Floyd Cardoz made my lunch for this episode. He used a selection of vegetables from the beautiful Union Square Green Market to prepare a special treat for me: a Bombay-style vegetable Frankie (or wrap). The flat bread he used was made at the bread bar. Chef Floyd then coated the bread in beaten egg. Once the egg was cooked, the wrap was filled with chutney and roasted vegetables mixed with toasted spices. Floyd told me his still vivid memories of riding his bike through the streets of Bombay as a kid, steering with one hand, holding on to his Vegetable Frankie with the other. (see recipe on opposite page)

● **Bread Bar at Tabla, 11 Madison Avenue, New York, NY, (212) 889-0667**
● **The Greenmarket at Union Square, Broadway at 14th Street, New York, NY, (212) 477-3220**

Vegetable Frankie

Vegetables:

1/2 cup yellow squash, quartered lengthwise and cut into 1/4-inch thick dice

1/2 cup zucchini, quartered lengthwise and cut into 1/4-inch thick dice

3 tablespoons canola oil

Salt and freshly ground black pepper

1 teaspoon ground cumin

1 large onion, peeled and sliced thin

1 tablespoon minced fresh garlic

1 (1-inch) piece fresh ginger, peeled and minced

1/2 teaspoon turmeric

1/2 cup English peas, shelled and blanched in salted water

1/2 cup sugar snap peas, blanched in salted water

1/2 cup (1-inch pieces) haricots verts, blanched in salted water

Frankie:

2 eggs

1 tablespoon chopped cilantro leaves

1/4 cup canola oil

4 (12-inch) whole wheat flour tortillas

Salt and freshly ground black pepper

Chaat masala (an Indian spice blend, available at gourmet markets or spice shops)

Fresh mint sprigs

Fresh cilantro sprigs

1 fresh chile pepper, sliced thin

Chutney

1 red onion, sliced thin, for garnish

● Prepare the vegetables: Preheat oven to 350°F. Toss yellow squash and zucchini with 1 tablespoon oil and salt and pepper, to taste. Place on a cookie sheet or roasting pan. Roast until tender, 10 to 15 minutes.

● In a large sauté pan, place the remaining 2 tablespoons canola oil and heat over medium heat for 2 minutes. Add cumin and cook for 2 more minutes. Add onions and continue to cook until lightly caramelized, about 5 minutes. Add garlic, ginger, and turmeric and cook for 3 more minutes. Season well with salt and pepper and let cool. Combine the onion mixture with the peas and beans and mix well. Keep warm until ready to use.

● Make the Frankie: Beat eggs in a bowl and mix in cilantro. In a large sauté pan, heat a very small amount of oil. Add a tortilla and a quarter of the beaten eggs. Lift tortilla up so that the eggs run underneath the tortilla. Once the eggs on that side are cooked (1 minute), flip the tortilla and cook the eggs on the other side. Remove the tortilla from the pan and place on an individual plate. Repeat with the remaining tortillas and eggs.

● Place some vegetables on top of each tortilla and season with salt, pepper, and chaat masala, to taste. Place a few sprigs of mint and cilantro on top of the vegetables. Add a few slices of chile and top with chutney. Roll and slice in half. Serve with sliced red onions.

sweet

I first read about this remarkable place in the City section of the *New York Times*. It was a piece on the effects of 9/11 on a young entrepreneur who was to open his tiny ice cream shop in late summer 2001 in an old ferryboat ticket shack just under the Brooklyn Bridge. His plans were postponed, but he did in fact open shortly thereafter, and today, Mark Thompson's small ice cream business is booming! To get there, I like to walk over the Brooklyn Bridge from Manhattan and reward myself at the other side with a scoop of the purest vanilla ice cream on earth. *The Times* called Mark the ice cream sommelier because he knows his ice cream so well. Mark uses just a few tablespoons of sugar in each 5-gallon batch

of his 10 pure flavors because he likes the natural sweetness of the cream to shine through. Many fine dining rooms and restaurants have asked to buy wholesale from him, yet Mark turns them down. He prefers to keep his batches small, just 5 gallons of each flavor on hand at a time. Oh, one last thing, I didn't have the time to mention on the show—Mark keeps a killer collection of vinyl records next to his old stereo right in the middle of the shop, so you can spin a disc of choice and let your ears and mouth take in some tasty licks at the same time!

● **Brooklyn Ice Cream Factory, Fulton Ferry Landing Pier, Brooklyn, NY, (718) 246-3963**

❝ When the live musicians take a break, Mahar plays selections from his vast collection of jazz recordings, some very rare. ❞

CLEOPATRA'S NEEDLE

MEDITERRANEAN CUISINE
LIVE JAZZ

2485 BROADWAY AT 92ND ST.
NYC 10025
www.cleopatrasneedleny.com
(212) 769-6969

dinner

I love jazz. So does Mahar Hussain, owner of Cleopatra's Needle. This is the kind of neighborhood joint you can find only by word of mouth. My friends Cal and Hiroko Kiiffner invited me to join them and it was quite a find! Mahar is a very kind man and the regulars who play here are fantastic! In our episode, Eric Lewis, the jazz pianist and Monk Prize recipient performed for us. They were cool! When the live musicians take a break, Mahar plays selections from his vast collection of jazz recordings, some very rare. There is no cover charge and as if this weren't

enough, Mahar is a wonderful cook whose menu is built largely around his Egyptian grandmother's recipes. I love the mixed Mediterranean platter with hummus, baba ganoush, and grape leaves. Also, the moussaka, both with and without meat, is terrific. Mahar makes a mean béchamel sauce! On the show, I believe I had the vegetarian moussaka with eggplant, chickpeas, greens, and tomatoes.

● **Cleopatra's Needle, 2485 Broadway, New York, NY, (212) 769-6969**

65

Hey, Rocky! I followed in your foot steps. For this episode, I went to a boxing gym and worked out on a heavy bag. I then recreated one of the greatest scenes in movie history by running up "the steps" and at the top, I jumped up and down on Rocky Balboa's sneaker foot prints. My camera man and the director made the run with me and we were all devastated that none of this made it to air; the network had concerns about my being seen in my workout gear. (They got over that, though. You see me in much less in Hawaii). Anyhow, now you know: I love to box, I love Rocky, and I am fit enough, despite all my dining out, to run up the museum steps in Philly. Yo, Adrian!

breakfast

I started my day at the Reading (pronounced red-ing) Market. It's huge and wonderful, especially if you're like me and love wandering in and around food for hours. Unlike some markets, this one also has many terrific sit-down restaurants. If you're an old fan of The Food Network from back in the day, perhaps you'll remember Jack McDavid, the owner of the Down Home Diner who shot many episodes with Bobby Flay. For our show, Jack cooked me up a wonderful plate of corn cakes (called Johnny Cakes in my family) and some homemade turkey sausage patties with maple syrup. Everything was down-home good!

● **Down Home Diner, Reading Terminal Market, 12th & Filbert Streets, Philadelphia, PA, (215) 627-1955**

❝ Everything was down-home good! ❞

recipe	courtesy Down Home Diner	$40ADAY

APPT - SOUP/SAL - **ENTREE** - VEG/POT - DESSERT - BEV

Corn Cakes
MAKES 10 CAKES

Corn Cakes

1 cup fine-ground yellow cornmeal
1 cup self-rising flour
4 tablespoons sugar
2 eggs
2 cups buttermilk
3 ounces (6 tablespoons) corn oil
2 cups fresh corn kernels

● Heat a griddle or large non-stick skillet over medium-high heat.
● Place cornmeal, flour, and sugar in a large bowl and mix together. In a separate bowl, combine eggs, buttermilk, oil, and corn and stir until blended. Fold liquid ingredients into dry, gently stirring just until incorporated; do not over-mix.
● Spray the griddle with cooking spray. Ladle 4 ounces (1/2 cup) of corn mixture onto the hot griddle. Cook over medium heat for 3 to 4 minutes on each side or until cooked through. Repeat until no batter remains. Serve immediately.

lunch

I will not be popular for saying this, but I truly believe
that with such heated competition in the Philly cheesesteak market, the handful of
places "famous" for their steaks are all very, very good. Make your way around
town and taste for yourself. For our taping, we chose to eat at Jim's, where I had
a warm, juicy steak sandwich with onions and provolone. I do not care for that
hot, yellow, artificially flavored and colored "cheesefood" sauce that is said to be
the authentic topping of choice. For me, with provolone and onions and a quick
dip of the roll in au jus, a Philly cheesesteak can be a beautiful thing.

● **Jim's Steaks, 400 South Street, Philadelphia, PA, (215) 928-1911**

sweet

Barry Shane takes his candy very seriously. I went to his shop to buy some candies
for souvenirs. Barry and his family have a long history as consummate producers of
fine confectionaries. After talking with Barry, I became fully aware that while
sweets are sweet for consumers, for producers they are hard work, more a science
than an art. I have a full appreciation now of the work and care that
goes into each delicious bon bon that I simply pop into my mouth.

Vanilla Butter Cream

● **Shane Candies, 110 Market Street, Philadelphia, PA, (215) 922-1048**

dinner

Villa di Roma is a nice family
place in South Philly, in the heart
of the old Italian neighborhood.
Their recipes go back generations
as do the members of the kitchen
and dining room staff. The food is
old-school and the atmosphere,
elbows-on-the-table comfortable.
I had Chicken Sicilian with hot
and sweet peppers. My mom, who
is Sicilian, would have liked it very
much, too.

● **Villa di Roma Restaurant, 936
South 9th Street, Philadelphia,
PA, (215) 592-1295**

recipe *courtesy of Villa di Roma* $40ADAY

APPT - SOUP/SAL - **ENTREE** - VEG/POT - DESSERT - BEV

Chicken Sicilian

SERVES 4

4 (8-ounce) boneless chicken breasts
Olive oil, for sautéing
1 cup chopped onion
4 cherry peppers, seeded and sliced
16 mushrooms, chopped
3 cups black oil-cured olives and capers
Dash paprika
3 to 4 ounces butter (6 to 8 tablespoons)

● Cut chicken into 1-inch pieces. Heat a sauté pan
over medium-high heat. Add enough oil to lightly
coat the bottom of the pan. Add chicken and brown
on all sides. Add onion and cherry peppers. Drain
off any excess oil. Add mushrooms, olives and
capers, paprika, and butter. Continue to cook over
medium-high heat until the butter is completely
melted, mixing to keep the butter from separating.

WASHINGTON, D.C.

I think every American should pay a visit to our nation's capital. Regardless of how you voted in the last election, you will be moved by the sight of the White House and the Capitol, and the surrounding monuments, especially on a first visit. This is clearly a serious place. After you're done touring, however, you'll discover that in and around the District, the scene can be lively and diverse.

Teaism Chai

breakfast

This place is a much needed refuge in a very pressured town. You come to Teaism to mellow out. Here you can sip teas ranging from delicate to daring and enjoy wonderful organic foods, from bento boxes to stir-fry to ginger scones. (see recipe on opposite page) Put a little Zen in your cup and check it out.

● Teaism, 2009 R Street NW, Washington, DC, (202) 667-3827

Teaism Ginger Scones

1 cup all-purpose flour

1 cup cake flour

1 tablespoon sugar

1/2 teaspoon dried ginger

1/2 teaspoon salt

1/2 teaspoon baking soda

1 teaspoon cream of tartar

4 tablespoons unsalted butter, cut in pea size cubes

2 ounces chopped, crystallized or candied ginger

3/4 cup milk

1 egg yolk, beaten with 1 teaspoon cold water to make an egg wash

Sugar, for sprinkling

● Preheat the oven to 450 °F.

● You can mix by hand or with a food processor or mixer, but be careful not to over-mix the dry ingredients. If you over-mix, your scones will be tough and chewy. Put the 7 dry ingredients in a bowl and add the cubes of butter. With your fingers, or with 2 knives, blend the butter into the dry ingredients until it resembles course corn-meal (some large pieces of butter should remain, as this will make your scones light and fluffy). If you are using a food processor, pulse briefly. Stir in the ginger pieces. Add the milk and incorporate quickly with a fork. The dough should be soft and lightly moist; do not over-mix. Turn the dough out onto a floured work surface and gently pat down until it stands about 1/2-inch thick. Cut into 8 triangles with a dough cutter or a knife and arrange on an ungreased baking sheet. Brush the tops of the scones with the egg wash and sprinkle with some sugar. Bake for 10 minutes or until golden. Let cool briefly before serving.

lunch

The menu cover has a cartoon of a donkey and an elephant dining together, and in looking around this joint at lunch time, that's an accurate rendering of the clientele. This place is crawling with G-men and suits (women, too)! The food is very good and the atmosphere non-partisan: all are welcome here. I had a steak. Red meat seemed appropriate. The steak was tender and the summer veggie ragout, farm fresh. Prices were tasty, too.

● **Clyde's of Georgetown, 3236 M Street NW, Washington, DC, (202) 333-9180**

❝ **This place is crawling with G-men and suits (women, too)!** ❞

recipe	SERVES 1	courtesy Clyde's of Georgetown	$40ADAY

APPT - SOUP/SAL - **ENTREE** - VEG/POT - DESSERT - BEV

Grilled Sirloin Steak with Summer Vegetable Ragout and Steak Fries

Tomato Mushroom Sauce:

1 tablespoon olive oil

1 tablespoon chopped garlic

1 tablespoon chopped shallots

1/2 cup corn kernels

2 blue foot mushrooms, white mushrooms or shiitake mushrooms, sliced

1 cup demi-glace

6 sun gold tomatoes, halved, or any yellow cherry tomato

6 sweet 100's tomatoes, halved

1 tablespoon butter

Salt and pepper

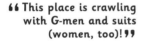

Sirloin Veggies and Fries

Tom's Steak Fries:

1 Idaho potato

Vegetable oil, for frying

8 ounces grilled sirloin steak

1 cup raw baby spinach, cleaned

1 red onion, julienned

A1 Ranch Dressing (recipe follows)

● Tomato mushroom sauce: Heat olive oil in a saucepan over medium heat. Add garlic and shallots and sauté until tender, about 4 minutes. Add the corn, mushrooms, and demi-glace and bring to a simmer. Reduce by 1/4. Add tomatoes and remove from heat. Swirl in butter and season with salt and pepper, to taste.

● Tom's Steak Fries: Place potato in salted, cold water and bring to a boil. Reduce heat and simmer for approximately 20 minutes. Drain and cool potato. Meanwhile, fill a large heavy pot halfway full with oil and heat oil to 350°F. Cut potato into quarters and fry until golden brown. Remove from oil, drain on paper towels, and sprinkle with salt and pepper.

● To assemble dish: Place grilled steak in the center of the plate. Spoon tomato-mushroom sauce over steak. Top with spinach and onion and drizzle with A1 dressing.

A1 Ranch Dressing:

1 cup ranch dressing

1/4 cup steak sauce (recommended: A1)

2 tablespoons whole-grain mustard

Salt and pepper

● Combine all ingredients in a small bowl. Season with salt and pepper, to taste.

dinner

Ole! What fun! This joint jumps! Here you can enjoy flamenco music and dancers, a hopping bar scene, and terrific tapas all in the same place! What's great about tapas (the little appetizer-size dishes of Spain) is that you can mix and match small portions of many dishes to match your taste and budget. The calamari was especially tender.

● **Jaleo, 480 7th Street NW, Washington, DC (202) 628-7949**

Calamari

recipe	SERVES 4	courtesy Jaleo	$40ADAY

APPT - SOUP/SAL - ENTREE - VEG/POT - DESSERT - BEV

Endives with Oranges Almonds & Goat Cheese

1 bunch endive leaves, cored and cleaned

8 tablespoons orange segments

4 tablespoons sliced almonds, toasted

8 ounces Spanish goat cheese

2 tablespoons chopped chives

Salt

4 tablespoons Vinagreta de Ajo Tostado (recipe follows)

● Set endive leaves on a plate. Arrange oranges, almonds, and cheese around plate. Sprinkle with chives and salt. Drizzle with Vinagreta de Ajo Tostado and serve.

Vinagreta de Ajo Tostado:

1/4 cup garlic cloves, peeled

1/4 cup extra-virgin olive oil, plus 1/2 cup

2 tablespoons sherry vinegar

1 tablespoon chopped shallots

Salt and freshly ground black pepper

● Preheat the oven to 350°F.
● Place garlic and 1/4 cup olive oil in a small baking dish and roast until garlic is very tender, about 20 minutes. Allow to cool slightly. Transfer to a blender. Add sherry vinegar, shallots, salt, and freshly ground pepper. Blend until smooth. Gradually add remaining 1/2 cup olive oil through the feed tube while blender is running.

Endives

sweet

This place has an awesome view of the Washington Monument from the terrace. On the show they gave me a banana flambé, an item normally served indoors, away from the wind. In short: come here for the view, just order something else.

● **Sky Terrace at Hotel Washington, 515 15th Street NW, Washington, DC, (202) 638-5900**

south

ATLANTA
CHARLESTON
SAVANNAH
ORLANDO
MIAMI
FLORIDA KEYS
NASHVILLE
MEMPHIS
NEW ORLEANS
DALLAS
AUSTIN
CORPUS CHRISTI

ATLANTA

I had a blast here! It was hot (like 100°F or so) and the state bird (the mosquito) had its way with my flesh, and still, I had a great time. Shopping is fantastic. The neighborhoods are diverse, colorful, and easy to navigate. There are tons of young people here, giving the city great energy and keeping the food prices fair because that's what a young market demands.

breakfast

The biscuits here are 4 inches thick and so light you really believe they could fly. The restaurant is funky, covered in brightly colored murals of crazy gardens, and the food, affordable and fun to eat. I had fried green tomatoes (see recipe on opposite page) and some biscuits, of course. The tomatoes were spicy and had a rocking cashew salsa on them. The Flying Biscuit rules!

Fried Green Tomatoes

● **The Flying Biscuit Cafe, 1655 Maclendon Avenue, Atlanta, GA, (404) 687-8888**

❝ The biscuits here are 4 inches thick and so light you really believe they could fly. ❞

Lunch at the Horseradish Grill

Fried Green Tomatoes

6 cups canola oil

4 medium green tomatoes

3 cups all-purpose flour

2 & 1/2 cups milk

2 large eggs

1/2 cup cornmeal

1 tablespoon kosher salt

1 tablespoon celery salt

1 & 1/2 teaspoons cayenne pepper

1 tablespoon freshly ground black pepper

1 teaspoon onion powder

Pinch paprika

2 cups The Flying Biscuit Cashew Relish (recipe follows)

4 ounces goat cheese

● Heat oil in a large pot to 350°F.

● Meanwhile, prepare the dipping process for the tomatoes: You will need a slotted spoon to drop the tomatoes into the hot oil. Core tomatoes and slice the ends off. Slice tomatoes 1/2-inch thick and set aside in a medium bowl. In a small bowl, set aside 1 & 1/2 cups all-purpose flour. In a medium bowl, mix milk and eggs.

● Make the cornmeal breading: In a large bowl, combine remaining 1 & 1/2 cups flour, cornmeal, and salt. Add celery salt, cayenne pepper, black pepper, onion powder, and paprika.

● Line a sheet pan with parchment paper. Line up the reserved 1 & 1/2 cups all-purpose flour, egg wash, and breading in a

row. Dredge tomatoes one by one in flour, then the egg wash, and finally the cornmeal breading mixture, placing dredged tomatoes on prepared sheet pan. Repeat this process until all the tomatoes are breaded. Fry tomatoes in batches until golden brown. They will float to the top when finished cooking. Drain on paper towels. Garnish with cashew relish and finish with a dollop of goat cheese.

The Flying Biscuit Cashew Relish

1 & 1/2 cups cashews

2 large red jalapenos, stemmed and roughly chopped

1/3 cup fresh cilantro leaves

3/4 cup honey

1/3 cup white vinegar

● Combine cashews, jalapenos, and cilantro in a food processor and pulse until combined. Do not puree; it should be a rustic mix. Pour mixture into a bowl; add honey and vinegar and mix thoroughly.

75

lunch

The Horseradish Grill is a classy, gorgeous-looking restaurant in a huge renovated barn. The food was fantastic. At lunch the menu offered many Blue Plate Specials for just $10. I had the pan-fried chicken and my choice of several side dishes; the green beans were my favorite. The chicken was so good, it must have been cooked in lard, but I have a "don't ask, don't tell" policy about my food! I remember thinking, while licking my fingers, that if I were to live in this area, I would come here for lunch three times a week and probably weigh an extra fifty pounds. And it might be worth every ounce!

● The Horseradish Grill, 4320 Powers Ferry Rd, Atlanta, GA, (404) 255-7277

❝ I remember thinking, while licking my fingers, that if I were to live in this area, I would come here for lunch three times a week and probably weigh an extra fifty pounds. ❞

recipe	SERVES 6	courtesy The Horseradish Grill	$40ADAY

APPT - SOUP/SAL - **ENTREE** - VEG/POT - DESSERT - BEV

Southern Pan-Fried Chicken

3 pounds bone-in chicken, cut into pieces

2 quarts cold water

1/2 cup kosher salt

1 quart buttermilk

1 & 1/2 cups all-purpose flour

1 & 1/2 teaspoons fine sea salt

1/2 teaspoon freshly ground black pepper

1/4 cup cornstarch

2 tablespoons potato flour

1 pound lard

1/2 cup (1 stick) unsalted butter

1/4 pound bacon or smoked pork shoulder

● Rinse chicken under cold running water. Mix water and kosher salt in a large bowl, stirring until salt dissolves. Cover chicken with salt-water brine and refrigerate overnight (minimum 4 hours).

● Remove chicken from salt water brine and immerse in buttermilk. Allow to marinate in the refrigerator overnight (minimum 4 hours). Remove chicken from buttermilk, holding each piece to drip excess buttermilk back into bowl. Lay chicken on a wire cooling rack set over a sheet pan.

● Mix all-purpose flour, sea salt, pepper, cornstarch, and potato flour in a large bowl. Dredge chicken parts in flour mixture, shaking off excess. Lay chicken parts on the wire cooling rack.

● Using a large cast iron or heavy skillet, melt lard and butter together over medium-high heat and add bacon. When the mixture is hot (but not smoking), add the chicken, 1 piece at a time, in a single layer, skin side down. The chicken should be half submerged. Cook each piece 10 to 12 minutes per side, turning once, or more often if necessary to brown evenly. Dark meat cooks more slowly than white meat; to check for doneness, cut a thigh to the bone and check for redness (there should be none). When evenly browned, removed the cooked chicken and place on cooling rack. Serve hot or allow to cool to room temperature.

sweet

I love browsing large markets when I travel: I can see the fresh ingredients used in the regional cooking, I can enjoy samples of local fruits, vegetables, and often cheeses and condiments, and I don't have to pay the overhead of a restaurant with table service. I stopped at the Sweet Auburn Bread Company and met the owner, Sonya Jones, who once made her sweet potato cheesecake for President Clinton. On this day, she made it for me. Bill and I are two of the luckiest people on earth. We've both tasted Sonya's cheesecake!

● **Sweet Auburn Bread Company, 2457 Martin Luther King Jr. Drive SW, Suite J, Atlanta, GA, (404) 696-5676**

Sweet Potato Cheesecake

MAKES TWO 9-INCH CHEESECAKES

Sweet Potato Cheesecake

1 medium sweet potato

1 loaf pound cake, cut into about 20 thin slices

3 (8-ounce) packages cream cheese, room temp.

1 cup sugar

3 eggs

1 cup heavy cream

1 teaspoon lemon extract

2 teaspoons pure vanilla extract

2 teaspoons ground nutmeg

● Boil sweet potato until tender, 20 to 30 minutes. Cool, peel, mash, and set aside.
● Preheat oven to 350°F. Line two 9-inch pie plates with pound cake slices. Firmly press into bottom of pans. Set aside.
● In a large bowl, beat cream cheese with an electric mixer on medium-high speed until fluffy. Gradually mix in sugar and blend well. Add eggs, 1 at a time, beating well after each. Pour in cream and mix well. Mix in mashed sweet potato, then lemon extract, vanilla extract, and nutmeg. Pour into lined pans. Bake until center is almost set, 45 to 55 minutes. Remove from the oven and cool at least 2 hours. Remove from pans, if desired (invert onto plates, then invert again onto serving platters); refrigerate until ready to serve.

dinner

Here I suffered yet another indignity when my crew saw fit to air me singing The $40 a Day Blues, badly, after one too many beers. But I ate well, too. Matt's food is good. The ribs were smoky, spicy, and dripping with sauce. I had a cold, local beer. Many nights, the shack rocks with live music and every night the prices are just right!
● **Fat Matt's Rib Shack, 1811 Piedmont Rd. NE, Atlanta, GA, (404) 607-1622**

CHARLESTON

Truth be told, I just do not buy this whole "palmetto bug" thing they sell in Charleston. I am from New York, where a roach is a roach! We stayed at one of the finest hotels in the South and still, we all had experiences with "palmettos" in our beds, towels, and showers. I awoke thinking I had gone blind because I had cocooned myself so tightly in my sheets to protect me from the bugs that I could not see through the covers when my alarm went off. Here, people take these HUGE bugs as a part of life. They make cards, postcards, tee shirts, and hats that boast and spoof the palmettos: they even have chocolate-covered palmettos in some of the gift shops! How oogie can you get? Fortunately, I got over them, and discovered that Charleston has lots more to offer. There is dramatic beauty in this part of our country: weeping willows, rolling hills, lots of horses, and green pastures. Charleston is, of course, of great importance in American history. Beyond that, Charleston has some incredible food, and I for one am ready for seconds!

breakfast

Joseph is one lucky man! He is surrounded by beautiful women. The restaurant, a family affair, is run by three generations: his mom, his wife, his mom-in-law, too, as I remember. Jennifer, his wife, works alongside her handsome hubby in the open kitchen, serving great, eclectic fare. Joseph's has a creative, inexpensive menu; it became one of our crew's favorite places, too. We filmed breakfast here and I

Sweet Potato Pancakes

woofed down a pile of sweet potato pancakes (see recipe opposite page). They were delish! Once we wrapped, we all sat down and I ate again: lunch!

● Joseph's Restaurant, 129 Meeting Street, Charleston, SC, (843) 958-8500

lunch

> **❝ Everything here is good because it's all made with two important ingredients, history and love. ❞**

The owner of this restaurant is not Jestine, but Dana. Dana was, however, raised by a lovely, big-hearted woman, a wonderful cook, and her name was Jestine. The restaurant's location on Meeting Street perfectly describes the place; it's a great place to meet. The food is healthful, with deep Southern roots. The gumbos and soups, the chicken and corn bread are all derived from Jestine's original recipes. The kitchen crew and dining staff have been with Dana for years. Everything here is good because it's all made with two important ingredients, history and love.

● Jestine's Kitchen, 251 Meeting Street, Charleston, SC, (843) 722-7224

Sweet Potato Pancakes

1 sweet potato
1 cup all-purpose flour
1 cup whole wheat flour
4 teaspoons baking powder
2 tablespoons firmly packed brown sugar
1 teaspoon ground cinnamon
Pinch ground nutmeg
2 cups milk
4 teaspoons melted butter, plus more for skillet
2 eggs, beaten
Pecan Butter (recipe follows)
Maple syrup, for serving

● Bake, boil, or steam sweet potato until tender. Peel and puree it.

● In a large bowl, combine sweet potato, white and whole wheat flours, baking powder, brown sugar, cinnamon, nutmeg, milk, melted butter, and eggs. Whisk until smooth. Place a skillet over medium-high heat and grease with butter. Cook pancakes in batches, regreasing pan in between, until bubbles form on the surface, then flip and cook until dark golden brown. Serve with pecan butter and maple syrup.

Pecan Butter:

1/4 cup finely chopped pecans, toasted and cooled
1 cup (2 sticks) butter, softened
1/2 teaspoon ground cinnamon
1 teaspoon pure vanilla extract
1 tablespoon firmly packed brown sugar
1 tablespoon honey

● Mix all ingredients together with your hands (use rubber gloves). Place pecan butter on a piece of parchment paper, roll into a log, and freeze. Cut into slices and use to top sweet potato pancakes.

Chef Joseph Passarini of Joseph's Restaurant

" The restaurant has a beautiful view and is set out in a mysterious wetland. **"**

sweet

This is the kind of big, sweeping plantation that I daydreamed I might find in the South. What a looker this place is! You can stay here, or just visit for a long walk or a delicious meal. The grounds cover several acres with many buildings and

Pecan Pie

miles of paths and dirt roads connecting them all. Rooms are very modern and the architecture, though sleek, blends in well with the surroundings. The restaurant has a beautiful view and is set out in a mysterious wetland; you cross a hanging wooden bridge and wander through the brush to get there. I had a delicious slice of pecan pie in the late afternoon and it was sweet, rich, and loaded with buttery nuts.

● Middleton Place, 4300 Ashley River Road, Charleston, SC, (843) 556-6020

dinner

Chef Robert Stehling takes hominy grits and all of the other typical elements of Southern cuisine to a whole new level. The restaurant itself is charming—light, bright, and homey. The food is even better! Meals are unpretentious, but with complex, surprising fare. I had sesame-crusted catfish with geechee peanut sauce and sautéed okra. The prices were so reasonable that I felt guilty paying so little and getting so much.

● Hominy Grill, 207 Rutledge Avenue, Charleston, SC, (843) 937-0930

Sesame-Crusted Catfish with Geechee Peanut Sauce and Sautéed Okra

1 cup sesame seeds

2 cups cornmeal

Salt and freshly ground black pepper

Peanut oil

4 skinless catfish fillets

1 cup sliced fresh okra

Geechee Peanut Sauce (recipe follows)

1/2 cup small diced celery

1 cup small diced onion

1/2 teaspoon salt

1/8 teaspoon white pepper

2 tablespoons red wine

1 & 1/2 cups tomato puree

1/2 cup chicken stock

2 tablespoons peanut butter

● In a spice grinder, grind 1/2 cup sesame seeds into a rough powder; leave the other 1/2 cup whole. Combine sesame powder, whole sesame seeds, cornmeal, salt, and pepper in a shallow bowl.

● Place a skillet over medium-high heat and coat with peanut oil. Dredge catfish fillets in sesame-cornmeal mix and sauté in hot peanut oil until golden brown. Remove catfish to a platter and keep warm. Empty skillet, of oil and crusty cornmeal. Add more oil to hot pan and sauté okra until slightly brown, about 8 minutes.

● Place the geechee sauce on the plate and put catfish fillets on top. Add another ladle of geechee sauce and top with sautéed okra.

Geechee Peanut Sauce:

2 tablespoons butter

1 tablespoon all-purpose flour

1 tablespoon bacon fat

1/4 cup small diced green bell pepper

1/4 cup small diced red bell pepper

● Make the brown roux: Melt butter in a sauté pan over low heat. Add flour and stir to combine. Cook slowly over low heat, stirring constantly, until the roux gets dark brown, 15 to 20 minutes. Don't rush it or the roux could burn and become bitter tasting. Set roux aside.

● Make the sauce: Place bacon fat in a skillet and add bell peppers, celery, and onion. Cover and cook over low heat until onions are translucent, about 15 minutes. Season with salt and pepper. Add red wine and cook until reduced by 1/3. Add tomato puree and stock. Whisk in 1 tablespoon roux, setting the rest aside for another use, and the peanut butter. Check seasoning. Let simmer for 30 minutes.

HOMINY GRILL

207 Rutledge Ave.
Charleston, SC 29403
843-937-0930

Catfish and Okra

SAVANNAH

When I think about the run of cities we went on in the South, one word comes to mind: HOT. We visited Savannah, Atlanta, and Charleston in the late spring and WOW it must have been 100°F every day. As a Northerner, I never really adjusted to the heat. However, considering I have a Cajun-Creole daddy from Louisiana, I took great comfort in the food, the drawls, and the hospitality of Southern ladies and gentlemen. I guess one might say I adapt well to the kindness of strangers.

lunch

Collard Greens

My favorite memory of the South as a whole is of Mrs. Wilkes. She was a remarkable woman who worked at her business into her nineties, literally until the time of her passing. I consider myself very privileged to have made her acquaintance. We visited her dining room just months before she passed away. Mrs. Wilkes had a boarding house in Savannah and for decades she cooked breakfast and dinner (a.k.a. "lunch" to northerners) for her boarders daily. Over the years, the boarding house became famous for the quality of her cooking, and it evolved into a restaurant. There were Wilkes' House Rules to be followed during meals: you bowed your head for grace, said by Mrs. Wilkes

Collard Greens
SERVES 4 TO 6

1 bunch fresh collard greens

1 medium piece salt pork

1 cup water

1 teaspoon salt, plus more to taste

1 tablespoon bacon drippings, butter, or margarine

Pinch sugar (optional)

● Strip the leaves from the stems (unless they are very tender), discard the stems, and wash the leaves thoroughly. Place greens in a saucepan and add pork, water, and salt. Cook, covered, over medium heat until tender, about 45 minutes. Remove pork and drain greens through a colander. Place greens in a pan and chop, using 2 knives like a scissors. If necessary, add more salt to taste. Keep hot and stir in the bacon drippings and a pinch of sugar, if desired.

Mrs. Wilkes' Dining Room

Brown Rice
SERVES 6

3 strips bacon

1/2 cup chopped scallions, including green tops

1 cup diced celery

1 cup sliced button mushrooms

3 cups cooked white rice

2 tablespoons soy sauce, plus more to taste

1 egg, lightly beaten

● Fry the bacon in a large skillet until crisp and golden brown. Drain on a paper towel, and crumble. Sauté onions and celery in the bacon drippings until tender. Add mushrooms, rice, and soy sauce. Cover, and cook 10 minutes over low heat, stirring occasionally. Stir in beaten egg and cook until egg is just set. Add bacon and mix well. Extra soy sauce may be added, to taste.

herself; you would say "please" and "thank you" and be generally courteous of your fellow diners. Lastly, you were expected to clean up by scraping your plates and placing them in the proper bins to be washed. Dinner (served 11 to 3) was served family-style around large communal tables. Staples included Mrs. Wilkes' famous fried chicken, greens, potatoes, and biscuits. The menu would vary slightly from day to day, even from table to table. You would eat what you were served and love it! The recipes were simple and simply delicious. Walls were covered with pictures of famous movie stars and celebrities who no doubt were expected to be well-behaved guests, too.

● Mrs. Wilkes' Dining Room, 107 West Jones Street, Savannah, GA, (912) 232-5997

❝ There were Wilkes' House Rules to be followed during meals: you bowed your head for grace, said by Mrs. Wilkes herself. ❞

Sweet

I don't eat much candy. My mom would occasionally give us a piece of bitter-sweet chocolate or a little ice cream, but we did not grow up with candy bars as treats. It was all about pasta, cheese, and vino at our house. But, I have always admired the color and look of candy stores. I remember a class trip in the third or fourth grade to Quincy Market in Boston, where we went into a huge candy shop that seemed like an out-take from Willy Wonka and the Chocolate Factory. I was so taken aback by the variety—so many colors and shapes—I spent half of my money buying candies, of which I never ate a single piece. Instead, I saved them. I coveted them, looked at them adoringly from time to time, until one summer's day in August, when, alas, my perfect colorful candies finally succumbed, and melted. My trip to the Savannah Candy Kitchen reminded me of that childhood trip more than 20 years ago. I was, all at once, a kid again. At the Kitchen, they make many sweet, wonderful treats right before your eyes. I helped make some and then tried my hand at displaying bits-o-brittle on the candy counters. They also have buckets, barrels, and bins of every kind of candy in any color or shape you can imagine, all here for the taking in small or glutton-sized quantities. Next time you visit, bring your sweet tooth, but pack your toothbrush, too.

● **Savannah Candy Kitchen, 225 East River St., Savannah, GA, (912) 233-8411**

66 This is the place to lose your edge and find your manners by enjoying the Southern tradition of afternoon tea. 99

afternoon tea

Gracious is the first word that comes to mind when I think of the Hamilton-Turner Inn. I remember it fondly as a lovely, quiet place to retreat to from the heat and grit of the day. This is the place to lose your edge and find your manners by enjoying the Southern tradition of afternoon tea. Made by two generations of talented bakers and cooks, the finger sandwiches, scones, and assorted treats were divine and the tea cups and accessories impressive as the selection of teas themselves. Afternoon tea is included with your room fee, if you are smart enough to stay here on your next visit to town. Make sure to take a carriage ride, too. I hailed my horse and buggy just outside the inn.

● **Hamilton-Turner Inn, 330 Abercorn Street, Savannah, GA, (912) 233-1833**

recipe adapted from Hamilton-Turner **$40ADAY**

APPT - SOUP/SAL - ENTREE - VEG/POT - **DESSERT** - BEV

Ashley's Scottish Shortbread

SERVES 10 TO 15

1 pound (4 sticks) butter, softened
1 & 2/3 cups sugar, plus more, for sprinkling
4 cups all-purpose flour, plus more for dusting
1 & 1/3 cups cornstarch

Shortbread

● Preheat oven to 350°F. Line a small baking sheet with parchment paper.
● Using an electric hand-mixer, cream butter and sugar until fluffy, 3 to 4 minutes. In a separate bowl, mix flour and cornstarch. Slowly stir the flour mixture into the butter and sugar, and mix until blended and a dough is formed. Press the dough into the prepared baking pan, using plastic wrap to help, so the dough is 3/4-inch thick. Bake until lightly brown, about 1 hour. Remove from the oven and sprinkle with sugar while still warm. Cut into 1-by-3-inch pieces. Can be stored in an airtight container for up to 1 week.

dinner

The Crab Shack is a fun time, plain and simple. Good crab, good people, good cold beer. The shack sits on the water's edge, so it can be a bit buggy. Wear some Off. When you sit outside you can hear the cicadas in the trees. You feel an element of danger: at any moment, a large winged insect could fly into your hair or worse yet, your crab. Beware of fake bugs. The night I visited the Shack, they had a magician roaming from table to table. He played a nasty trick on me involving a BIG, black spider. I made a BIG, loud noise, more like a blood-curdling shriek! I would like to thank our director, our camera man, and our editing team for allowing me to relive this banner moment in my life, over and over again. So happy it made it to air. Thanks, guys!

● **The Crab Shack, 40 Estill Hammock Rd., Tybee Island, GA, (912) 786-9857**

" Good crab, good people, good cold beer. "

Well, I'm not a huge fan of crowds and I don't have the patience to endure long lines; therefore, theme parks have never been high on my list of must do's. My sister Maria has been to Disneyland enough times to meet quotas for the whole family. In fact, it was in part her descriptions of the high pricing of food and drink inside the uber-theme parks that convinced me to come up with some choices for hungry travelers in Orlando, but outside of these parks.

Blinchiki

breakfast

Lacomka is a charming Russian bakery that looks as if it belongs in an ethnic area of a more metropolitan city, on a side street of lower Manhattan or on the outskirts of the North End in Boston. A family operation, run by a loving mother and her devoted son, Lacomka features pastries, cakes, and cookies made from authentic family recipes that go back generations. Other retail items include small Russian arts and crafts. Sergei, the son, invited me and the $40 crew into Mama's kitchen in the back of the bakery where she made blinchiki (cheese and fruit blintzes) for all of us. I wish I had known how to say "yummy" in Russian, but I think the hug and kiss I gave her made the translation for me.

● **Lacomka Bakery, 2050 North Semoran Boulevard, #140, Winter Park, FL, (407) 677-1101**

recipe courtesy Lacomka Bakery $40ADAY

APPT - SOUP/SAL - **ENTREE** - VEG/POT - DESSERT - BEV

Blinchiki
SERVES 4

3 eggs
1/2 teaspoon salt
1 tablespoon sugar
1 cup milk
2 cups all-purpose flour
1 tablespoon vegetable oil, plus more for pan

● Combine eggs, salt, and sugar in a bowl and mix until thoroughly blended. Stir in milk. While mixing, add flour, a little at a time, until a thick batter is formed. Add 1 tablespoon vegetable oil and combine.

● Heat a 12-inch, oiled skillet over medium-high heat. Pour all of the batter into the hot skillet and fry until golden on 1 side. Carefully flip over and brown the other side. Fill with cottage cheese or fruit.

LACOMKA
Bakery & Deli
Russian Cuisine
We make cakes for weddings, birthdays, and other occasions
Casselton Corner
2050 N. Semoran Blvd. #140 • Winter Park, Florida 32792
407-677-1101

lunch

The White Wolf Cafe is my kind of find! It is a large, unique antique market that also happens to serve delicious, healthful foods. Now, anytime I can combine my two favorite activities—shopping and eating—well, I'm yours forever, or, at least yours for lunch! White Wolf did not disappoint as a restaurant or antique store. On the eating end of things, I had a vegetarian plate of hummus and other spreads with vegetables and pitas and it was delicious! The portions were very generous. I especially enjoyed the black bean hummus. Terrific flavor combo in the taboule salad as well: the nutty cracked grains contrasted with the sweet, chewy bite of chopped bits of dried apricots—tasty. On the shopping end-of-things, well, let's just say I was tempted to part with way more than $40!

● **White Wolf Cafe, 1829 North Orange Avenue, Orlando, FL, (407) 895-9911**

recipe adapted from White Wolf Cafe **$40ADAY**
APPT - SOUP/SAL - ENTREE - VEG/POT - DESSERT - BEV

Hummus
SERVES 12 TO 16

4 cups cooked garbanzo beans, drained
1 cup tahini
1 cup fresh lemon juice
3/4 cup minced garlic
1/2 cup canola oil
1 teaspoon salt
1 teaspoon freshly ground black pepper

Hummus

● For a chunky hummus, place all ingredients in a mixing bowl. Mix vigorously by mashing with a potato masher and then whisking until well combined.
● For a totally smooth hummus, puree the cooked and drained beans in a food processor or in a blender. Transfer to a large bowl, add remaining ingredients, and whisk until well combined.
● Transfer hummus to a large plastic container with a lid, and refrigerate, covered, until ready to serve. Bring to room temperature before serving.

Black Bean Hummus:
4 cups cooked black beans, drained
1 cup tahini
3/4 cup fresh lemon juice
3/4 cup minced garlic
1/4 cup canola oil
1 teaspoon salt
2 teaspoons freshly ground black pepper

Black Bean Hummus

● Follow directions above.

66 **The White Wolf Cafe is my kind of find! It is a large, unique antique market that also happens to serve delicious, healthful foods.** 99

| recipe | SERVES 8 | courtesy Café Tu Tu Tango | $40ADAY |

APPT - SOUP/SAL - ENTREE - VEG/POT - DESSERT - BEV

Cuba Libre Jamon
RUM-AND-COLA-CURED PORK TENDERLOIN

1/4 cup kosher salt

1/4 cup firmly packed brown sugar

1/4 cup rum

1 & 1/2 cups cola

1/4 cup honey

2 pork tenderloin

Cilantro-Lime Mustard (recipe follows)

● In a baking dish just large enough to fit the pork, combine salt, sugar, rum, cola, and honey; whisk until salt, sugar, and honey are completely dissolved. Add pork tenderloin and let marinate, covered, in the refrigerator 4 to 8 hours, turning the pork occasionally if the marinade does not cover it completely.

● Preheat a grill. Cut pork into 2-inch medallions and grill for 7 to 9 minutes on each side, until cooked to medium. Transfer to a serving platter and let rest for 5 minutes before slicing. Serve with Cilantro-Lime Mustard on the side.

Cilantro-Lime Mustard:

1 cup stone-ground mustard

1/3 cup freshly squeezed lime juice

2 tablespoons finely chopped cilantro

1 teaspoon ground cumin

● Place all ingredients in a mixing bowl and stir to combine completely. Chill for 1 to 2 hours before serving.

❝ Going to Tu Tu's is like taking the family to Ringling Brothers, only less expensive and no safari-like smell. ❞

dinner

Cuba Libre Jamon

Café Tu Tu Tango is part of a privately owned restaurant group that hires certified Executive Chefs for their restaurants across the country, so their standards are high. All have a common theme. Visiting Tu Tu Tango's is like hanging out in an artist's loft. From caricature artists to belly dancers, magicians to flame throwers, Tu Tu's has a circus of talent enthralling the dinner crowds each night. For a restaurant in this affordable price range, the menus are creative and ambitious. The menu items work like tapas in that you can mix and match two or three different items to make your meal. Going to Tu Tu's is like taking the family to Ringling Brothers, only less expensive and no safari-like smell. For our $40 episode, I had rum-and-cola cured pork and sweet potato salad. Tu Tu menus change often, so what I actually ate on TV is long-gone. However, the crew had some of everything —it all looked great (and tasted even better!)

● Café Tu Tu Tango, 8625 International Drive, Orlando, FL, (407) 248-2222

sweet

Colorado Fondue Company might seem an odd choice for the state of Florida, but that brings us back to the amusement-park showmanship of Orlando: detailed, believable, pseudo-authentic facades are an art form in this town. This restaurant, part of a chain, looks the part of a Colorado mining town. The concept is cute and kitschy—and fondue can be a fun way to get fussy eaters to eat their meat and veggies. Also, any child of the late sixties or

Chocolate Toffee

seventies (when fondue ruled) will find this place a retro, blast-from-the-past! At Colorado Fondue you can dip it all: breads, meats, seafood, vegetables, fruits, nuts, cakes, and candies in all sorts of coatings, from cheesy and saucy, to sweet and syrupy. For our taping we chose to share a dessert fondue of white chocolate and toffee with a family of four, The Garfinkles. Surrounding the fondue pot were fresh and dried fruits, bite-sized pieces of cakes and cookies. Honestly, this fondue was just too sweet for me. But, the Garfinkles were terrific (even though their youngest son kept tickling me during my closing delivery for the show). And I admit that I'm really more of a cheese fondue fan. So, if I ever return, I'll give the Colorado Fondue Co.—via Florida—another dip!

● **Colorado Fondue Company, 1016 East Semoran Blvd., Casselberry, FL, (407) 767-8232**

recipe | SERVES 6 | courtesy Colorado Fondue Co. | $40ADAY

APPT - SOUP/SAL - ENTREE - VEG/POT - **DESSERT** - BEV

Mocha White Chocolate Fondue with Chocolate Toffee Candy

8 ounces white chocolate
1/4 cup freshly brewed coffee
2 ounces chocolate-covered toffee, such as a Heath bar, crushed
Miscellaneous bite-sized fruits and cake pieces, for dipping

● Combine white chocolate and coffee in the top of a double boiler. Stir until white chocolate is melted and the mixture is creamy. Add the crushed toffee bar and stir to incorporate. Serve with bite-sized assorted fruits and cake pieces for dipping.

MIANI

I've had many of my life's firsts in Miami: my first mojito, my first taste of Columbian cuisine, and my first time dancing on a bar. Looking back, I think the last could have remained off the list. Prior to my $40 a Day trip here, my only knowledge of Miami was through Crockett and Tubbs. I dislike pastels, heat, neon, tropical drinks, and pink flamingos, so why would I like Miami, right? Wrong. It does grow on you, really. I just went there for a Food and Wine festival and I left town wishing I could spend a few extra hours on South Beach. The shopping is great. Cuban food, drink, music, and culture are fascinating, forbidden, and delicious. The faces and bodies are all tan and very fit! The hotels are stunning! My favorites are the sleek Delano and the art deco-style Loews. The food—WOW! I could just live at Emeril's and Nobu on alternate nights. Both offer many little dishes, so if you think you can't afford to go, think again! Just think appetizers rather than entrees.

early lunch

❝ I enjoyed some delicious garlic crab that was so fresh it was jumping out of the pan, literally! ❞

For our show, we went to Captain Jim's Seafood, a market that I would shop at often, if I lived here. At first I felt the shop was too far off the main drag, and for the average traveler not easy to find (and I am very average). However, once we found it, Jim's was worth the trip. I enjoyed some delicious garlic crab that was so fresh it was jumping out of the pan, literally! Also, I was very impressed with the prices. The displays were gorgeous, full of seafood that had come off Captain Jim Hanson's boats that very same morning!

● **Captain Jim's Seafood, 12950 W. Dixie Hwy, N. Miami, FL, (305) 892-2812**

snack

Ortanique on The Mile is right in the middle of Miracle Mile, a shopping mecca! The Coral Gables area is a girl-must-see stretch of fantabulous stores, and the Miracle Mile is the main artery. When you shop-till-you-want-to-drop, you need a place to replenish. Ortanique is it! The food and drink are Cuban, colorful, delicious, and reasonably priced, considering the area and high level of preparation. I had a spiny lobster cake with mango relish that was rich but light. The bartender had a gorgeous guayaberra shirt and a fabulous smile. He made me the first, and to this day the best, mojito I've ever had (see recipe on next page). This drink is a muddle of lime, mint, sugar cane, and rum, and man, I guarantee you that it will be at least nine-times tastier than any tropical, syrupy, sticky, pastel-colored cocktail you've ever had on vacation!

● **Ortanique on the Mile, 278 Miracle Mile, Coral Gables, FL, (305) 446-7710**

West Indian Curried Crab and Lobster Cakes

MAKES 14 CAKES

1 egg

1/2 cup mayonnaise

1 tablespoon whole-grain mustard

1 tablespoon Worcestershire sauce

2 tablespoons Javin brand curry blend (more or less, to taste, based on brand used)

2 scallions, chopped

1/4 cup diced red bell pepper

1/4 cup diced yellow bell pepper

1/4 cup chopped red onion

2 tablespoons chopped fresh flat-leaf parsley

Salt and freshly ground black pepper

1/2 pound jumbo lump crabmeat

1/2 pound spiny lobster, cooked and chopped

1 cup panko (Japanese-style) bread crumbs (found in Asian food markets)

Vegetable oil, for pan frying

● Combine egg, mayonnaise, mustard, Worcestershire, curry, scallions, bell peppers, red onion, parsley, and salt and pepper in a mixing bowl. Taste for seasoning. Gently fold in crabmeat and lobster, being careful not to break up crabmeat too much. Fold in panko, adding enough so that the mixture is not too tight.

● Heat 2 tablespoons oil in large skillet over medium-high heat. Form 1 crab cake, and sear on both sides until golden brown, about 3 minutes on each side. Taste and adjust the seasoning if necessary. Form the remaining mixture into fourteen 2 & 1/2-ounce cakes. Heat 3 tablespoons oil over medium-high heat. Add the remaining crab cakes, in batches as necessary, and sear on both sides until golden brown, about 3 minutes on each side. Serve immediately.

Crab Lobster Cakes

Ortanique Mojito

2 limes, halved and then scored

16 to 24 Cuban mint or spearmint leaves, halved

3 to 4 ounces simple syrup

8 to 12 ounces light rum

4 splashes soda water

4 sugarcane sticks, for garnish (optional)

● Make a simple syrup by combining an equal amount of sugar and water in a saucepan. Bring to a simmer and cook just until the sugar is dissolved. Remove from the heat and let cool before using.

● In each glass, combine 1/2 lime, 4 to 6 mint leaves, and 3/4 to 1 ounce simple syrup by muddling the lime and mint together. Add ice to fill each glass, then add 2 to 3 ounces rum to each glass, and stir well. Add a splash of soda water and garnish with a sugarcane stick, if desired.

Ortanique Mojito

Mango's Tropical Cafe

dinner

At Mama Vieja's, a Columbian restaurant, the ceiling is covered with a collection of hats and sombreros. If they like your hat well enough, they'll trade you a plate of food in exchange for your hat, which they add to the collection. I brought in a very loud hat, definitely not to everyone's taste, and it rated a Countryman's Plate, a Bandeja Paesa, as a trade-in supper. The host was very nice to me. I wanted to like and enjoy my meal—very generous portions—just to please him and other on-lookers. If you want to see an interesting selection of hats or if rice and beans with cracklin', eggs, and fried steak sound tasty to you, go and enjoy! I'll probably be over at Emeril's eating some sweet shrimp with rosemary gravy.

● Mama Vieja, 235 23rd Street, Miami Beach, FL, (305) 538-2400

sweet

The Ice Box Café was my savior! What a wonderful way to end my day! Robert Siegmann has a way with cakes, and people, too. His creations are so original. The Ice Box cakes are fun, comforting, and familiar twists on old-fashioned treats. I had peanut butter ice-cream cake and it was worth every calorie. Run, don't walk, to Ice Box and burn off enough calories to have a second slice of heaven!

● Ice Box Café, 1657 Michigan Avenue, Miami, FL, (305) 538-8448

Ice Box Café Peanut Butter Ice Cream Cake

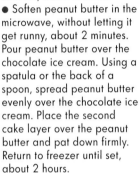

Ice Cream Cake

Chocolate Cake:

Butter, for pan

1 cup vegetable oil

2 cups sugar

3 eggs

1 teaspoon pure vanilla extract

1 cup milk

1 cup strong-brewed coffee

1 cup Dutch-process cocoa powder

2 cups all-purpose flour

1 teaspoon baking powder

2 teaspoons baking soda

Pinch salt

Ice Cream Cake:

1 pint chocolate ice cream

2 cups creamy peanut butter

1 pint vanilla ice cream

Melted chocolate, for garnish (optional)

Whipped cream, for garnish (optional)

● Make the chocolate cake: Preheat oven to 350°F. Grease a 10-inch round with butter; line the bottom with parchment paper. Combine oil and sugar in the bowl of an electric mixer and blend until well combined. Add eggs and vanilla extract and continue to mix until well combined. Blend in milk and coffee.

● Sift cocoa powder, flour, baking powder, baking soda, and salt together in a bowl. Add the dry ingredients to the wet ingredients in three batches, blending well after each addition. Pour the batter into the prepared pan and bake until a skewer inserted into the cake's center comes out clean, about 45 to 50 minutes. Allow to cool to room temperature. Unmold and cover with plastic wrap. Refrigerate overnight to allow it to cool thoroughly.

● Make the ice cream cake: Cut the chocolate cake horizontally to make 2 layers and slide 1 of the layers onto a plate or cake board, being careful not to break the layers. Line the same pan you used to bake the chocolate cake in plastic wrap (the plastic will help you remove the ice cream cake from the pan once it is set, so make sure to use a piece large enough that the edges hang over the sides). Slide 1 of the layers of chocolate cake into the pan. Make sure that it rests firmly in the bottom of the pan; if the plastic wrap has slipped inside, adjust it so that it spills over the sides of the pan. Empty a pint of chocolate ice cream into the bowl of a mixer and mix to soften until it is spreadable; do not let it become runny. Pour ice cream over choco-

late layer in the mold and spread evenly with a spatula or the back of a spoon. Return to freezer until set, about 2 hours.

● Soften peanut butter in the microwave, without letting it get runny, about 2 minutes. Pour peanut butter over the chocolate ice cream. Using a spatula or the back of a spoon, spread peanut butter evenly over the chocolate ice cream. Place the second cake layer over the peanut butter and pat down firmly. Return to freezer until set, about 2 hours.

● Empty a pint of vanilla ice cream into a mixer and soften it until it can be easily spread. Spread over chocolate layer with a spatula or the back of a spoon. Return to freezer and allow to set overnight.

● To unmold, simply invert the cake onto a cake board or plate and place a warm towel over the pan for a couple of minutes. The cake should slide out without any problems; grab a hold of the ends of the plastic wrap and give it a tug if it is stubborn. Invert back onto a serving plate so that vanilla ice cream is on top. Decorate with drizzled melted chocolate or dollops of whipped cream.

93

THE FLORIDA KEYS

If life is a series of memorable experiences, then a trip to the Florida Keys is a must, at least once in a lifetime. You'll either thrive here or just barely survive, but whichever, you'll never forget the visit and you'll wear the experience like a Girl Scout badge. Next time you're in Miami with time to spare, buy a Jimmy Buffet CD, rent a convertible and keep heading south, till you see rooster-crossing signs and blue-green water under the mile-long bridges. Here, parrots flap past sky blue-pink sunsets and a huge, bullet-shaped monument pointedly marks road's end as the "Southern-Most Point in The United States of America." You can't miss it—it's right next to the guy who sells the petrified, unborn baby sharks and devil fish. Oh, and if you're in the Keys during the holiday season, as we were, try not to miss the Christmas parade. Here you'll see tan, bare-chested strapping men, with antlers on their heads, parading down the main-drag, 10-point bucks, in tight, red velvet, fur-cuffed pants with satin "hooves." Prancer leads, next to Rudolph, but these guys are anything but "tiny" in their performance of Santa's reindeer! They're HOT-HOT-HOT! A word of caution: be careful not to walk too close to Key lime trees, or even in the tall grass. This is how our crew caught chiggers, mites that nest in your flesh. Repeated coats of clear nail polish will smother them. You're forewarned!

Kristi's Key Lime Pie

- 1 cup Key lime juice or regular lime juice, or 6 to 8 sliced Key limes plus 2 cups water
- 1 (14-ounce) can sweetened condensed milk
- 1/2 cup sour cream
- 2 large eggs
- 1 (9-inch) pre-made graham cracker crust
- 1 cup whipped topping

● If using key limes instead of lime juice, place 2 cups water in a blender or food processor, set processor on puree, and with processor running, drop lime slices in one at a time. Key limes are very tough—do not drop in too many at one time; drop in 8 to 10 slices. Process completely, then pour through strainer into another container; make sure to press out all of the juice. Discard lime remains; then pour the lime juice back into the blender. Drop in remaining lime slices, repeating the above process until you have processed all of the limes. Set aside 1 cup of the resulting lime juice.

● Preheat oven to 350°F. In the bowl of a mixer, beat lime juice with sweetened condensed milk on medium speed. Add sour cream and beat on medium speed until combined. In a separate bowl, beat eggs, and then add to the lime mixture and beat for 1 minute. Pour the mixture into prepared graham cracker crust. Bake 10 minutes. Remove from the oven and cool pie completely, about 1 hour.

● Top with whipped topping and place the pie in the freezer. Freeze at least 3 hours or overnight. Remove from the freezer 10 minutes before serving. For easier cutting, wet the knife in hot water before slicing.

66 According to USA Today, Key Largo's Crack'd Conch has the best Key lime pie in the whole state. **99**

Key Lime Pie

breakfast

According to *USA Today*, Key Largo's Crack'd Conch has the best Key lime pie in the whole state. So, because it was the first Key I came upon, I had pie for breakfast. I don't know that it was my favorite-ever, but it was quite good and very unusual in that the pies are frozen and served very cold. They are made with key lime juice and some condensed milk.

● Key Largos' Crack'd Conch, 105045 Overseas Highway (MM 105), Key Largo, FL, (305) 451-0732

recipe	SERVES 4	courtesy Blue Heaven	$40ADAY

APPT - SOUP/SAL - **ENTREE** - VEG/POT - DESSERT - BEV

Tortilla with Jerk Chicken

2 boneless, skinless chicken breasts, sliced lengthwise into "fingers"

2 cups Jerk Marinade (recipe follows)

2 tablespoons olive oil

2 cups cooked rice

2 cups cooked black beans

4 fresh (8-inch) flour tortillas, warmed

1 cup grated white cheddar cheese

2 cups shredded romaine lettuce

4 dollops sour cream

4 large spoonfuls salsa

1 avocado, sliced

8 jalapeño slices

● In a covered bowl, marinate chicken in jerk marinade in the refrigerator 4 to 5 hours.

● Preheat a broiler. Heat oil in a large skillet over high heat. Add marinated chicken strips and sauté over high heat, until cooked through, about 3 minutes on each side; discard any marinade left in bowl. Place 1/4 of the rice and beans on each tortilla. Top with cooked chicken and the cheese, dividing each evenly among the 4 tortillas. Place tortillas on a sheet pan and then place under the broiler until the cheese is melted. Remove from the broiler and top with shredded lettuce, sour cream, salsa, avocado, and jalapeño slices.

Jerk Chicken Marinade:

4 teaspoons ground allspice

4 teaspoons dried thyme

3/4 teaspoon cayenne pepper

1 tablespoon freshly ground black pepper

1 tablespoon ground sage

1 teaspoon ground nutmeg

1 teaspoon ground cinnamon

2 tablespoons salt

4 & 1/2 teaspoons garlic powder

4 teaspoons sugar

3 tablespoons olive oil

3 tablespoons canola oil

6 tablespoons soy sauce

1 cup white vinegar

3/4 cup freshly squeezed orange juice

3 tablespoons freshly squeezed lime juice

1 small Scotch bonnet pepper, finely diced

3/4 white onion, chopped

1/3 cup chopped scallions

3/4 tablespoon chopped fresh garlic

● Mix all ingredients together in a bowl. Refrigerate, covered, until ready to use.

Jerk Chicken

❝ So, what does Heaven look like? It is, indeed, blue. It's a house that used to be a brothel upstairs, and the place where Ernest Hemingway boxed, downstairs. ❞

BLUE HEAVEN
YOU DON'T HAVE TO DIE TO GET THERE!

lunch

Blue Heaven is among my top favorite locations in all of the Southeast. It's an ultra cool playground for grown-ups and kids alike, depending on the hour of day and amount of alcohol in your icy beverage of choice. Blue Heaven has an incredible history—and oh, they serve really good food, too. So, what does Heaven look like? It is, indeed, blue. It's a house that used to be a brothel upstairs, and the place where Ernest Hemingway boxed, downstairs. Today, you can buy great American folk art inside, and run completely wild among the cats, chickens, roosters, and super-cool rope swing outside. There's a big, ole tree running up through the bar, and a tree house and water tower. A few carnival games and a bowling alley complete the activity scene. When you're done playing around, sit down at the community picnic tables and enjoy some healthful, tasty, organically grown and artfully prepared plats du jour! The couple that owns Blue Heaven started by making lunch for their hungry, poor, vegetarian artist friends. Lucky us! This is my favorite hangout in the Keys. (see recipe on opposite page)

● **Blue Heaven, 729 Thomas Street, Key West, FL, (305) 296-8666**

dinner

Bahama Mama's is "small restaurant, with big heart!" Cory, the cook and owner, serves up his family's recipes, island style. I had Cory's conch curry. Now, the Keys are called "The Conch Republic," so no trip here is ever complete without dining on a meal of conch. Many shy away from the task or take the whoosy-way-out by ordering a conch chowder or soup. Conch can be a challenge; it lends itself to being tough, like chewing on an eraser. Cory tenderizes the conch by beating-the-heck out of it before chopping. Then, he stews it in sherry and a hot-'n-spicy curry sauce. Yumm-o! This meal's not for those of tender palates, but if you're gonna get conched-out, Cory's kitchen is one great place to do it!

● **Bahama Mama's, 324 Petronia Street, Key West, FL, (305) 294-3355**

drink

Rum Runner

BillyFish is the best spot to watch the sun set over the water, so much so, they now call the place Sunset Pier. I had a rum runner—a mix of rum and banana and blackberry liqueurs.

● **BillyFish Bar & Grill (now called Sunset Pier), Zero Duval Street, Key West, FL, (305) 296-7701**

NASHVILLE

More music! Yeah! I love the South, really, because the heat and the history has, for better or worse, through sickness and health, and war and social revolution, produced uniquely American music: jazz, Gospel, rock and roll, and country. I remember not too long ago hearing a country music guy define country music very neatly. He said that for him, rock and roll is the soundtrack of weekends, and country music is the stuff that gets a working man or woman through the week. Nice. While you're in town, make sure you make a trip to the Country Music Hall of Fame. Whether you consider yourself a fan or not, you'll learn something about yourself and your nation here. Also, don't miss the original home of The Grand Ole Opry, the Ryman Auditorium. Go also to Gruhn Guitars on Broadway. It's a Mecca for me, and I don't even play! Just about every top rock, pop, and country icon has purchased guitars from Gruhn's and there's a reason behind that level of respect. Gruhn Guitars is as much a museum as it is a retail business. Among the priceless collection of guitars on display here, you can see those once played by everyone from Hendrix to Elvis, as well as an eclectic collection of hundreds of one-of-a-kind string instruments of historical importance from around the globe.

breakfast

> **The coffee drinks and food menus are truly original and the prices are literally half of a trip to Starbucks.**

There are islands in the river of Starbucks that flows across our nation and Bongo Java is one of them. It is full of good-looking college kids who are really well-trained baristas. The coffee drinks and food menus are truly original and the prices are literally half of a trip to Starbucks. There are games, newspapers, and magazines, cozy niches and nooks, and it can be a lively or a quiet place to start or end your day. I had a Cherry Bomb latte thing in a huge cup and an egg sammy on an English muffin. Good.

● Bongo Java, 2007 Belmont Boulevard, Nashville, TN, (615) 385-5282

lunch

Roasted Chicken Salad

Nashville has a quiet, cultured side hiding in plain sight, and the Nashville Public Library on Church Street is a wonderful example. Now when you're traveling for pleasure, library visits probably don't make your list of sights to see, but make this place an exception. The architecture, the painted ceilings, the gourmet food are worth a stop. Within the library is an eat-in or take-out place called Provence Café that is packed with customers each day for lunch. The salads, sandwiches, and baked goods are all tray gourmet, as a friend of mine would say. I had a chicken-salad sandwich flavored with fresh lavender on warm, freshly baked, rosemary focaccia. Go browse or look something up, then grab a bite at Provence Breads & Café.

● **Provence Breads & Café, 1705 21st Avenue S., Nashville, TN, (615) 386-0363**

dinner

This place, outside the center of town, was filled only with locals. I went for the late-night special when, after 9 PM, entrees are priced at fifty percent off. It's a good deal. There's live jazz in the bar and I had a delicious sweet potato gnocchi at half price in the beautifully lit dining room. I'm sure menus change often here, but all of the food looked good. If you are in the neighborhood of Crestmoor Road late at night, it's a worthy stop.

● **F. Scott's, 2210 Crestmoor Road, Nashville, TN, (615) 269-5861**

drink

Broadway is packed with music clubs. You can't miss Legend's Corner. The band that played the night I was in town was the best I heard on the entire strip. The place is huge and has great atmosphere. I had an Electric Lemonade made by a gorgeous and very sweet barmaid. Fellas, you would especially like it here. The lemonade was good. It made me smile!

● **Legend's Corner, 428 Broadway, Nashville, TN, (615) 248-6334**

recipe   courtesy Legend's Corner $40ADAY

APP - SOUP/SAL - ENTREE - VEG/POT - DESSERT - BEV

Honky Tonk Lemonade

SERVES 1

Honky Tonk Lemonade

1/2 ounce vodka
1/2 ounce triple sec
1/2 ounce blue curaçao
1/2 lemon, juiced
Splash lemon-lime soda
Splash sweet-and-sour mix
2 teaspoons sugar
Maraschino cherry, for garnish, optional

● Mix all ingredients in a shaker and pour over ice. Garnish with cherry, if desired.

south

MEMPHIS

Graceland, Beale Street, Sun Records, Rock and Soul Museum...hey, if you love rock n' roll, if you got soul, you got a home in Memphis. Just say "Memphis" slowly, let it roll off your tongue, and you'll have an instant, sexy drawl. "Ya'll come down, now."

San Diegan Omelet

breakfast

If you're a glass-half-empty skeptic, you need to know about Brother Juniper's. Named for a generous monk, this restaurant is as small as a small business gets. It's a healthy marriage of family, faith, and community. Brother Juniper's encourages people to be mindful of each other, caring, and giving, too. This family-run business considers those in their community part of their family, too. Every morsel that passes your mouth is made with pure love, from whole foods that are grown, delivered or manufactured by other small, local producers. The bread made here is served with breakfast and prepared by members of social services programs who are building a better future by making some of the best breads you'll ever have! I had a delicious omelet called the San Diegan, accompanied by chewy, whole-grain bread. (see recipe on opposite page) The omelets are huge and open-faced, like frittatas. Go to Brother J's for a most satisfying meal.

● Brother Juniper's College Inn, 3519 Walker Avenue, Memphis, TN, (901) 324-0144

❝ Every morsel that passes your mouth is made with pure love, from whole foods that are grown, delivered or manufactured by other small, local producers. ❞

lunch

Yummy. This is a local joint that's packed at lunch. It's not fancy, it's just good. I hate to fall back on a cliché, but you really do lick your fingers here. Located in a cinderblock building, Gus's is easy to find, and worth a trip. Come hungry and bring quarters for the juke box.

● Gus's Fried Chicken, 310 South Front Street, Memphis, TN, (901) 527-4877

dinner

I remember that there is more than one Neely's and some sort of on-going family feud. This particular Neely's draws celebs, politicians, and locals alike. I thought the ribs were tasty and Mr. Neely told some very colorful stories to match.

● Jim Neely's Interstate Bar-B-Que, 2265 South 3rd Street, Memphis, TN, (901) 775-2304

San Diegan Omelet

2 small red potatoes

1 tablespoon margarine, plus more for pan

1 tablespoon butter

3 slices bacon

Sprinkle granulated garlic

1/4 cup diced yellow onion

Salt and freshly ground black pepper

1/2 cup diced portobello mushroom

3 eggs

2 to 3 tablespoons sour cream

1/2 cup diced tomatoes

2 to 3 tablespoons crumbled feta cheese

● Boil red potatoes until almost cooked through; cool in the refrigerator until cold. When potatoes are cold, cut into 1/2-inch chunks. In a large skillet, sauté the potato chunks in margarine and butter. Meanwhile, in a separate skillet, cook bacon until crisp, cut into small pieces and set aside. Just before potatoes become browned, add the garlic, onion, salt, and pepper; stir to combine. Drain off excess oil. Remove potatoes and set aside. In the same skillet, sauté mushrooms; set aside.

● In a bowl, whisk eggs together. Grease a 10-inch omelet pan or nonstick skillet with margarine and place pan over medium heat. Have all other ingredients ready to assemble quickly after the eggs are cooked. Pour eggs into pan and cook slowly over medium heat: With a spatula, push eggs to the center of the pan. As the eggs begin to seal on the bottom, keep folding the loose eggs under the cooked portion. This is an open omelet, so do not fold over. When almost all the loose egg is cooked, flip the eggs over and cook for 1 minute longer. Lay the cooked eggs flat on a plate. Spread with sour cream, then place potatoes on top, followed by the mushrooms, tomatoes, and bacon. Top with feta cheese.

Blueberry Hill

SERVES 1

3/4 ounce rum (recommended: Bacardi)

3/4 ounce raspberry liqueur

2 ounces sweet-and-sour mix

2 ounces lemon-lime soda

Maraschino cherry, for garnish, optional

● Mix all ingredients and pour over ice. Garnish with a cherry, if desired.

drink

On Beale Street you'll catch acts ranging from Elvis impersonators to one of my favorite rock bands ever, Queens of The Stone Age. There is always music happening on Beale Street. At Rum Boogie, you'll recognize the signatures of anyone and everyone in rock, from The Allmans to Billy Joel. The drinks are cool, too. I had a Blueberry Hill, some kind of glowing, sweet cocktail. It went down smoothly. The music was hot.

● Rum Boogie Cafe, 182 Beale Street, Memphis, TN, (901) 528-0150

NEW ORLEANS

My daddy, Jim Ray, is from Louisiana, so I was raised with a good ear for jazz and a taste for spicy food and hot times! I must admit, I never liked the heat and humidity, though, and I would say that this is never the summer-place-to-be. When I was little, my mama and daddy brought me down here one August to visit my Nanny to celebrate both our birthdays and I cried from the time I entered the state until I left. In other months of the year, you'll love this place, one of the greatest party towns in the entire world! The iron work, the verandas, and colorful buildings in the Garden District make for especially vivid memories. And New Orleans is one of the few cities where you cannot get "bad" food. However it's generally very pricey, so check out the following for some affordable picks.

breakfast

> 66 The beignets were hot, light, and crisp and I felt as if I could have eaten ten of them! 99

Café du Monde is the most famous spot for chicory coffee and beignets (doughnuts) but when the line is too long, go looking for a Café Beignet (three locations). I visited Royal Street, in the midst of it all, and have nothing but high praise for the place. It is really lovely, inside and out; there are delightful murals, and tiny wrought-iron tables and chairs. The beignets were hot, light, and crisp and I felt as if I could have eaten ten of them! The coffee was deep, rich, and strong, and I love its slightly bitter chicory taste.

● Café Beignet, 334-B Royal Street, New Orleans, LA, (504) 524-5530

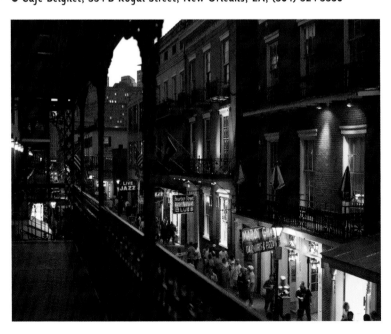

lunch

I grew up with muffaletta before I knew it was called a muffaletta. A muffaletta is a sandwich on a large, flat, crusty, round loaf of bread that is split open and slathered with olive relish (originally made from the bits at the bottom of the olive barrel), then filled with provolone, sliced ham, and salami. My Gran'pa Emmanuel from Sicily slapped meat, cheese, and olives together often—he called it a panino. Hey, whatever you call it, you can't go wrong with a salty, fatty sammy in between crusty bread. Stand on line at Central Grocery, said by many to be the creators of muffaletta in N'Awlins. You can buy half or whole. Ask for extra olive salad, too.

● **Central Grocery Company, 923 Decatur Street, New Orleans, LA, (504) 523-1620**

dinner

Broiled Fish and Shrimp

This is among our top ten finds of all time—really. Fabulous food, charming surroundings and four- or five-star dining at one- or two-star prices. The restaurant is in a wonderful old house. Frank Brigtsen is the chef and co-owner with his wife, Marna. The menu changes daily and I had a delightful three-course, prix fixe meal featuring broiled fish with shrimp and a jalapeno-smoked corn burre blanc. Some days, I get so spoiled! I can't believe this is my job!

● **Brigtsen's, 723 Dante Street, New Orleans, LA, (504) 861-7610**

drink

When it's hot, nothing beats cool jazz and cold beer. That's what you get at this classy joint. Enough said.

● **The Jazz Parlor at Storyville, 125 Bourbon Street, New Orleans, LA, (504) 586-9022**

DALLAS

As an adolescent of the '80s from the Northeast, I must confess that my only references to Dallas were the Dallas Cowboy cheerleaders and the nighttime soap, "DALLAS." When I thought of, well, not just Dallas, but of the state of Texas in general, I thought only of big hair, oil rigs, baby-blue suits, and 10-gallon hats. How naive was I! Dallas is a hip, vibrant, cosmopolitan city with fantastic food, boutique hotels, and something I've been chasing in my dreams for years, a true supper club. Definitely worth a visit. Y'all go, now. Ya hear?

breakfast

People are strange. We don't get many "hate-mail" letters, thank goodness, but you guys can be tough. In my opening to $40 a Day, I used to review the "rules" of my personal budget challenge: breakfast, lunch, and dinner with a drink or snack or dessert thrown in, all for $40 bucks, "no fast food allowed." Well, I had no idea that La Madeleine was a chain restaurant, until I got a bunch of grumpy letters! Some even wrote about "personal disappointment" in my "resorting" to a

Savory Crepes

chain. Guys, really, this is taking it all way too seriously. In my rules, I had said "no fast food" because I didn't want to go to drive-thru restaurants or food courts just to make our budgets. A good chain restaurant is another matter. Listen, if you are able to visit this particular La Madeleine in Dallas, then you are fortunate to have access to good, affordable French food. At the time of our taping, the chef was a French national and a terrific cook. We shot here, then wrapped the equipment and quickly sat down to eat again! The crepes, soups, breads, and omelets were all light on the palate, yet filling and savory. I ate nothing that came out of a pouch or was microwaved. Bottom line: don't be a food snob. Your eyes and nose can spot good food, and if you need further recommendations, do what I do, ask some local folks.

● La Madeleine, 3072 West Mockingbird Lane, Dallas, TX, (214) 696-0800

Tiny and smoky are the first thoughts that come to mind, though delicious is not far behind. I have never left a restaurant, even a barbecue joint, smelling so much like a big piece of beef jerky. Lucky for Sonny's BBQ, the meat is far better than jerky. This is seriously smoky, tender meat on a white hamburger bun. You squirt on the special BBQ sauce as you like, and then sit down at old school desks to chat up the friendly locals who come to Sonny's in droves.

● **Sonny Bryan's Smokehouse, 2202 Inwood Road, Dallas, TX, (214) 357-7120**

recipe courtesy Sonny Bryan's $40ADAY

APPT - SOUP/SAL - ENTREE - **VEG/POT** - DESSERT - BEV

Sonny's Onion Rings

SERVES 12 TO 14

Sonny's Onion Rings

4 pounds white colossal onions, peeled
2 eggs, beaten
1 quart whole milk
1 (12-ounce) can beer
5 & 1/2 cups all-purpose flour
2 tablespoons baking powder

Vegetable oil, for frying

● Crosscut onions into 1/2-inch rings, discarding onion hearts. Combine eggs, milk, and beer in a bowl. Mix flour and bakinpowder thoroughly in separate bowl.
● Heat oil in a deep, heavy pot or deep fryer to 360°F. Make sure pot is not more than half full with oil as the oil will expand once the onions are added. Soak onions in milk mixture for 15 minutes, then coat in flour, shaking off the excess. Dredge onions in the flour a second and even third time to ensure that they're entirely covered with flour. Fry onions until golden brown. Transfer to a paper-towel-lined plate to drain. Serve hot.

66 Tiny and smoky are the first thoughts that come to mind, though delicious is not far behind. **99**

105

recipe	SERVES 8	courtesy Monica's Aca Y Alla	$40ADAY

APPT - SOUP/SAL - **ENTREE** - VEG/POT - DESSERT - BEV

Mexican Lasagna

12 (8-inch) corn tortillas
1 cup homemade or store-bought marinara sauce
1 (8-ounce) can corn
1 (14-ounce) can black beans
14 ounces Monterey Jack cheese, grated, plus more for topping
Salt and freshly ground black pepper
16 ounces cooked chicken, cubed

● Preheat oven to 350°F. Prepare tortillas by soaking them in hot water until they are slightly soft. Coat the bottom of a 9-by-13-inch pan with about 1/2 of the marinara sauce. Arrange 4 tortillas on top of the sauce in the pan. Top the tortillas with about 1/3 of the corn, beans, and cheese. Sprinkle to taste with salt and pepper. Top with 1/3 of the chicken. Place 4 more tortillas on top and make another layer of corn, beans, and cheese. After you have made 3 layers, spread the remaining marinara sauce and top with more cheese. Bake for 45 minutes, or until cheese is bubbly and golden brown.

Mexican Lasagna

"You can conga, samba, and mambo, all-night long to a 13-piece orchestra playing on the bandstand."

dinner

This place is more than just another good restaurant; Monica's is a destination in and of itself. Go to enjoy great food and drink at outrageously reasonable prices, but beyond that, go to Monica's on a weekend night and you'll be walking into a real-live supper club. Just like back-in-the-day, you can conga, samba, and mambo, all-night long to a 13-piece orchestra playing on the bandstand. Monica herself is a classy, smart, and unusual woman! Her matchbooks coin many of her infamous sayings and isms. To paraphrase, "I may not be the most beautiful and on the phone I sound like Ricky Ricardo, but baby, I can cook!" You have to meet Monica to fully understand and appreciate her, but that's easy to do. She spends most of her time in Aca Y Alla (which translates to Here and There, I think) and its sister restaurant. Monica cooked for me personally. I had divine, surprisingly light Mexican lasagna made of tomato and tomatillo sauces, shredded chicken, spiced vegetables, flour tortillas and Asadero cheese. What a creation! (And so is she!) I miss you, Monica! I'll bring John and we'll come to conga soon!

● Monica's Aca Y Alla, 2914 Main Street, Dallas, TX, (214) 748-7140

sweet

Get your ZaZas and your YaYas out! I was completely knocked out by this boutique hotel's design. The guest room Za-sign especially was sleek, but unlike other "hip," Ian Schrager-ish properties I have stayed in, these rooms were actually huge and fully appointed right down to paperclips and cups of sharpened pencils at my high-speed internet-wired desk! At night, fairies came to my room and they turned down my covers and my lights, left jazz on the stereo, and sweet treats on my pillow, all for a price lower than some Best Westerns I've stayed at! Nice. The lobby was so sexy, I would have dated it. The restaurant was ultra-loungy and so posh, I worried about prices and food quality. When it comes to food, I've sometimes found that lots of glam can hide a sham. The Dragonfly buzzed-over my worries and surpassed my expectations. I only had time and budget to enjoy a dessert here, a special, delicate lemon grass soup. If I'd had the chance, I'd have eaten four courses here!

● **Dragonfly at Hotel ZaZa, 2332 Leonard Street, Dallas, TX, (214) 550-9500**

Lemongrass Soup

AUSTIN

Love, love, love at first sight. Every second I spent in Austin was better than the last! There are so many reasons to love this place. For example, there's Bob Schneider, an Austin musician, whose recordings I discovered at Waterloo Records, years after seeing part of an Austin City Limits episode; the music, art, film, and theater scene in general, which rivals even NYC; the clubs, restaurants, hip hotels, even the bats (yup, flying, winged, black, blind-as-a...that kind). Shopping is great, and the Salt Lick (see below) is nearby, and catch the Hot Club of Cow Town (buy their CD, too) if you can.

breakfast

Migas Taco

You cannot miss this place because it has a huge papier-maché statue of Maria on the roof with arms opened wide, Evita-like. Owner Maria Corbalan has many friends, including Bob Schneider who wrote taco=love on the wall here. Covered with signatures of famous musicians, movie stars, and taco lovers from around the globe, the colorful walls indicate that Maria's is Austin central: you never know who will walk through the door next. The great music never stops. Maria herself is a delight—off the cool-factor meter and man, does she have tales to tell! The Mexican fare is fresh and delicious, surprisingly light and healthful, and the prices are completely unreal—so inexpensive! I had a local favorite: Migas tacos with egg and salsa, because it was breakfast time. Tacos=love.

● **Taco Xpress, 2529 South Lamar Boulevard, Austin, TX, (512) 444-0261**

recipe courtesy Taco Xpress

$40ADAY

APPT - SOUP/SAL - ENTREE - VEG/POT - DESSERT - BEV

Migas Taco
SERVES 1

1 (12-inch) flour tortilla

1 small handful lightly crushed tortilla chips

1 tablespoon chopped jalapeños

2 tablespoons diced tomatoes

2 tablespoons diced onion

1/2 cup Mexican Blend cheese

1 egg, lightly beaten

Salsa (optional)

● Put tortilla in a skillet over low heat to stay warm throughout the process. Watch carefully so the tortilla doesn't burn or harden. Mix chips, jalapeños, tomatoes, and onions and sauté in a separate, large nonstick skillet over medium heat until the onions are mostly translucent (don't let the chips burn).

● Push the veggies to one side and, on the other side of the skillet, add cheese and heat until melted, while cooking the rest of the dish. Add the egg to the vegetables, scramble together and heat until the egg is cooked. Scoop the egg mixture on top of the cheese. Use a spatula to scoop up the cheese and egg and place it on the warmed tortilla. Top with salsa, if desired.

❝ Covered with signatures of famous musicians, movie stars, and taco lovers from around the globe, the colorful walls indicate that Maria's is Austin central. ❞

109

lunch

This restaurant is a vision of loveliness: soft, brightly hued rooms; cozy, classic decor; plants; small tables with white cloths; bistro fare on white plates; people of all ages, eating, smiling—it was just pleasant and relaxing to enter and be seated here. The food made it an even richer experience. I ordered a soup and salad lunch, thinking I would keep it simple, but I'd never dined at Josie's before. One thing they don't do is simple! The flavors in my soup were complex and layered: fresh, buttery artichokes mixed with rich homemade stock, dollops of herb pesto, and croutons of crusty bruschetta (charred garlic toast). Wow! I also had a Caesar salad that would have brought Caesar himself to his knees.

● **Café Josie, 1200-B West 6th Street, Austin, TX, (512) 322-9226**

recipe	SERVES 4	courtesy Café Josie	$40ADAY

APPT - <u>SOUP/SAL</u> - ENTREE - VEG/POT - DESSERT - BEV

Artichoke Bisque

Artichoke Bisque

4 whole artichoke hearts

4 Roma tomatoes

1 red bell pepper

Vegetable oil, for brushing

1 tablespoon butter

1 small onion, chopped

4 large garlic cloves, minced

1 & 1/2 cups vegetable stock

1 cup cream

Several sprigs fresh cilantro, leaves picked and chopped

1 tablespoon cornstarch

1/2 cup water

1/2 teaspoon salt

Pinch freshly ground black pepper

Manchego cheese, for garnish

Toasted pumpkin seeds and pine nuts, for garnish

● Preheat a grill. Skewer artichokes. Coat tomatoes, bell pepper, and artichoke hearts lightly-with oil, place on grill just away from the hottest spot. Turn occasionally with tongs to sear all surfaces. Cook until the artichokes are tender and the skins of the tomatoes and peppers are black and blistered. Remove to a dish to let cool; reserve any juices that accumulate. Once peppers and tomatoes are cool, peel the skins off both and seed the peppers. In a food processor, small chop and set aside.

● In a large saucepan over medium heat, melt butter and sauté onion and garlic, stirring, until onion is translucent. Add vegetable stock, cream, grilled vegetables, and reserved juices, and cilantro. Bring to a simmer; stir to heat evenly. Combine cornstarch and water in a small bowl to make a slurry. Slowly add the slurry to the saucepan while stirring to combine. Bring to a simmer and allow sauce to thicken slightly, 1 to 2 minutes. Be careful not to boil for too long or the cornstarch will lose its thickening ability. Add salt and pepper, to taste. Serve with cheese, pumpkin seeds, or pine nuts, if desired.

dinner

You can smell this place from miles away—then you drive faster! Just outside Austin city limits, in Driftwood, is a place so beloved by every person I met in Austin, I bet any of them would have chauffeured me here person-  ally. I rented at Hertz. Out in the country, on a huge piece of land with an old split-rail fence is, for my money, the best barbecue pit in Texas. When you walk into the cavernous dining area you'll find it surprisingly warm and inviting with communal bench seating at beautiful, old, dark-stained wooden tables, and a huge stone fire- place, fire blazing. You'll be awe struck by the huge, brick and

Salt Lick Brisket

stone pit covered with meat. Fires flare, men slice gigantic slabs of meat and serve up mounds of chicken, sausages, and rib racks, too. The aroma is intoxicat- ing. You will eat until you feel a need to pass out. When you go to Austin, make sure to get in your licks!

● **Salt Lick, 18300 Fm 1826, Driftwood, TX, (512) 894-3117**

drink

Across from my favorite hotel, San Jose Hotel, is the coolest, hottest club in town! Live music, nightly, the Continental pours a stiff drink and keeps the dance floor loose. I was lucky enough to hit the Continental  on a big night: Hot Club of Cowtown was playing. These are three of the most talented musicians on the planet: bass, fiddle, and guitar, all with voices of angels, all easy on the eye, too! Their music is eclectic: swing, jazz, folk, western, American pops, all mixed up in a blender. They know how to get feet tapping and crowds clapping! Good drinks, too. Try the Margatinis!

● **Continental Club, 1315 South Congress Avenue, Austin, TX, (512) 441-2444**

CORPUS CHRISTI

All over town local people kept asking us why we were filming in Corpus Christi. They had us worried. I think they meant why were we here filming out of season. This place is a hopping, hot (very hot) spot in the spring and summer. In winter, when we showed up, it was cold and really pretty deserted. We dressed it up with some footage of warmer months and left with some good food and funny stories under our belts.

breakfast

This place is very homey, though in a strip mall. Everyone in town can tell ya how to get here. Inside, the food is good and the conversations a dull roar. The prices and food quality keep them rolling in the door most mornings. I got hooked on Migas (eggs) in Austin, so I had them again here at Andy's. They were very tasty and the salsa topping on my eggs gave me a jump start to my day.

● **Andy's Kitchen, 5802 South Staples Street, Corpus Christi, TX, (361) 993-0251**

lunch

What a crazy place! It is out near a beach where I saddled up and went horseback riding, so I stopped in. The restaurant is attached to a funky candle shop. The food looked great and the place was packed with locals! I had a jerk pork sandwich which was spicy, lean, and delicious! Prices were right and out back, a lovely garden, too.

● **Laffite's, 15605 South Padre Island Drive, Corpus Christi, TX, (361) 949-2428**

sweet

This restaurant, again nestled among the strip malls, was surprisingly cozy. Its decorative antiques and artifacts have been collected from all over the world by the owners.
The menu is vast and everything looked lovely, even the free bar buffet of Mexican snacks. Crystal's also has a confectionary bar where I had a dessert called a Mexican Hot Fudge Hat, which was ice cream and fudge spilling over a crisp tortilla. It was yummy.

● **Crystal's Restaurant and Confectionary Bar, 4119 South Staples Street, Corpus Christi, TX, (361) 857-8081**

Hot Fudge Hat

❝ The menu is vast and everything looked lovely, even the free bar buffet of Mexican snacks. ❞

dinner

Brad and Liz Lomax have started quite a trend in their part of town on North Water Street. Thanks to their vision and hard work, a cluster of cool shops, restaurants, and bars has taken root. The Seafood Company, an old factory made new with great design, architecture, and style, is a feast for the eyes and a real culinary find, too. I had a jambalaya and pasta dish that rocked and a huge iceberg lettuce wedge covered in a bright cilantro vinaigrette. I paired it with a slightly spicy Texan red wine and it was party time for me.

Seafood Pasta Jambalaya

● **Water Street Seafood Co., 309 North Water Street, Corpus Christi, TX, (361) 882-8683**

---

recipe | SERVES 4 | courtesy Water Street Seafood Co. | $40ADAY

APPT - SOUP/SAL - ENTREE - VEG/POT - DESSERT - BEV

Seafood Pasta Jambalaya

1/2 cup (1 stick) butter

1 chicken breast, cut into strips (about 1 cup)

16 (21–25 count) shrimp, peeled and deveined, tails removed

1/2 cup crawfish tails

1/2 cup sliced andouille sausage

1/3 cup sliced yellow onion

1/4 cup sliced red bell pepper

1/3 cup sliced green bell pepper

1/3 cup sliced zucchini

1/3 cup sliced yellow squash

1 cup diced Roma tomatoes

1 quart Andouille Cream Sauce (recipe follows)

4 cups cavatappi pasta

1/2 cup sliced scallion

1/2 teaspoon chopped fresh flat-leaf parsley leaves

● Melt butter in a large sauté pan over medium-low heat. Increase heat to medium and add chicken, shrimp, crawfish, andouille, onion, and bell peppers. Sauté until shrimp and chicken are just cooked through. Add zucchini, yellow squash, and tomatoes, cook 2 minutes. Add andouille cream sauce, toss well, and bring to a boil. Remove from the heat and keep warm.

● Cook cavatappi in boiling salted water until al dente; drain well.

● Pour sauce over pasta, and toss, pulling shrimp, chicken, and crawfish to the top. Evenly sprinkle scallion over pasta. Sprinkle parsley around rim of bowl and serve.

Andouille Cream Sauce:

1 teaspoon canola oil

1/4 cup diced yellow onion

2 tablespoons chopped garlic

3 ounces andouille sausage, such as Sysco brand, casing removed

2/3 cup crushed tomatoes, such as Machacado's

2/3 cup cold water

3/4 tablespoon chicken base

2 teaspoons cornstarch

1 cup heavy cream

2 teaspoons blackening seasoning 1/4 teaspoon cayenne pepper

1/4 cup jalapeño-Jack cheese, grated

● Place oil in a saucepan over medium heat. Add diced onion and sauté 3 to 4 minutes. Add garlic, stir well, and sauté 2 minutes. Add andouille sausage and sauté 2 more minutes. Add crushed tomatoes and mix well to thoroughly combine.

● In a mixing bowl use a wire whisk to combine water, chicken base, cornstarch, and cream. Add liquid to the onion mixture. Bring to a boil, reduce the heat, and simmer 8 to 10 minutes. Add blackening seasoning and cayenne and mix well to incorporate. Add grated cheese to the sauce and blend well. Allow to simmer until all the cheese has melted, 2 more minutes.

CHICAGO
MILWAUKEE
CLEVELAND

CHICAGO

Now, here's a looker! Chicago is one of the most beautiful cities in the world. The wide avenues remind me of Paris, as do the stone bridges and huge touring boats that glide under them. I love the unusual way buildings are sited; downtown goes off on so many different angles, and many buildings are masterpieces of architecture. There are massive outdoor sculptures by Miro and my favorite, a Picasso, so large that small children run, jump, and slide all over it. Make sure to go on a walking architectural tour, as I did. It was fast, informative, and entertaining. Museums here are fantastic, too. My favorites: The Field Museum and The Art Institute of Chicago. At night, check out Blues Alley. You'll find that standards are high. I am a huge baseball fan and I love both ball parks equally—they are so different. Wrigley Field is charming, homey, and, like Fenway Park in Boston, it's surrounded by residences and businesses. Comisky Park is a whole other thing. It's got a carnevale vibe about it. I love the food here! You can get corn, scraped fresh off the cob, which are then topped with your choice of twenty spices and toppings. I always get chili-lime corn. In the stands, men with sombreros and backpacks serve frozen Cuervo margaritas right at your seat! Cool! When it comes to shopping, this is the home of The Miracle Mile, so get those credit cards polished up! At Marshall Field's I browse my way from the bottom of the store to the top, then relax for afternoon tea in the dining room. This place is more than a store, it's an institution.

breakfast

Of all the places I've filmed, more than 200 now, I find myself telling strangers about a select few over and over again because they are such personal favorites. Kitsch'n is one such place. I had a ball here! The chef became a friend and I hear he's opened a second location. I can't wait to go! I have written recipes for my own cooking show that pay homage to the kitschy food that Jon Young has created. Kitsch'n is retro-metro, funky, and chic. It's filled with actual kitsch from the '70s, my era. From fondue pots to lava lamps and mod-squad lunch boxes, Jon's joint brings me back-in-the-day. On TV, watch Foxy Brown, Shaft, Starsky and Hutch, HR Puffinstuff. I brought in a Syd and Marty Croft character to add to his collections. The menu is gourmet-for-everyday and include's Jon's fancy TV dinners and dressed up Mac and Cheese. At breakfast, I tried his Green Eggs and Ham. I've seen versions of this before, playing on the Seuss book title, the "green" refers to whatever you mix or top the eggs with, like green salsa or guacamole, or, in Jon's case, pesto sauce. Jon made me a spinach pesto, mixed with eggs and chopped ham. Alongside, he served thick-cut Texas toast. It was delicious and so is this place!

● Kitsch'n On Roscoe, 2005 West Roscoe Street, Chicago, IL, (773) 248-7372

Green Eggs and Ham

recipe · SERVES 1 · courtesy Kitsch'n On Roscoe · $40ADAY

APPT - SOUP/SAL - **ENTREE** - VEG/POT - DESSERT - BEV

Green Eggs and Ham

2 tablespoons clarified butter (butter melted slowly over low heat and foam skimmed)

1/2 cup fresh spinach greens, washed and dried

1/4 cup diced smoked ham

2 tablespoons chopped scallions

3 eggs, beaten

1 heaping tablespoon Spinach Pesto (recipe follows)

Salt and freshly ground black pepper

● Heat butter in a medium skillet over medium-high heat. Add spinach, ham, and scallions, stirring with a wooden spoon to combine. Cook 2 minutes, then pour eggs over the spinach mixture. Allow the eggs to begin to set, then add pesto, salt, and pepper. Stir together until eggs are cooked evenly.

Spinach Pesto:

1 & 1/2 cups packed fresh spinach greens, washed and dried

1/4 cup fresh basil leaves

4 roasted garlic cloves, chopped

1/4 cup grated Parmesan, optional

1 cup extra-virgin olive oil

Salt

● Place spinach, basil, garlic, and Parmesan, if using, in the bowl of a food processor and pulse. Slowly add olive oil while the processor is running on low speed. Pulse until the ingredients are blended into a smooth sauce, being careful not to overmix. Season, to taste, with salt.

Tip: Pesto can be made ahead of time and stored in the refrigerator for 1 day.

lunch

Polenta Lasagna

The Backstage Bistro at the Culinary Institute of Chicago has a wall of glass so you can watch the future rock star chefs of America toil away over your meal. The menu changes daily and is always fairly priced, ridiculously so. For a few bucks, you can eat some of the most artfully prepared food in the country as it is being created under the hawk eyes of supervising master chefs. I have enjoyed eating in the dining rooms of many culinary schools, but I thought the restaurant design here was a real step-up. I had an amazing polenta and vegetable lasagna stack with a fire-roasted tomato sauce. Rock on!

● **Backstage Bistro, 180 North Wabash Avenue, Chicago, IL, (312) 475-6920**

dinner

Chicago has a huge Greek Town. Greek Islands is the largest of all the restaurants in this section of town and for a good reason: everyone eats here because it's the best. They must serve thousands a day here, really. The white-washed, tiled interiors go on and on forever. You're on a Greek island or so it seems! I sat up in a small turret overlooking a dining room ablaze with a huge wood-burning oven and could see that the open kitchen operated like a well-orchestrated stage show.

Because of volume, prices are very reasonable. I had a delicate lemon and artichoke appetizer and a stuffed lamb loin for dinner. Greek food is much more than a feta-covered salad and grape leaves. Go Greek in Chicago!

● **Greek Islands, 200 South Halsted Street, Chicago, IL, (312) 782-9855**

sweet

If you have kids, check out the Navy Pier. There are carnival rides, lots of bright lights and sweet treats, of course. The Popcorn Palace is a family-run business offering as many popcorn coatings as Jelly Belly makes for their beans! The list is really endless. I munched on some macadamia butter toffee corn and it was crazy sweet, nutty, and delicious!

● **The Popcorn Palace, 700 East Grand Avenue, Navy Pier, Chicago, IL, (800) 873-2686**

recipe courtesy The Popcorn Palace $40ADAY

APPT - SOUP/SAL - ENTREE - VEG/POT - DESSERT - BEV

Macadamia Butter Crunch Popcorn

SERVES 4 TO 6

12 cups popped popcorn
3 cups whole macadamia nuts
1 cup firmly packed brown sugar
1/2 cup (1 stick) unsalted butter
1/4 cup light corn syrup
1/2 teaspoon salt
1/2 teaspoon baking soda

● Preheat oven to 200°F. Divide popcorn and nuts between 2 ungreased 9 by 13-inch rectangular pans, making sure popcorn and nuts are evenly mixed.
● In a medium saucepan over medium heat, cook brown sugar, butter, corn syrup, and salt stirring constantly until bubbly around the edges. Continue cooking for 5 more minutes, then remove the pan from the heat. Stir in baking soda until the mixture becomes foamy. Pour the mixture over the popcorn and nuts, stirring until they are well coated. Bake, uncovered, for 1 hour, stirring every 15 minutes.

❝ The Popcorn Palace is a family-run business offering as many popcorn coatings as Jelly Belly makes for their beans! ❞

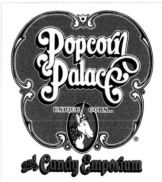

MILWAUKEE

Now, I am a Harley-Davidson-loving girl from way back, so I was really excited to visit the home of one of my favorite American institutions. My trip to the Mac-Daddy Harley D Store out on Silver Spring Road coincided with their 100th Anniversary celebration and it was

hopping! What an amazing selection of bikes they have! Years ago, I even dated a guy with a dog named Harley (after his Sportster). It didn't work out, the thing with that guy, but riding on the back of that bike was way-cool and so was the dog! Milwaukee is really a fun place to hang out, and to my surprise, a great weekend vacation spot, too.

Miss Katie's Diner

breakfast

Three Cheese Omelet

Next to having Sunday breakfast at home or at Sutton's Market Place, near my little cabin in the woods, the next-best-place to start any day is a good diner. I'm not a fan of hibernating in my hotel room with overpriced room service (well, maybe once in a while...). I like to hit a local joint first thing, just to get a feel for the area, usually an elbows-on-the-table place, away from the tourist strip. Miss Katie's Diner is off the beaten path and lots of fun. It is very retro and even has a game room. I played tabletop shuffleboard with a local, while they made me one of their menu favorites, the three-cheese omelet. After all, Wisconsinites are affectionately called Cheeseheads! The omelet was ooey, gooey, and delicious!

● Miss Katie's Diner, 1900 West Clybourn Street, Milwaukee, WI, (414) 344-0044

❝ I played tabletop shuffleboard with a local, while they made me one of their menu favorites, the three-cheese omelet. ❞

recipe courtesy Miss Katie's Diner $40ADAY

APPT - SOUP/SAL - ENTREE - VEG/POT - DESSERT - BEV

Three-Cheese Omelet
SERVES 1

2 tablespoons butter
3 large eggs, well beaten
1 ounce mild Cheddar, grated
1 ounce aged provolone, diced
1 ounce aged Swiss cheese, diced

● Melt butter in an 8-inch, nonstick skillet over medium heat. Add eggs. As eggs begin to set, sprinkle the 3 cheeses evenly over the eggs. As cheese begins to melt and before the eggs get brown, flip egg mixture over. Continue to cook until the cheese melts. Flip omelet again. Slide onto a plate, folding in half, and serve immediately.

lunch

Mader's is a destination in and of itself. It has been in Milwaukee, serving the best bratwurst around (Usinger's) for decades. To dine here is to enjoy the best of the "brats" in style! I've never had a plate of sausage so well prepared or so delightful to look at: Fanned, crisp-skinned brats cut on a bias formed a carefully balanced sculpture over a chiffonade of cabbage with mustards and wedges of hearty rye points. This was truly gourmet bratwurst like no other! (see recipe on next page)

Bratwurst and Knockwurst

● Mader's Restaurant, 1037 North Old World Third Street, Milwaukee, WI, (414) 271-3377

Bratwurst & Knockwurst with Rye Toast Points

1 teaspoon sea salt

8 to 10 new red potatoes

4 bratwurst (recommended: Usingers')

4 knockwurst (recommended: Usingers')

2 tablespoons butter

1 tablespoon minced chives

Salt and freshly ground black pepper

4 slices rye bread

1 tablespoon herb butter, recipe follows

8 ounces sauerkraut, drained and warmed in a saucepan

4 ounces German mustard, for serving

● Bring a medium pot of water to a boil; add salt. Add potatoes and cook until tender, about 10 minutes. Remove potatoes from water and keep warm; reserve hot water over medium heat.
● Preheat a grill or grill pan. Poach bratwurst and knockwurst in reserved simmering water until cooked through, about 10 minutes; drain.
● Grill bratwurst and knockwurst until golden brown and cooked thoroughly, about 10 minutes.
● While the sausages are browning, cut potatoes in half. Melt butter in a sauté pan over medium heat. Add potatoes and chives and cook until the potatoes are well coated. Season with salt and pepper, to taste.
● Cut crusts off rye toast and brush on herb butter. Grill until toasted. Cut into "points" (2 diagonal slices, like an "X"). To assemble plate, place 2 ounces of sauerkraut in center of each plate. Place halved potatoes around; slice bratwurst and knockwurst, arranging with toast points. Serve with mustard.

Herb Butter:

2 sticks unsalted butter, softened

1 tablespoon finely chopped fresh chives

1 tablespoon finely chopped flat-leaf parsley

Salt and freshly ground black pepper

● In a large bowl, mix all ingredients with a rubber spatula until combined. You can also use a food processor to combine all the ingredients. Use as needed.
● To store: Place the butter on the bottom end of a large piece of plastic wrap. Fold the bottom edge of the wrap over the butter and roll the enclosed butter forward until completely wrapped to form a log, about 1 & 1/2 inches in diameter. Twist the ends and refrigerate to chill. Slice rounds as needed. Store in the freezer for up to 1 month.

drink

I have never had such a hard time finding a place that was hiding in plain sight as I did finding The Safe House. Created at the peak of the 007 James Bond-era, it is a spy-spoof hoot! Just to get in, you'll need help and directions from several locals—they have fun torturing tourists with hints. Once you're in on the joke, it becomes funnier. You make it into the place by passing some tests administered by Miss Moneypenny. They measure your ability to impersonate people, animals, or states of being—important traits for spies, don't ya know. Meanwhile, you're on candid camera downstairs in the bar. When you finally make it in, you are given the password. Once in, you think the tough part is over, but then you walk into the bar. You're greeted and graded by the crowd, mocking you and your performance while holding up scorecards. It's fun for them, horrible for you, until you get to do it to the next guy. There is no other way in. Once in, have fun with it all. I can't tell you all that's inside. It's a secret. I could put many lives in jeopardy. You must go to The Safe House, soon, or there will be much danger. The password is....

● **The Safe House, 779 North Front Street, Milwaukee, WI, (414) 271-2007**

❝ It's fun for them, horrible for you, until you get to do it to the next guy. There is no other way in. ❞

dinner

Look for the Schlitz globe on the rooftop, and you'll find a family restaurant housed in an old, warm house. Owner Branko Radicevic is the welcoming host. His beautiful daughter and loving wife work here as well. The food, which has some similarities to Hungarian and Polish cuisines, and the atmosphere are so comforting, you'll want to stay on well after the meal. I had an amazing, meat-filled pastry called a burek. I have no idea what's in it or how to make it. It's a family secret that belongs to Branko's mother. I would recommend having the burek as a starter or a side dish, rather than a meal, and then sharing it two to four ways, because it is so very rich! As I looked around, I saw other delicious-looking plates of well-prepared food, and diners smiling and happy, which is always a good sign.

● **Three Brothers Serbian Restaurant, 2414 South St. Clair Street, Milwaukee, WI, (414) 481-7530**

CLEVELAND

Cleveland is the home of The Rock and Roll Hall of Fame because Cleveland ROCKS! I've loved this town ever since my first trip here, several years ago. My friend, David Moss, the movies and cool-stuff reporter for Fox News, lives here. Moss Man is reason enough for me to visit, but for you guys, I recommend going during baseball season. Jacob's Field has had a facelift and it is now one of my favorite ball parks in the country. And The Hall of Fame never disappoints. There's always a new show; my favorite to date, the U2 exhibit I caught while we were taping $40 a Day. Plan a whole day around the R&R Hall of Fame and try to catch all of the movies and multimedia rooms. Next door is a science museum that is really fun and interesting for kids and adults. I loved the West Side Market, too. My favorite food in the whole Market was the falafel that came from a stand in the back corner. It's the best I have ever tasted. The sauce is a secret recipe and it takes the owner's wife days to make up a batch. So good.

breakfast

This restaurant is outside the city and you'll need a car to get here. Rent one. Tommy's is the gathering place for all the locals for miles around. It's '70s-looking, bright and light with lots of local art, a great soda fountain, and a beautiful glassed-in dining room. I loved it all, down to the funky tee shirts that my boyfriend and I wear all the time. The menu is HUGE, clever, and eclectic, with lots of whole foods and vegetarian choices. I especially loved the whole-wheat calzones filled with veggies and cheese. Yummy. I had my own veggie omelet, mixing up ingredients from several offerings on the menu, many named after some of the regulars. This restaurant is another of my all-time favorites, along with Tommy himself. He's quite a guy, a true original!

● Tommy's, 1824 Coventry Road, Cleveland, OH, (216) 321-7757

> **❝ If you think NYC is the home of the best deli sandwich, Slyman's will set you straight. ❞**

lunch

If you think NYC is the home of the best deli sandwich, Slyman's will set you straight. This is by far the best corned-beef sandwich I have ever tasted in my life. It is a mile high and half the price of any I've had at any of NYC's big, famous delis. The meat was lean and warm and the mustard, light brown and spicy. At lunchtime, the place is a zoo and the line for take-out stretches out the door. Still, do not go to Cleveland without having the greatest sandwich in America. Sorry NYC, but you still have that Broadway thing going for ya!

● Slyman's, 3106 St. Clair Ave., Cleveland, OH, (216) 621-3760

snack

The West Side Market is a great place to get an overview of all the great foods of Cleveland. You can sample lots of locally produced sausages, meats, cheeses, vegetables, and of course, pierogis. How can you go wrong with potato dumplings? At the Pierogi Palace you can find pierogis filled with anything and everything in them, from mushrooms to fruit. And they only cost a buck a pop.

● **Pierogi Palace, Westside Market, Stand E-5, 1979 West 25th Street, Cleveland, OH, (216) 566-5187**

drink

If you are in the Market, the Brewing Co. is just across the street. Head over to sample a few of the brews before you decide. I went with a Burning River Ale, delicious and crisp. Stop in for a cold one.

● **Great Lakes Brewing Co., 2516 Market Ave., Cleveland, OH, (216) 771-4404**

dinner

Neighborhoods like Little Italy are always fun and I go looking for them in different cities because I know the food will be fresh, home-made, and fairly priced. At Trattoria Roman Gardens, a nice family-run business (of course), they offer half portions for half the price! I

had a fantastic and very generous half-portion of linguini with pesto and scallops. The pesto, bursting with fragrant fresh basil, held it's color well, and the scallops were sweet and cooked to perfection.

● **Trattoria Roman Gardens, 12207 Mayfield Rd., Cleveland, OH, (216) 421-2700**

w.est

SANTA FE
SEDONA
TUCSON
GRAND CANYON
PARK CITY
SUN VALLEY
TELLURIDE
DENVER
ASPEN
LAS VEGAS
SAN DIEGO
LAGUNA BEACH
PALM SPRINGS
LOS ANGELES
SANTA BARBARA
SAN FRANCISCO
MONTEREY
SONOMA
PORTLAND
SEATTLE
VANCOUVER

SANTA FE

This city is a wash of stucco, laid over old, large wooden beams, wrapped in hand-made brightly colored textiles, and dotted with beautiful ceramic tiles. You want to stay outside all day here, wandering, taking it all in. The air is crisp and dry, and I did not notice the heat. The shops and plazas are filled with beautiful art objects, from jewelry to pottery, serapes to rugs, all produced by local Native Americans and craftsmen. The Eldorado Hotel was a cool place to stay and to hang around. Have a drink at the La Fonda, upstairs on the rooftop, to check out the view. Visit the Georgia O'Keefe Museum and one of the surrounding pueblos to learn about true American history from Native Americans. Each pueblo, by the way, is a separate nation from the US, completely independent of Federal laws and government. (How utopian can you get?). I loved my kickball game in the Pueblo of Tesque.

breakfast

Tamal Dulce

Cafe Pasqual's makes my all-time favorites list of places to dine out on the planet. It's a small space made large, open, and airy by bright colors, banners, and artwork. Each dish is a masterwork of Southwestern and/or Mexican cuisine. Kudos to owner Katharine Kagel for the research and love which must have gone into the creation and operation of this business. Compliments to chefs Gabaldon and Lopez for my breakfast of Tamal Dulce, a sweetened corn-meal delight. I could have three meals a day here and never tire of it.

● **Cafe Pasqual's, 121 Don Gaspar, Santa Fe, NM, (505) 983-9340**

lunch

COWGIRL
BBQ &
Western Grill

319 South Guadalupe Street
Santa Fe, NM 87501
505•982•2565

Fun and funky are the first two words that come back to my mind when I remember this restaurant. I had a barbecue special, and it was good. But it was the crazy décor that made this joint memorable. At night, inside small brightly painted rooms, the Cowgirl turns honky tonk with live music and rowdy crowds. By day, the courtyard out front is the most popular dining area. Old metal furniture is mixed in among wagon wheels and graveyards of memorabilia. It is charming. My quirky cowgirl waitress was a filmmaker who had just completed a film about waitresses. Like I said, fun and funky.

● **Cowgirl BBQ & Western Grill, 319 South Guadalupe Street, Santa Fe, NM, (505) 982-2565**

dinner

Coyote Cafe has been famous for some twenty years now. I remember buying their products wholesale for gourmet marketplaces I worked in many years ago. I remember their cookbook back in the '90s, when Sante Fe cuisine was all the rage, coast to coast. Coyote Cafe is still going strong, still cutting edge in Southwestern cuisine. The Rooftop Cantina is a terrific budget-minded alternative to the main dining room; its delicious offerings incorporate all the signature flavors and techniques used in the main Cafe. It is a perfect choice for lunch to late-night light bites. I had the vegetable enchiladas, which were amazingly good and inexpensive, too.

Coyote Cafe

Vegetarian Enchilada

● **Rooftop Cantina at Coyote Cafe, 132 West Water Street, Santa Fe, NM, (505) 983-1615**

❝ **The Rooftop Cantina is a terrific budget-minded alternative to the main dining room.** ❞

sweet

Had I another day here, I would have gone to The Shed for dinner. It is charming and warm, the artwork fantastic. Courtney, the owner, is gorgeous, hard-working, and sweet (she was then eight months pregnant!) The entrance is set back and the doorway tiny, as are all the winding, connected dining rooms. Prices are beyond reasonable and the menu was very creative, innovative, and fresh-sounding. I had a divine, delicate lemon soufflé that was under five dollars and worth two to three times that price. Yumm-o!

● **The Shed, 113 1/2 East Palace Avenue, Santa Fe, NM, (505) 982-9030**

THE SHED
CREATIVE COOKING
Family Owned & Operated Since 1953
Courtney and Linnea Carswell
113 1/2 East Palace Avenue • Santa Fe, New Mexico 87501
www.sfshed.com   Fax 982-0902   Phone 982-9030

SEDONA

I am superstitious. I am sentimental. I still believe my dolls have feelings and my dog is human. I believe my grandfather watches over me and that when we die we go somewhere or become a part of something larger than ourselves. This is as far as I can go into The New Age. I don't believe that colored rocks and crystals heal people; I think they keep people in physical or emotional stress either from dealing with it or worse, away from medicine and doctors who could help them. I do not believe in tarot card readers or psychics. I think some of these people lie either collectively to themselves and others or worse, knowingly deceive people who are feeling lost. I do believe that devout practitioners of many Eastern religions and disciplines can achieve higher levels of consciousness than the rest of us. I do not

think that the bored or the unemployed can suddenly channel ancient guides and take you along for the ride. I bring this rant up because Sedona is saturated with The New Age and its minions. It is the industry here, so be prepared. When we asked some New Agers to sign releases to appear in our program, more than one wanted to know whether to give their real names or the names given to them by their channel guides. Wow. Sedona is ground-zero for these followers because of the supposed vortices that occur here. A vortex is a place of heightened magnetic energy in the earth's magnetic field. I watched a professor in a recent television program measure the magnetic field at one vortex and he found it had a lower magnetic field than at another point outside the vortex. Further, whether these vortices exist or not, magnetic energy has never had an effect on my love life or job. All of this being said, Sedona is still one of the most beautiful places I have ever seen in my lifetime (and I've been around)! The red rocks are really red, the sunsets fantastic. The dessert is beautiful, truly awesome and the rock formations, humbling and inspiring. You must take a jeep tour ride around the rocks and the Cococino National Forest and parks. This is one bumpy, crazy, exciting ride and it's fun for all ages. Check it out.

breakfast

I stayed at L'Auberge and we filmed here. It was so relaxing and delightful, I felt as if I were in a storybook, living in an enchanted forest. My room was a tiny cottage with a wood-burning fireplace and a dreamy bed. My breakfast was served al fresco alongside a babbling brook (or a singing stream); the water was full of ducks, all paired off, further proof of the romance in the air here. My breakfast was sweet and delicious; I had ground almond-crusted French toast. I wouldn't change a thing about the food or this place or even the prices. It was all simply perfect.

● **Terrace on the Creek at L'Auberge de Sedona, 301 L'Auberge Lane, Sedona, AZ, (928) 282-1667**

Pain Perdu

recipe courtesy Terrace on the Creek $40ADAY

APPT - SOUP/SAL - ENTREE - VEG/POT - DESSERT - BEV

Pain Perdu

SERVES 6

6 eggs
1 cup cream
1/4 teaspoon salt
1 tablespoon ground cinnamon
1 tablespoon pure vanilla extract
12 thick slices bread, preferably brioche
2 cups coarsely ground almonds
2 tablespoons butter
Confectioners' sugar, for serving
Sliced seasonal fruit, for serving

● Beat eggs lightly in a shallow bowl with a fork or whisk; add cream, salt, cinnamon, and vanilla. Submerge the bread slices in the egg mixture for 5 minutes. Lay both sides of the bread in the almonds to coat.

● Heat butter in a large, heavy skillet over low heat until the foam subsides, then add a few slices of bread. Cook until delicate brown; flip and brown other side. Transfer to a plate. Sprinkle with confectioners' sugar and garnish with sliced fruit; serve hot. Repeat with the rest of the bread slices.

lunch

Downtown Sedona looks like an old Western movie set and the Cowboy Club is the head honcho. They make great grub here, not just grits and ribs, but fine food, done cowboy style. I had a surprising offering, venison enchiladas. It was the daily special and it was spicy, but not too hot; the meat was very tender and flavorful, and it came wrapped in a red flour tortilla. (see recipe on next page) This restaurant was fun, casual, and affordable, considering the high quality food.

● **Cowboy Club, 241 North Highway 89A, Sedona, AZ, (928) 282-4200**

Venison Enchiladas

1/4 cup canola oil, plus more for dish

2 pounds venison stew meat, cubed

1 medium yellow onion, diced

2 tablespoons chopped garlic

Salt and freshly ground black pepper

1 tablespoon chili powder

1 tablespoon firmly packed brown sugar

1 bunch fresh cilantro, leaves picked and chopped

1/2 cup reduced (double-strength) chicken stock

5 cups grated colby-Jack cheese

12 (8 to 10-inch) corn tortillas

Red Enchilada Sauce, recipe follows

Venison Enchilada

● Heat oil in a large heavy skillet over high heat until almost smoking. Carefully add venison, onion, and garlic; season with salt and pepper and brown the meat, stirring occasionally. Add chili powder, brown sugar, and cilantro. Add chicken stock and stir, scraping up any browned bits from the pan. Remove from heat and allow to cool, about 20 minutes. Stir in 3 cups grated cheese.

● Preheat oven to 375°F. To soften the tortillas, wrap them in a damp cloth, place in a microwave oven, and cook on high until pliable, 10 to 20 seconds. Spoon 2 to 3 tablespoons venison mixture into the center of each tortilla and roll. Place rolled enchiladas into a lightly oiled baking dish, seam side down. Smother with Red Enchilada Sauce and sprinkle remaining grated cheese, to taste. Cover and bake until cheese is melted and bubbly, about 20 minutes.

Red Enchilada Sauce:

1 red bell pepper

2 tablespoons canola oil

1 & 1/2 medium onions, chopped

6 garlic cloves, chopped

10 (6-inch) corn tortillas, torn into bite-size pieces

3/4 cup chili powder

1/2 tablespoon ground cumin

1 tablespoon cocoa powder

2 tablespoons freshly ground black pepper

2 tablespoons salt

5 cups chicken stock

2 cups brewed coffee

1/2 cup orange juice concentrate

1/2 cup semisweet chocolate, chopped into small pieces

● Roast bell pepper over the flame of a gas burner until skin is blistered; place in a bowl and cover with plastic; allow to cool. Peel, seed, and chop bell pepper.

● In a heavy skillet, heat canola oil over medium-low heat. Sauté onions, bell pepper, and garlic until onions are lightly caramelized. Add tortilla pieces. Add chili powder, cumin, cocoa powder, pepper, and salt, cooking and stirring to release oils in the spices, about 1 minute; take care not to burn the spices.

● Add chicken stock, coffee, orange juice concentrate, and chocolate. Bring to a boil then lower heat; simmer for about 45 minutes. Remove from heat and allow to cool for at least 5 minutes. In batches, carefully blend in a food processor or blender until smooth (sauce should be thick). When using a blender, do not fill blender more than halfway. Release 1 corner of the lid; this prevents the vacuum effect that creates heat explosions. Place a towel over the top of the machine, pulse a few times then process on high speed until smooth. Adjust the consistency with additional chicken stock, if necessary.

dinner

Up in the hills is a crazy old western town called Jerome, where you can find some fantastic art galleries, folk art, and crafts shops. Everything closes at three in the afternoon, so go early. When the town shuts down, head to the local hangout, the Haunted Hamburger, for some great comfort food: burgers, chicken, meat-loaf, pastas. Nothing is greasy or pre-made. All of the plates looked terrific. I had a killer Italian-style meat loaf, incorporating some ham and cheese. It was great with garlic smashed potatoes, especially. Cakes and desserts, made in-house, too, looked tempting, but the meatloaf was very filling.

● Jerome Palace Haunted Hamburger, 410 North Clark St., Jerome, AZ, (928) 634-0554

Italian Stuffed Meatloaf

recipe SERVES 10 courtesy Jerome Palace $40ADAY
APPT - SOUP/SAL - ENTREE - VEG/POT - DESSERT - BEV

Italian Stuffed Meatloaf

2 pounds ground beef

2 eggs

1 to 1 & 1/2 cups bread crumbs

1 cup grated Parmesan

1 tablespoon Italian seasoning

1 tablespoon freshly ground black pepper

2 tablespoons chopped fresh flat-leaf parsley

2 garlic cloves, minced or pressed

1 onion, diced

1/2 cup ketchup

1/4 cup Worcestershire sauce

1 cup milk

Vegetable-oil cooking spray

8 slices Cheddar

8 slices baked ham

8 slices bacon

● Preheat oven to 350°F. In a large mixing bowl, combine ground beef, eggs, 1 cup bread crumbs, Parmesan, Italian season-ing, pepper, parsley, garlic, onion, ketchup, and Worcestershire. Mix well, gradually adding the milk.*
● Spray a large roasting pan with cooking spray. Press the meatloaf into a 1 & 1/2" thick circle. Layer cheese slices and ham down the center, then fold the sides over the middle and tuck in the ends, form-ing an oblong loaf. Criss-cross the surface of the loaf with bacon strips, to cover. Bake until a meat thermometer inserted into the cen-ter reads 160°F, 35 to 45 minutes. Let rest 15 minutes. Cut and serve.

* If it seems too moist, add more bread crumbs until it will hold a loaf form.

recipe courtesy Olive 'R Twist $40ADAY
APP - SOUP/SAL - ENTREE - VEG/POT - DESSERT - BEV

Chocolatini

SERVES 1

1 & 1/4 ounces coffee liqueur (recommended: Kahlua)

1 & 1/4 ounces dark crème de cacao

1/2 ounce vanilla vodka

● Shake all ingredients with ice in a cocktail shaker. Pour into a glass and serve immediately.

drink

This seemed to be "the place" to hang out and have cocktails. There was music, every seat filled, and the spe-cialty martini list, very long and reason-ably priced. I had a chocolatini, recom-mended as a house favorite. It was too sweet for me, as I like my martinis "dirty" these days, with olive juice and olives, but I would go back anytime. It's a cool place for a cool cocktail.

● Olive 'R Twist, 1350 W. Highway 89A, Sedona, AZ, (928) 282-1229

TUCSON

My trip to Tucson felt like a class trip or camp because I learned so much. I went on a long walking tour of the city and learned about its rich history and the history of the American railroad, so key to Tucson's existence. Take the walking tour called the Downtown District Tour and you'll understand why. Stay and hang out at the Hotel Congress. It's cool. I met the actor/director John Waters in the parking lot, proving my point. The Saguaro National Park, so named for a type of cactus, was eye-opening to an upstate New Yorker who knew nothing of the dessert. You can spend many hours here wandering, learning, and getting exercise, too. I petted snakes, fed birds, spied on mountain lions, and saw countless types of plants and creatures I had no idea even existed. I left feeling almost as smart as my 12-year-old niece, at least for a moment.

breakfast

Breakfast is done well here. Home fries weren't greasy, eggs were fluffy, and the coffee hot and strong. Prices are fine, and the service fast and polite. But again, you should go to the Hotel Congress for the scene. Lots of smart, talented artists, actors, musicians, and poets have stayed here over the years and their cool vibes are everywhere. (see recipe on opposite page)

● Cup Café at Hotel Congress, 311 East Congress Street, Tucson, AZ, (520) 798-1618

Hotel Congress
311 East Congress
Tucsun, AZ 85701
520-622-8848
fax 520-792-6366
free 800-722-8848

R/R Crossing

Potatoes:

2 cups large-diced red bliss potatoes

2 tablespoons canola oil

1/2 cup medium-diced red bell pepper

1/4 cup medium-diced green bell pepper

1/4 cup medium-diced red onion

2 teaspoons salt

2 teaspoons freshly ground black pepper

2 teaspoons dried thyme

Sandwich:

Butter, for pan

2 eggs, lightly beaten

4 ounces sliced deli ham

1 medium croissant, sliced horizontally

2 slices Swiss cheese

● Prepare the potatoes: Cook them in boiling water for 7 minutes, then drain into a colander and pat dry with paper towels. Heat 1 tablespoon oil in a large skillet over medium-high heat. Slowly add potatoes to the hot skillet and cook until golden and crisp. In a separate large skillet, heat the remaining 1 tablespoon oil over medium-high heat. Add bell peppers, onion, and seasonings, and sauté until vegetables are tender yet still crisp. Remove both skillets from the heat, and combine the potatoes and vegetables in a large bowl, tossing until they are completely mixed.

R/R Crossing

● Make the sandwich: Melt a little butter in a nonstick pan over medium-low heat. Cook the 2 eggs, stirring, until they are just firm and cooked through; set aside. Place ham in a large skillet and heat over medium-low heat, flipping ham to warm it on both sides. Meanwhile, toast croissant in a toaster or in the oven for a minute. Place ham on the toasted croissant, and top with cheese and scrambled eggs. Serve with potatoes on the side.

lunch

Suzana Davila is the great chef and owner of this find-of-a-lifetime. She is so happy, healthy, and inspired, that she glows. And so does her restaurant; there are vibrant colors everywhere, including the food on your plate. I had a well-orchestrated mélange of vegetables and roasted chicken and spice. If I lived within a hundred miles I would come to this restaurant twice a week to get myself adjusted and inspired. Her fruit and flower iced tea is reason enough to make a cross-country pilgrimage.

● Café Poca Cosa, 88 East Broadway, Tucson, AZ, (520) 622-6400

❝ If I lived within a hundred miles I would come to this restaurant twice a week to get myself adjusted and inspired. ❞

dinner

The biggest thing going for this lovely bistro is actually the wine selection, which is amazing and very reasonably priced. There's a reason for that. This little restaurant is attached to a huge retail wine shop offering fine wines at fair prices. I carried home several that are hard to find on the East Coast. The restaurant itself has terrific dishes served at the bar, including a delicious mussel stew, my choice. All the food looked fabulous, but make sure to partake in the fantastic selection of wines by the glass! That's the real dish on this place!

Sauteed Mussels

● **The Dish Bistro & Wine Bar, 3200 East Speedway Boulevard, Tucson, AZ, (520) 326-1714**

❝ Make sure to partake in the fantastic selection of wines by the glass! That's the real dish on this place! ❞

recipe	SERVES 1	courtesy The Dish Bistro & Wine Bar	$40ADAY

APPT - SOUP/SAL - ENTREE - VEG/POT - DESSERT - BEV

Sautéed Mussels

3 to 4 cups black mussels

1/2 cup Saffron Base, recipe follows

2 tablespoons butter

1/4 cup diced tomatoes

1 tablespoon chopped fresh oregano leaves

1 tablespoon chopped fresh basil leaves

1 tablespoon chopped garlic

Salt and freshly ground black pepper

● Heat a large skillet over medium heat. Add mussels to the dry skillet and then immediately add the remaining ingredients. Toss mussels with a wooden spoon while they are cooking. The mussels are ready when they have all opened and the butter has melted. Discard any mussels that did not open.

Saffron Base:

1/2 teaspoon saffron threads

2 cups white wine

4 cups fish stock from a white fleshed fish

Salt and freshly ground black pepper

● Mince saffron and place in a dry stockpot. Carefully toast saffron over low heat until it is heated through but has not changed color. Add wine and fish stock and raise heat to medium-high. Let cook until the liquid has reduced by 3/4, adjusting the heat as necessary. Season, to taste, with salt and pepper.

Berry Patch Pie

Berry Patch Pie

Dough for 2 (9-inch) pie crusts, rolled out
1 & 1/4 cups sugar
1 orange, zest grated
Pinch salt
1/2 teaspoon fresh lemon juice
2 tablespoons unsalted butter, cut into small pieces
1 & 1/2 cups fresh blueberries, rinsed and picked over
1 & 1/2 cups fresh blackberries, rinsed and picked over
1 cup fresh raspberries, rinsed and picked over
1 & 1/4 cups fresh strawberries, rinsed, hulled, and sliced

● Line a 9-inch pie pan with 1 of the pie doughs and place in the refrigerator.
● Preheat oven to 400°F.
● In a large bowl, stir together sugar, orange zest, salt, lemon juice, and butter until combined. Gently add berries, and gently toss a few times until most are coated with the sugar mixture. Pour the berry mixture into the unbaked pie shell. Top with the second pie dough, folding the edges under and crimping together by pinching with the thumb and forefinger of 1 hand. With a sharp knife, cut a few slits in the center of the top crust. Refrigerate until the dough is firm, 20 minutes.
● Bake until crust is golden all over, 15 to 20 minutes, then reduce the oven temperature to 350°F and bake until berry juices bubble at center slits, another 40 to 50 minutes. If crust darkens too quickly, cover it with aluminum foil. Let pie cool on a wire rack before serving.

THE B LINE

621 N 4TH AVE • TUCSON, AZ • 85705
882-7575

sweet

Funny, it's on the B line of transportation and that's also what you want to make to the dessert case upon entering, a beeline! It was impossible to decide what to have here, all too good to be true or even real! Desserts were gorgeous, just like my grandma never used to make. I had the berry patch pie. Well, they just gave me one slice, but I could have had a berry patch pie to myself; it was that good.

● **The B Line, 621 North 4th Avenue, Tucson, AZ, (520) 882-7575**

Well, it's big. Upon reaching the rim, I felt a bit like Chevy Chase in one of my favorite comedies, Vacation. I stood at the rim, bobbed my head up and down and said "Nice. Can we go now?" While I really do understand the fascination of the thousands of tourists who travel to the Grand Canyon each year, I just have never been that spellbound myself. The last time I went camping I was 11 and I got sent home early for causing trouble. I had a party, because I was bored and cranky from all the bug bites, and in the middle of things, one of my friends broke her arm, so we had to get help, and we got busted. I was sad about the arm, but thrilled to leave! Many friends of mine think I am "nature girl" because I live in the Adirondack mountains. It's quite the contrary. I love living in the woods because I can appreciate the beauty from the inside looking out. I have never been a fan of bugs, dirt, dust, or sleeping among any of the three. My director on this episode, Jeff Weaver, loves the canyon and one of his favorite memories is hiking down at 2 AM and camping out. He said it was a beautiful and spiritual experience. Me, I need plumbing. The hotels here, including the finest, El Tovar, have modest rooms that reminded me of a college dorm, but their lodge and dining room are magnificent, like being at a fancy camp for grown-ups. I did soften up a little after a helicopter ride in the canyon. That was truly amazing and I would recommend it highly. Flights are reasonably priced and the up-close views of all of the rock formations are truly awesome. Also, do not miss Verkamp's, a retail store that faces the El Tovar. The jewely and statues by local American Indian designers on

display are so intricate and beautiful that shopping here is like visiting a museum. Lastly, the people I met on this trip, at every one of our locations, were extremely accommodating, making the trip memorable with their warm and friendly hospitality. To our tour guides and rangers in the park, to the great salespeople at Verkamp's, to the dining staff at Tovar, to Miss Maggie at Happy Trails, and all the performers at The Canyon Star, my compliments and sincere thanks.

breakfast

This is the finest hotel in the park and it's all about the lobby and the dining room. They are stunning. The lodge is massive. It looks as if a giant might live here. Breakfast and lunch menus are well put together, creative, and fairly priced. I had an Navajo breakfast taco made on Indian bread, topped with spiced stewed meat, black beans, and vegetables. The bread was fried and heavier than I expected and the breakfast itself was so generous it could have fed four. The meat, however, was very tasty, spicy, but not too hot or too salty.

● **El Tovar Dining Room at El Tovar Hotel, 10 Albright, Grand Canyon, AZ, (928) 638-2631**

snack

This joint is really fun! It is a bakery, snack and lunch counter, and a fantastic shop with great jewelry, tee shirts, arts and crafts, and textiles all made in the region. Maggie, the owner, makes an awesome tea and has some of the tastiest home-made trail-mix ever! (see recipe on next page) It has clusters of nuts and coconut mixed in with spiced dried fruits and whole nuts. YUMM-O! This place rocks! Stop in here on your way to the park on highway 64. You can't miss it. Happy Trails, to you!

● **Happy Trails at Grand Canyon, 114-A Highway 64, Grand Canyon, AZ, (928) 638-0400**

recipe courtesy Happy Trails $40ADAY

APPT - SOUP/SAL - ENTREE - VEG/POT - DESSERT - BEV

Trail Mix
MAKES 14 CUPS

1/2 cup butter
1/3 cup honey
1 teaspoon vanilla
1/2 cup packed light brown sugar
1/3 cup toasted flaxseed
1 cup chopped, toasted pecans
1 cup soy grits
1 cup toasted wheat germ
2 cups shredded coconuts
6 cups rolled oats
2 cups dried cranberries
1 teaspoon cinnamon
1 teaspoon grated nutmeg
2 oranges, zested

● Melt butter on low heat. Add honey vanilla and brown sugar. Stir until melted. Turn off heat and add rest of ingredients. Stir until dry ingredients are completely covered. Let cool.

❝ It is a really happening dining room with tons of live entertainment from good country music singers and bands to local tribal dancers, singers, and musicians who perform in traditional dress. ❞

dinner

This place is packed with locals! It is a really happening dining room with tons of live entertainment from good country music singers and bands to local tribal dancers, singers, and musicians who perform in traditional dress. The food is great, too! I had a tender, lean, smoky buffalo brisket that I devoured in less than 5 minutes! I can't imagine having a better home on the range than The Canyon Star at night.

● The Canyon Star at The Grand Hotel, Highway 64, Tusayan, AZ, (928) 638-3333

Sweet

This lodge, out on the rim, is very convenient and open long hours. I had a tasty homemade apple crisp called "apple grunt," topped with a Perry's brand ice cream made especially for the Grand Canyon, Canyon Crunch Ice Cream. WOW! The Canyon Crunch made this dessert! It was too good. I could have eaten a gallon! It was a sweet way to end the day, indeed.

● **Arizona Room at Bright Angel Lodge, 10 Albright, Grand Canyon, AZ, (928) 638-6296**

❝ I did soften up a little after a helicopter ride in the canyon. That was truly amazing and I would recommend it highly. ❞

PARK CITY

I go to Park City for the Sundance Film Festival. It's one of the few film festivals at which all screenings and events are open to the general public, not just industry insiders. Park City has perfect weather and I love the landscape, mountains that mix rock and foliage. My favorite pastimes here: watching films in old theaters, horseback riding, gallery-walking, skiing. When I go to town, I rent a condo and actually cook my own meals more often than not. However, when I do go out, I have many favorite restaurants. Two worth mentioning, in addition to those on the show, are Karleen's and Chimayo. Karleen's is my favorite for a simple lunch. It's tiny, just a few seats tucked under the Treasure Island motel. Karleen and her cute daughter Niven work the counter. These ladies rock! Their soups and sandwiches are the best on the planet, especially the soups. Everything is made fresh daily from original recipes using ingredients such as wild mushrooms and lots of fresh herbs. Brownies and cookies are homemade, too. Karleen hangs a sign during the film festival that I love: Reel food for Reel people! Chimayo is gorgeous! It's a very chic, funky, Mexican-influenced gourmet restaurant on Main Street. Its walls are stucco and tile and there is a real wood-burning fireplace, too. The food is surprisingly delicate, and the margaritas just right, not too sweet. Though pricey, Chimayo is worth the splurge!

> **I always eat breakfast here and I always have the same thing, The Morning Ray.**

breakfast

I have been coming here for years. It moved a few years ago from a tiny spot to a huge spot, yet it's still packed all the time! I never get too weary to wait it out. How could I not like a place called the Morning RAY! Jason Sanford, the owner and a great cook, is as cool as his menu and this place is as laid-back as you can get! They had a great tee shirt designed for the film festival last year that read on the front, "Do you know know who I am?" and on the back, "That makes us even!" A classic. I always eat breakfast here and I always have the same thing, The Morning Ray. I usually get a half-order (huge), but, if I've skipped dinner the night before, I order a full. The dish is a pile of potatoes, peppers, onions, and mushrooms, topped with cheese and an egg. It's served with salsa and guacamole and bread. I love this meal so much, I made a few versions of it for my other show, 30 Minute Meals, giving Jason full-credit on air! The coffee here is some of the best I've ever had, too. It's low-acid organic with good, round, full flavor.

● **The Morning Ray Café, 255 Main Street, Park City, UT, (435) 649-5686**

lunch

This place is a huge favorite of the locals in town. Lunch here can get crazy! Sandwiches and salads are really killer and the breads are all baked on the premises. The restaurant, though not downtown, is easy to get to; free local buses take just a couple of minutes and when it's not cold out, you could totally walk, too. When I was very small, we lived in New England where clam chowder was king. Me, I preferred corn chowder (always the rebel!). I loved corn so much that my mom has a picture of me in my high chair at three, sucking on a cob! The Southwestern Corn Chowder here at Windy Ridge made me love corn even more!

recipe	SERVES 6	courtesy Windy Ridge Café	$40ADAY

APPT - **SOUP/SAL** - ENTREE - VEG/POT - DESSERT - BEV

Southwestern Corn Chowder

10 Roma tomatoes

Olive oil

2 pounds frozen corn

1 medium red pepper

Salt and freshly ground black pepper

1/4 small yellow onion, diced

3 garlic cloves, sliced

2 tablespoons butter

2 tablespoons flour

3 cups chicken stock

2 cups half-and-half

5 small white corn tortillas fried crispy, chopped

Dash cumin

Pinch chili powder

1 & 1/2 teaspoons salt

1/2 teaspoon pepper

1 medium avocado, small diced

● Preheat the oven to 500°F. Preheat a grill or grill pan.
● Rub the tomatoes with olive oil and place on a cookie sheet. Roast for 10 to 12 minutes until skin blisters and blackens. Remove from oven and cool. When cool enough to handle, peel the tomatoes and set aside.

● Lay the corn out on a cookie sheet. Season with salt and pepper. Roast until lightly browned, about 10 minutes.
● Rub the red pepper with olive oil. Grill until skin is black and blistered. Place in a resealable plastic bag and refrigerate until cooled. Peel, seed and dice and set aside.
● In a large saucepan over medium heat, sauté the onion and garlic in butter until the onion begins to soften, about 4 minutes. Add the flour and cook for 2 to 3 minutes. Add chicken stock, roasted corn, peeled tomatoes, and half-and-half and bring to a gentle simmer. Add the fried corn tortillas and simmer 2 minutes.
● Puree with an immersion blender, or carefully with a regular blender. If you use a regular blender, do not fill the blender more than half way as hot liquids can expand and spurt out of the blender. Season, to taste, with cumin, chili powder, salt and pepper. Strain. Serve soup garnished avocado and roasted red pepper.

I wanted to lick the bowl, really! It had a sweet, smoky, and spicy flavor, a wonderful texture, and fabulous presentation. They should charge more. Go here soon, before they figure that out!

● **Windy Ridge Café, 1250 Iron Horse Drive, Park City, UT, (435) 647-2906**

Snack

Robert Redford is co-owner of this spirited, but relaxed restaurant. Drop-dead tasteful in its interior design, Zoom's menu features mostly gourmet twists on comfort foods. The seared greens and mac and cheese, for example, are both great. And the bar snacks are among the best I've had and are very reasonably priced. Overall, compared to other high-end restaurants in the area, Zoom is the most consistent. It delivers great food at a fair price. I especially enjoyed the all-American wine list! Rock on, RR! You made this RR feel more patriotic by just eating and drinking at Zoom! Star spotting: I went to the men's room because the line at the ladies' was too long and I bumped into Jake Gyllenhaal on my way out! Yikes! How classy am I? I eat everything here, but on the show, as a snack, I devour a pile of the Buffalo Rings, spicy jumbo onions rings. YUMM-O! Go for lunch or bar snacks if you are on a budget and still want in on the people watching. Go for dinner, if you can afford a splurge.

● **Zoom, 660 Main Street, Park City, UT, (435) 649-9108**

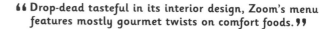

❝ **Drop-dead tasteful in its interior design, Zoom's menu features mostly gourmet twists on comfort foods.** ❞

dinner

I had a lunch meeting at a hotel restaurant and the waitress, M, just M, was a pistol! She said I should also check out a new steak house called Butcher's, located right at the base of the town ski lift. I asked M what I should have there, since clearly she knew me and my tastes so very well; her answer surprised me. She recommended the macaroni and cheese. In fact, the items she loves most on the menu are all vegetarian! So, off I went to the steak house for anything but steak! The steaks at Butcher's look thick, juicy, and mean! (I wish I had had one, on the side.) But let me tell ya, M knows her stuff! The mac and cheese here is made with Asiago, cheddar, and Parmigiano reggiano, and is topped with an herb crust! WOW! This is deep-dish delish! Go with friends to Butcher's and share some of everything: steak, mac 'n cheese and you MUST try the Yukon gold-potato chips with blue cheese, too. You'll work it off on the slopes, which are right in front of you!

● Butcher's Chop House & Bar, 751 Main Street, Park City, UT, (435) 647-0040

Macaroni & Cheese

1 pound penne pasta

6 & 1/2 cups milk

1/8 onion wedge

1 clove

1 bay leaf

1 sprig thyme

4 ounces unsalted butter

4 ounces flour

1/8 diced white onion

1/8 small diced carrot

1 pound extra sharp white cheddar cheese (we use Cabot), grated

4 ounces yellow cheddar cheese, grated

Salt

White pepper

Nutmeg

Breadcrumb mixture:

1/2 cup Asiago cheese

1/2 cup panko (Japanese-style) bread crumbs (found in Asian food markets)

1 tablespoon chopped assorted fresh herbs (thyme, oregano, rosemary, tarragon, basil)

● Preheat the oven to 350°F.
● Bring a large pot of salted water to a boil. Cook the penne until al dente. Drain and set aside.
● Place the milk in a large saucepan and set over medium heat. Press the clove into the onion wedge. Cut a small slit in the onion wedge and insert the bay leaf into the wedge. Add the onion and thyme to the milk. Bring to a simmer and simmer for 20 minutes, watching carefully and stirring so the milk doesn't scorch.
● In another saucepan, melt the butter over medium-low heat. When the butter is melted, add the diced carrot and onion and sauté for 3 minutes, just until the vegetables begin to soften. Stir in the flour to make a roux. Cook until the roux bubbles and resembles pancake batter, about 5 minutes. Be careful not to let the roux get any color.
● Strain the milk into the roux, stirring, and cook until thickened and smooth, about 10 minutes. Strain the thickened milk mixture into a heat-proof bowl. Stir in the cheddar cheeses and stir until the cheese is completely melted. Season with salt, white pepper, and nutmeg, to taste.
● Toss with the pasta and transfer into a greased baking pan. In a small bowl, combine the Asiago cheese, panko crumbs, and chopped herbs. Sprinkle the mixture over the pasta. Bake until the topping is golden brown and the macaroni and cheese is bubbly, about 35 to 40 minutes.

❝ WOW! This is deep-dish delish! Go with friends to Butcher's and share some of everything: steak, mac 'n cheese and you MUST try the Yukon gold-potato chips with blue cheese, too. ❞

SUN VALLEY

up, it's named Sun Valley for good reason. Even in winter with lots of snow it actually feels HOT by day, because of the intense sunlight and dramatic mountainous terrain. I can totally see why this place, the first American ski resort, continues to attract tourists from around the world. Confession: I am almost vampire-like in my habits and habitats. Because of my heavy work load, I don't see much daylight. Also, my home is in a forest set among 200-foot pine trees. The result: I live in the "twilight zone," literally, and that's why Sun Valley was a bit of a shock to my system. It took a few hours and some really cool Smith polarized sunglasses, before I could focus on the beauty of this light-filled valley. What's also cool about Sun Valley is that everyone hangs out with anyone, including those of us who are not "someone." CEOs talk sports and cars and chicks with undergrads; super models swap travel tips with car-pooling single dads. Me, I met a billionaire owner of a hotel and real-estate empire hanging out in a tiny tea house, while I was sitting next to a couple of students online, and a guy spontaneously strumming a six-string! Nice.

breakfast

Even without my telling you, you'd find the Kneadery in "downtown" Ketchum easily. Look for a large, cozy-looking cabin-like structure with a big wooden sign that has carved bear cubs crawling all over it. There are several reasons that make this a "go-to" place for tourists and locals alike. First, when you leave, you get edible parting gifts—some fruit and bottled water or freshly baked cookies and water, if you are in for lunch. Second, the food rocks and the menus are really unusual, like my eggs benedict with smoked trout and spinach—awesome! Lastly, it's the value. With the reasonable price of any breakfast, you receive a homemade muffin of choice, free. It's little things that show effort and caring which make a restaurant truly memorable. The Kneadery offers generous portions, home-baked goods, the freshest and highest quality ingredients, all for a fair price, not a tourist jack-up! I love the kneadery and if you have a family in tow, the kids will love it too!

● **The Kneadery, 260 Leadville Avenue North, Ketchum, ID, (208) 726-9462**

❝ It's little things that show effort and caring which make a restaurant truly memorable. ❞

recipe	SERVES 4	courtesy The Kneadery	$40ADAY

APPT - SOUP/SAL - **ENTREE** - VEG/POT - DESSERT - BEV

Rocky Mountain Benedict

16 ounces smoked Idaho trout or salmon

4 English muffins, split

8 eggs

2 tablespoons chopped fresh parsley or dill leaves

Paprika

Hollandaise Sauce (recipe follows)

● Toast or grill split English muffins and set aside. Fill a large shallow pan with 2 to 3 inches of water, and bring to a boil. Reduce heat to a simmer and gently break eggs into the boiling water. Poach eggs until yolks set to desired doneness, approximately 3 minutes. Remove eggs from heat and drain.

● Heat smoked trout or salmon in a nonstick skillet over medium high heat for 30 seconds. Arrange toasted English muffins on plates and top with trout or salmon. Using a slotted spoon, place 1 poached egg on top of each English muffin. Spoon warm hollandaise sauce over eggs and sprinkle with parsley and a dash of paprika to garnish. Serve immediately.

Hollandaise sauce:

1 pound butter

1/2 cup dry white wine

1 tablespoon lemon juice

1 tablespoon Tabasco sauce

6 egg yolks

● Melt butter over medium heat. Bring a saucepan with 2-inches of water to a boil. While butter is melting, whisk together white wine, lemon juice, and Tabasco in a large metal bowl that will fit over the saucepan of water. Whisk in egg yolks. Place bowl over the pot of boiling water and continue whisking until a custard consistency develops. Slowly whisk in melted butter. Continue whisking until sauce is rich and smooth.

lunch

I have a friend, Zemo Crisman, a true renaissance man, who lives in Sun Valley. I could not blow into town without seeing him, work or no work. Lunch was his pick. He chose Grumpy's. I know how the name came about. "Grumpy" is what you may become just looking for this place. I drove by it twice! Once you find it and go inside, the cool-factor of this joint goes way up! It's funky decor, made up of a collection of license plates and vintage beer and booze signs, is appealing, and Grumpy's is known to locals as the place to go for a burger, hands-down! But, I

ended up choosing a "fowl burger" (because of the name, of course) and basically, it was just a teriyaki chicken breast on a bun with veggies and a special sauce. I know, it sounds like a fast-food drive-through, but really, the sammy was super-tasty and the fries may be among the crispiest in the state! Thanks, Zemo! Nice call!

● **Grumpy's Burgers & Beer, 860 Warm Springs Road, Ketchum, ID, No telephone**

Fowl Burger

4 boneless chicken breasts

2 cups teriyaki sauce

2 tablespoons olive oil

4 slices Monterey jack cheese

Ketchup

Mayonnaise

4 seeded hamburger buns

1 tomato, sliced

1 yellow onion, sliced

4 large leaves lettuce

● Wash chicken and pat dry with paper towel. Put chicken in teriyaki sauce and marinate overnight in the refrigerator.

● Preheat the grill to 500°F.

● Remove the chicken from the marinade. Lightly oil the grill. Grill chicken on each side for about 3 minutes or the chicken is firm and almost cooked through.

Butterfly the chicken breast with a fillet knife about 3/4 of the way through the center, being careful not to cut all the way through. Place inside down onto the grill. Top the chicken with cheese and grill for 3 minutes or until the cheese is melted and the chicken is fully cooked and the juices run clear.

● In a small bowl mix mayonnaise and ketchup to make the secret sauce.*

● Toast seeded bun on grill or toaster. Coat each bun with special sauce. Add lettuce, sliced tomato and onion to bottom bun. Add chicken and top bun.

*Only the Grumpy's staff knows the exact proportions of the sauce. But they do provide one tip: "Make sure the secret sauce is not too pink and not too red"

drink

I love jazz and big band, swing and standards. At the Sun Valley Resort Lodge, halls are filled with photos of all the famous devotees of the area, from RFK to Hemingway, Lucy to Clint. In the bar, The Duchin Lounge, you see photos of past musical greats. Eddie Duchin was among the legends who played here. Today, jazz trios still make music happen in this happening place.

● **The Duchin Lounge at Sun Valley Resort, 1 Sun Valley Road, Sun Valley, ID, (208) 622-2145**

recipe courtesy Duchin Lounge	$40ADAY
APPT - SOUP/SAL - ENTREE - VEG/POT - DESSERT - **BEV**	

Hot Buttered Rum
SERVES 4

2/3 cup (packed) dark brown sugar
1/2 cup (stick) unsalted butter, room temperature
1/4 cup honey
1/2 teaspoon ground cinnamon
1/4 teaspoon ground nutmeg
1/8 teaspoon ground cloves
Pinch salt
3/4 cup spiced rum
2 cups boiling water
4 cinnamon sticks

● Using an electric mixer, beat first 7 ingredients in medium bowl until blended and smooth. Transfer mixture to 4-cup measuring cup. Add rum, then 2 cups boiling water; stir until butter mixture dissolves. Divide buttered rum among 4 mugs. Garnish with cinnamon sticks and serve.

❝ **The Duchin Lounge, you see photos of past musical greats. Eddie Duchin was among the legends who played here.** ❞

dinner

Ketchum has one of the best art scenes that I have found anywhere in the US. From jewelry to sculpture, abstracts to detailed photography, Ketchum has a gallery and a price tag to match your tastes and budget. Tucked in among the galleries is a tiny house that looks like magic! Appropriately, the name Strega means witch in Italian! Strega is many things: an unsurpassable tea house, a fine wine-by-the-glass bar, a gallery for art, photos, and jewelry by local artists, and last, but yummily, a bistro for very light fare. I had the Asian "momos," which were steamed, spiced turkey dumplings served with a side of baby greens. (see recipe on opposite page) I enjoyed a cup of Czar Nicholas tea with my meal, as well. I ate and shopped and went home with a pair of black pearl earrings, which were way over $40, but my shopping came out of a different budget, my plastic one! Oh, and the owner, Kim, she's a good witch, like Glenda.

● **Strega, 360 First Avenue North, Ketchum, ID, (208) 726-6463**

Momos

Dough:

1 cup warm water (105–115°F)

4 teaspoons dry yeast

2 tablespoons olive oil

1 & 1/2 teaspoons salt

3 cups organic flour

Pinch salt

Free-Range Turkey Filling :

1 pound ground free-range turkey

1/4 cup cilantro chopped

1/4 cup fresh dill chopped

1/2 bunch of green onions chopped (green part only)

1 teaspoon salt

Fresh ground pepper

Sauce:

2 tablespoons white wine

5 cloves garlic

3 large shallots

1 tablespoon dried cumin

1 tablespoon olive oil

1 pint organic cherry tomatoes

1/2 teaspoon salt

3 tablespoons chopped fresh cilantro leaves

1 tablespoon chopped fresh dill

● Make dough: Pour 1 cup warm water into large bowl; sprinkle yeast over. Let stand until mixture is foamy, about 10 minutes. Mix oil and salt. Place flour in a medium bowl. Stir enough flour mixture into yeast mixture, 1/2 cup at a time, to form a slightly sticky dough. Knead on floured surface until smooth and elastic, about 10 minutes. Oil large bowl; add dough and turn to coat. Cover bowl with plastic wrap. Let stand in warm area until doubled in volume, about 1 hour. While dough is rising, make filling.

● Filling: Mix all ingredients well together and set aside.

● Sauce: Heat a saucepan over medium heat. Add the white wine, chopped garlic, shallots, and cumin and cook just until shallots and garlic start to soften, about 2 minutes. Set aside.

● Place a sauté pan over high heat. Add the oil and heat. When the oil is hot, add the tomatoes and cook until the tomatoes split and the juice comes out. Add the salt, cilantro, and dill sauté for another 1 minute. Remove from the heat. Place the tomatoes mixture and the shallot garlic mixture in a food processor and process until the mixture is fairly smooth. Keep warm and set aside.

● Assemble and steam: Roll out a portion of dough very thin, about 1/8-inch thick. Cut out 3-inch circles with a cookie cutter. Place 1 tablespoon of the filling in the middle of dough and hold in one hand while you use the other hand to pinch the edges and seal into a half-moon shaped dumpling. If they stick to your fingers, use a little oil on your hands. Repeat with the remaining dough and filling.

● Oil a steamer insert surface and put in a few momos at a time so that none touch. Steam until the dough looks transparent, about 8 minutes. Serve with some of the dipping sauce on the side. Serve immediately.

TELLURIDE

As I have admitted before, though I grew up in upstate NY surrounded by ski resorts and mountains, I never learned to ski. I picked it up at 33 and today I still fall down and run into things a lot. I was scared to go to Telluride because I knew it meant getting out there on the slopes and from what I'd seen of this place on television, well, I figured odds were pretty good I could end up in a body brace of some kind. I bought some travel insurance and got on the plane. Then, I got on an even smaller plane which took me up, way up, to Telluride. Even the plane made me nervous. It looked like a toy. Less than 48 hours later, I was transformed. I was begging to stay out on the slopes after finishing my three-mile ski run; I only fell once, when I was actually standing still—smooth! My ski instructor rocked and looked like a Kennedy, which wasn't a bad thing either. In Telluride the slopes are so diverse and wide—they stretch for miles—that even a beginning skier can enjoy a life-transforming experience of a great day on the slopes. There are also scary cliffs and rocky terrains for fearless kids who hurl themselves down, but, if you're like me and you ski to take in the view and be outdoors, Telluride is your NIRVANA! I could live here. I will return, with my skis.

breakfast

Telluride is so small you can walk from one end of town to the other in fifteen minutes. Dotted along the main street, Colorado Avenue, are several really good little eateries, sandwich places and Mexican joints. I took a vote from the locals out early and started my day at Sofio's, a Mexican restaurant. Sofio's is bright, busy, and smells great, three good signs. I had a Mexican eggs benedict of sorts: grilled chorizo sausage layered with poached eggs and chipotle (smoked jalapeno) hollandaise sauce. This smoky, spicy meal was a really different way to start my day and it was rocking good! The sauce, more smoky than hot, was especially delicious. Telluride and Sofio's are both so friendly you will tell stories about it to all your cranky friends back home. It's a well-mannered, laid-back town. They have doggie parking and play areas all over the downtown. Some restaurants even welcome pooches in! A sharing box in the center of town encourages community members to swap goods. And at Sofio's, I saw children's pancakes in the shape of Mickey Mouse heads decorated with intricate fruit mosaics of banana, kiwi, and berries. That takes time and love! Telluride and Sofio's is like a big fuzzy bear hug! P.S. The crew had lunch here and loved every morsel!

● **Sofio's Mexican Cafe, 110 East Colorado Ave., Telluride, CO, (970) 728-4882**

---

recipe | SERVES 8 | adapted from Sofio's Mexican Cafe | $40 A DAY

APPT - SOUP/SAL - **ENTREE** - VEG/POT - DESSERT - BEV

Southwest Benedict

Chipotle Hollandaise:

6 egg yolks (in the restaurant, we use pasteurized egg yolks)

1 teaspoon red Tabasco sauce

1 teaspoon Worcestershire sauce

1/2 teaspoon salt

1/2 lemon, juiced

1 cup melted butter

1 tablespoon Chipotle puree (to taste) or 1 tsp dried ground chipotle

Benedict:

1 tablespoon white vinegar

2 pounds chorizo sausage

16 eggs

8 English muffins

● Hollandaise: Whip the egg yolks until foamy. Continue whipping while you add sauces, salt and lemon juice. Put in top of double boiler, and continue whipping by hand for approximately 2 minutes. After the sauce becomes slightly thicker, remove from heat and add butter. Add chipotle puree or powder, to taste. Keep warm.

● Benedict: Fill a saucepan with about 1 & 1/2 inches water. Bring the water to a gentle boil. Add the vinegar. Carefully break the eggs into small bowls or cups. Gently slide each egg carefully into the simmering water. Let cook 3 to 4 minutes, until whites are firm. Gently scoop each egg out with a slotted spoon and drain thoroughly.

● Preheat a grill or grillpan.

● Cut chorizo into 8 equal pieces. Cut each piece in half length-wise, and grill open-faced until fully cooked. Likewise, grill an English muffin, open-faced until slightly crisp.

● Place a piece of grilled chorizo on each half of the English muffin. Place one poached egg on top of the chorizo. Cover with the chipotle hollandaise.

● For a vegetarian option, use avocado slices, and slightly wilted spinach leaves in place of chorizo. Also, add a slice of tomato atop the poached egg before topping with the hollandaise sauce.

lunch

Up at the ski area in Mountain Village, there's a great little self-serve restaurant perfect for lunch when you don't want to get off the mountain. The Crunchy Porcupine is a ski-in place with great chili and gourmet sandwiches. I had a delicious, crusty baguette with chicken, pesto sauce, tomatoes, mozzarella, and arugula. It was delish and I got a free homemade oatmeal cookie with my meal!

● **The Crunchy Porcupine, 670 Mountain Village Boulevard, Telluride, CO, (970) 728-0677**

sweet

The flavors at this ice cream parlor, right in the middle of town, are named for locals and for employees who work in the shop—cool! The flavor combinations are dictated by the current inductee in the Case of Fame. I had a Diesel (he works here) in the flavor he loves most: banana cream pie! Yumm-o! I also tried so many great flavors on tester spoons that I could not keep them straight! Bottom line: there is nothing like this fresh, homemade ice cream. How sweet it is!

● **The Sweet Life, 115 West Colorado Avenue, Telluride, CO, (970) 728-8789**

dinner

When you come down from the slopes and back into town, Wildflour Cooking Company is there waiting for you with open doors! They have a wide, open bar and a very high-end and low-priced bar menu with everything on it from grilled shrimp to lamb stew. I had the stew and it was a masterpiece of root vegetables, fresh fennel, rich stock, lean tender lamb, orange zest, and fresh rosemary. (see recipe on opposite page) The prices were so fair, I felt guilty. If you're fresh off the slopes and you want to warm up from the inside-out, eat at Wildflour.

● **Wildflour Cooking Company, 250 West San Juan Avenue, Telluride, CO, (970) 728-8887**

Lamb Stew

For the broth:

4 yellow onions, peeled

1 turnips, peeled

4 carrots, peeled

Olive oil

6 quarts chicken stock

1/2 head garlic

1 quart orange juice

1 quart apple cider

1/4 cup coriander seed

1/8 cup fennel seed

1 star anise

2 tablespoons cumin seed

1/8 cup orange zest

1 tablespoon salt

1 & 1/2 teaspoons black pepper

For the lamb:

4 to 5 pounds boneless leg or shoulder lamb stew meat

1/2 cup cooking oil

1 & 1/2 cups dry white wine

For the stew garnish:

1 carrot, diced

1 yellow onion, diced

1/2 turnip, diced

1 fennel bulb, white part only, diced

2 tablespoons olive oil

Salt and freshly ground black pepper

1 & 1/2 teaspoons orange zest

1 tablespoon chopped fresh herbs (like parsley, thyme, basil, chives)

● For the broth: Preheat the oven to 500°F. Place a large roasting pan in the oven and preheat.

● Quarter the onions and turnips. Cut the carrots into 2-inch chunks. Toss the carrots, onions and turnips lightly in oil and Place in the hot roasting pan in 1 layer. Roast, stirring vegetables every 10 minuets, for 30 minutes or until vegetables are a very dark caramel color. Remove from the oven and place in a large pot with the rest of the ingredients for the broth. Reserve the roasting pan. Place over high heat and bring to a boil. Reduce heat to a gentle simmer and reduce by half, about 2 hours.

● For the Lamb: While the broth is simmering, remove excess fat and sliver skin from the leg of lamb and dice into one-inch cubes. Place on a wire rack or a clean towel to soak up excess moisture. Place a large heavy bottom sauté pans over high heat. Add the oil and heat until the oil just starts to smoke. Carefully add diced lamb, in batches, and sear until brown on all sides, about 3 minutes per side. Be careful not to crowd the pan or the lamb will steam and not sear. Remove the lamb to the roasting pan.

● Preheat the oven to 325°F.

● Carefully add the wine to your empty sauté pan, return to the heat and scrape the bottom of the pan with a wooden spoon. When wine is reduced to almost dry and the solids have come up off the pan, pour reduced wine over the seared lamb.

● Once you finish searing the lamb, your broth should be ready. Strain all solids from the broth and pour over the seared lamb in the roasting pan. Cover with a lid or parchment paper and braise in the oven until lamb is tender, about 1 & 1/2 to 2 hours. Remove from the oven and set aside. Raise the oven temperature to 500°F. Place a cookie sheet in the oven to heat.

● For the stew garnish: Toss the diced carrots, onions, turnips, and fennel lightly in oil, salt, and pepper. Roast them until they are almost fully cooked, about 15 minutes.

● Add the roasted vegetable garnish to the lamb stew and place the stew on the stove over medium heat. Bring to a simmer and cook for 10 minutes. Season, to taste, with salt and pepper. Stir in the orange zest and herbs. Serve with rustic bread on the side.

DENVER

Rocky Mountain air must be good because everyone in Denver is very healthy-looking. This mile-high city is very urbane. It has great shopping and art galleries. Parks are big and beautiful. It is culturally diverse, which surprised me, pleasantly, and there is a huge Rainbow Coalition presence. There was a massive parade promoting gay and lesbian tourism while we were in town taping. For such a liberal city, they are very small town in their deep devotion to all sports, including their baseball and football franchises, of course. Catch a game if you're traveling in season.

breakfast

New Mexican cuisine is very popular here in Denver. I was planning on a Denver omelet for breakfast, but thought that too much of a cliché. I ended up in this funky, cool, and inexpensive section of town with fantastic shopping; I knew what my after-breakfast exercise would be! Julia is young and beautiful and works the

Sante Fe Quiche

cafe everyday. Her menu is eclectic and yet works with classic combinations of ingredients. I had a New Mexican quiche, which proved to be colorful and tasty, just like the surroundings.

● **Julia Blackbird's New Mexican Cafe, 3617 West 32nd Avenue, Denver, CO, (303) 433-2688**

lunch

This place is owned by a sweet young Italian couple from Florence and they make insanely good food. A marketplace and deli with a few seats, it's perfect for lunch, like being back in Italy, really. I had a focaccia sandwich, the home-baked bread piled with prosciutto di Parma, hand-made mozzarella, and topped with an arugula pesto dressing. To wash it down, a bitter lemon soda. I was one happy Sicilian girl, let me tell you! Note: If you live in the Denver area, shop at Parisi, and eat there, too. You wouldn't want them running back to Italy any time soon!

● Parisi, 4401 Tennyson Street, Denver, CO, (303) 561-0234

---

recipe courtesy Parisi $40ADAY

APPT - SOUP/SAL - ENTREE - VEG/POT - DESSERT - BEV

Arugula Pesto

MAKES 2 CUPS

5 garlic cloves
2 anchovy fillets
1/4 cup capers
1/2 pound baby arugula
1/2 cup grated Parmigiano-Reggiano
1 & 1/2 lemons, juiced
1/2 cup extra-virgin olive oil
Salt and freshly ground black pepper

● Put garlic, anchovies, and capers in the bowl of a food processor and pulse until finely chopped. Add arugula, cheese, lemon juice, and olive oil and pulse until the mixture is completely combined and is the consistency of a classic pesto. Add salt and pepper, to taste. Spread on bread or crackers, or toss with pasta. Transfer any remaining pesto to a freezer-safe airtight container and freeze for up to 1 month.

Arugula Pesto

drink

This place offers a brew-house tour, free tastes along the way. Brews are good, cold, and varied in taste and texture. The staff was knowledgeable and the brew master funny and friendly. The food looked great and the beer went down easy. Beer is always a great treat because it fits into any budget.

● Wynkoop Brewing Company, 1634 18th Street, Denver, CO, (303) 297-2700

dinner

This place is like walking into Paris from a Denver city street. Tables are tiny, the spacious restaurant feels intimate with small rooms and rush seat chairs. The food is classic French, as is the wine list. Charming and intimate, I had some wine and pork tenderloin. (see recipe opposite page) Vive Le Central!

Pork Loin

● Le Central, 112 East 8th Avenue, Denver, CO, (303) 863-8094

❝ This place is like walking into Paris from a Denver city street. ❞

Pork Loin with Mushroom Fricassee

2 tablespoons minced shallots

1 tablespoon minced garlic

1 tablespoon minced fresh thyme leaves

1 teaspoon minced fresh oregano leaves

1 teaspoon minced fresh flat-leaf parsley leaves

1 (5-pound) pork loin

Spice Paste, recipe follows

1 cup chicken stock

Mushroom Fricassee, recipe follows

● In a small bowl, combine shallots, garlic, thyme, oregano, and parsley. Rub the mixture all over the pork, cover with plastic wrap, and refrigerate overnight.

● Preheat oven to 350°F. Place the pork loin in a roasting pan and bake for 30 minutes. Remove pork from the oven, and when cool enough to touch, spread the paste all over the loin. Return pork to the oven and cook until it has developed a crunchy crust on the outside and is cooked to desired degree of doneness, about 25 to 30 more minutes.

● Remove the pork from the roasting pan and let the pork rest a few minutes. Pour the juices from the meat into a fat separator. Pour the meat juices only—not the fat—and chicken stock into a small saucepan. Cook over medium-high heat until reduced to the consistency of a sauce. Meanwhile, make the mushroom fricassee.

● To serve, cut the pork loin into slices, pour the mushroom fricassee and sauce over, and serve immediately.

Spice Paste:

1 cup firmly packed brown sugar

2 teaspoons finely chopped garlic

2 teaspoons ground ginger

1/2 teaspoon ground cloves

1/4 teaspoon freshly ground black pepper

1 teaspoon kosher salt

● Combine all ingredients in a small bowl.

Mushroom Fricassee:

1/4 cup (1/2 stick) butter

1/2 cup thinly sliced morel or chanterelle mushrooms

1/2 cup thinly sliced shiitake mushrooms

1/2 cup thinly sliced portobello mushrooms

1/2 cup thinly sliced white mushrooms

1/4 cup tomato paste

Pinch ground cinnamon

Pinch ground nutmeg

Pinch ground cloves

Salt and freshly ground black pepper

● In a large skillet, melt butter over medium heat. Add all of the sliced mushrooms and sauté until just beginning to brown. Add tomato paste and stir to incorporate. Season, to taste, with cinnamon, nutmeg, cloves, salt, and pepper.

Why go here out of ski season, as I did? Because it's closer and less expensive than a trip to the Alps, which is what Aspen resembles, really. And, everyone speaks English. You'll find yourself humming the Sound of Music soundtrack in no time! The views and scenery come alive in summer and you'll be climbing, wandering, and breathing more deeply, every minute. Check out Jimmy's, which I didn't find until I was ready to leave town, so I couldn't tape there. Jimmy is brilliant and fun; his food rocks and every great chef and celebrity in the US and abroad has visited here and signed his wall in the bar. His many appetizers can serve as entrees for little money!

breakfast

This is The Place for breakfast. You'll find everyone in town, tourists and natives alike, here to start the day. I had eggs and toast because of the price, an early-bird special. Truth be told, I should have coughed up an extra couple of bucks and had a real meal. Everyone else's breakfast looked so much more exciting than my scrambled eggs, which were fine, but ya know, they were just scrambled eggs. Oh well. Eat there for me and have something more exciting than I did.

● Wienerstube Restaurant, 633 East Hyman Ave., Aspen, CO, (970) 925-3357

lunch

Thank God I have a HUGE mouth, because these people do not lie about the BIG in the Big Wrap! This is a tiny take-out joint with a line out the door everyday at lunch, for good reason! Every wrap sounds so healthful and fantastic that it's hard to decide, truly! I had a chicken, vegetable, and bean wrap with citrus tortilla chips on the side. I made a picnic for myself up on the top of a mountain and man, was it good and big, I mean the food AND the view. The Big Wrap is easy to find, right in the middle of town. It's

Caesar Chicken Wrap

inexpensive and the food is great and BIG so go there for lunch, in any season.

● **The Big Wrap, 520 East Durant Avenue, #101, Aspen, CO, (970) 544-1700**

❝ **This is a tiny take-out joint with a line out the door everyday at lunch, for good reason!** ❞

dinner

This little hide-away is not so hard to find. It is tucked away in a section of town laden with great bistros. The unique thing about this place is the depth of the bar menu. I ordered, from among many delectable choices, the rainbow trout and vegetables. No kidding. Right there in the bar for the same price as your average buffalo chicken pizza or basket of mixed fried things, I enjoyed light, lovely, sautéed trout and fresh, crisp vegetables. Nice.

Rainbow Trout

● **Cache Cache, 205 South Mill St., Aspen, CO, (888) 511-3835**

drink

A groovy, fun, country hideaway, a favorite of writer Hunter Thompson, this is where I enjoyed my favorite margarita made on US soil. Owner Shep Harris shares freely everything he knows about good quality tequilas, and he knows a lot. So, his margaritas are not syrupy slurpies with cheap alcohol, they are liquid meditations. I had a ball here. I would be a barfly if I lived close by. Then Hunter would write something creepy and weird about me, too.

● **Woody Creek Tavern, 2 Woody Creek Plaza, Woody Creek, CO, (970) 923-4585**

LAS VEGAS

w.e1t

I don't gamble, so I've never had a desire to travel to Vegas. I went to film a $40 episode two years ago, and I have made four trips there since! I am a Bellagio junkie now! John, my sweetie, and I run off there whenever we can find a spare weekend. I get the world's greatest pedicures at the salon, and we enjoy working out at the spa—they actually make it fun! The rooms are to-die-for and John always gets us one with a great view of my favorite Vegas attraction, the amazing dancing fountains. They should make an exception and give them a Tony! We recently taped a return to Vegas episode and it rocked! I should tell you about my favorites for nights when you may want to break the budget and blow your bank: Aqua at Bellagio has the best seafood menu and Le Cirque is a circus of gastronomic delights. For Valentine's Day, John took me to see a real circus, a Cirque du Soleil show (all three that play in Vegas are fantastique!), then to Le Cirque for a late supper. Guys: heads up! This is a really good idea! Also, please do not miss Fiamma at MGM Grand, which has the best Italian food in Vegas. Every item was as good as any meal I've enjoyed in Italy. The chef is remarkable, the dishes simple, but masterful. Two last words on Vegas: Tom Jones. I have had a crush on him since I was three and let me tell you, today, nothing has changed. I am still devoted and he is still one hot number!

breakfast

There is nothing more glorious than the dancing fountains out in front of the Bellagio, but at breakfast, the water is still resting. Before you head in to see the buffet, take time to stroll through my second favorite attraction at the hotel, the glorious, light-filled, glass-domed conservatory. Every few months the motif changes in this sprawling garden. In February, the theme was Chinese New Year and there were huge dancing Chinese boys and girls made of flowers holding giant fire crackers; dragon kites floating across the ceiling; and crazy monkeys climbing over vines and swinging from trees while water arches sprayed illusive arbors over the winding garden paths. When we taped a few weeks later, the theme had changed to butterflies. In the pond, giant hydrangea-covered swans were nesting. In the center of the conservatory, a netted gazebo housed hundreds of exotic butterflies in as many vibrant colors, all dancing and fluttering together. Up in the air, gigantic streams of artificial butterflies ribboned across the ceiling. Make sure you bring your camera! On your way to the buffet, take time to study the colors in the massive, blown-glass flowered ceiling created for the lobby. This buffet is more like an intricate food floor show, a live performance of a dozen chefs creating a truly special meal for you. The food is fantastic and couldn't be fresher; some items are created for you while you watch. A gourmet experience at a fast-food price, do not miss this buffet, especially at breakfast. It's really great value. I had an omelet, made to order, with crab, red bell pepper, and spinach; a slice of brioche French toast and berries; and smoked salmon with capers, red onion, and seared bok choy. That's what I call a full house for the stomach!

● **The Buffet at Bellagio, Bellagio Hotel & Casino, 3600 South Las Vegas Boulevard, Las Vegas, NV, (702) 891-3446**

lunch

I really love the Time Out guides for travel. They are hip, easy to read, and give you true insider info. I got the 411 on a steak and shrimp meal not listed on the menu at Lucky's in the Hard Rock Hotel and Casino. For $7.77 I got a real-deal surf and turf supper that rocked! Plus, as Lucky is there for you 24/7, you can eat dinner at 3 in the AM! Lucky's is a sure bet! The Hard Rock Hotel and Casino is just good times all around: great music, of course; Nobu for sushi; a man-made beach at the pool; and an awesome theater that books everyone who's anyone in rock, pop, or alternative music.

● **Mr. Lucky's, Hard Rock Hotel & Casino, 4455 Paradise Road, Las Vegas, NV, (800) HRD-ROCK**

drink

I love the strip, but there are other places off it that are worth checking out. A truly unique place that the locals and college students love, the Mediterranean Cafe and Hookah Lounge, is only a five-minute drive away and it's really easy to find. Outside, it looks like a strip-mall business in every way. Inside, well, it will blow your mind! It is lush with fabric-covered walls and carved, low chairs and ornate tables, paintings, and light fixtures. The mood is exotic, sexy, and relaxed. On the show I was in the Lounge where I enjoyed a really unusual Babylon spice cocktail with ginger, fruit juice, and rum. The food at the adjacent cafe with many Middle Eastern dishes, looked fantastic and healthful.

● **Mediterranean Cafe & Hookah Lounge, 4147 South Maryland Parkway, Las Vegas, NV, (702) 731-6030**

dinner

Again, this place is five minutes off the strip and packed with locals. It's brand new and all the buzz in local publications is what brought us here. Firefly is a super-luxe Spanish tapas bar. Tapas are perfect for budget-conscious meals because each little dish is modestly priced and you can buy as many or as few as your appetite and wallet allow. I had a spicy gazpacho soup and delicate artichoke hearts on toast; both were terrific. (see recipes on opposite page) Plus, each table is given an additional plate of olives, nuts, chick peas, compound butter and bread for snacks. The modern design of the restaurant is enhanced by live Spanish guitar music and a bright abstract art collection.

● **Firefly on Paradise, 3900 Paradise Road, Suite A, Las Vegas, NV, (702) 369-3971**

recipe | MAKES 20 PIECES | *courtesy Firefly on Paradise* | $40ADAY

APPT - SOUP/SAL - ENTREE - VEG/POT - DESSERT - BEV

Artichoke Toasts

Marinated artichokes:

1 (14-ounce) can quartered artichokes in water, drained

4 ounces lemon juice

4 ounces extra-virgin olive oil

1 tablespoon fresh ground black pepper

1 tablespoon kosher salt

1/2 cup chopped fresh parsley

2 tablespoons whole coriander seeds

Dash Tabasco

Aioli:

2 eggs

1/2 lemon

Kosher salt

1 tablespoon sriracha sauce (Thai chili-garlic sauce)

1 tablespoon minced garlic

1 cup extra-virgin olive oil

1 loaf baguette, sliced 1/2 inch thick, brushed with a mixture of olive oil, garlic, salt, black pepper, rosemary, time, then grilled or broiled

1 ounce basil chiffonade (very thinly sliced)

1 roasted red pepper, peeled, seeded, and sliced

● Combine artichokes, lemon juice, olive oil, pepper, salt, parsley, coriander seeds and a dash of Tabasco and mix well. Cover and marinate in refrigerator overnight.
● To make aioli, add eggs, lemon juice, a pinch of salt, sriracha, and garlic to a blender. Blend to combine, then slowly pour in olive oil until mixture is thick and creamy.
● Spread grilled bread generously with aioli, top with marinated artichoke, a strip of red pepper, and sprinkle with basil.

recipe | SERVES 5 | *courtesy Firefly on Paradise* | $40ADAY

APPT - SOUP/SAL - ENTREE - VEG/POT - DESSERT - BEV

Gazpacho

4 ripe tomatoes, concasse* see below method

1/2 cup extra-virgin olive oil

2 ounces cider or sherry vinegar

2 cups tomato juice

1 cup diced stale or lightly toasted baguette bread

2 cucumbers, peeled, seeded, and chopped

1 red pepper, seeded and chopped

1 red onion, chopped

1 tablespoon minced garlic

1/2 bunch chopped parsley

1/2 bunch chopped cilantro

1 tablespoon minced jalapeño, seeded and deveined

Kosher salt

Sliced or diced avocado, for garnish

● To concasse tomatoes: Bring a large pot of salted water to a boil. Cut a cross into the top and bottom of the tomatoes. Boil tomatoes for 20 to 30 seconds or until skin begins to peel back. Drain tomatoes and immediately plunge into ice water to chill and to stop the cooking. Peel and seed tomatoes, then chop.
● In a bowl, mix the olive oil, vinegar, and tomato juice. Add the bread and soak for 10 minutes, or until softened.
● Combine the tomato concasse, cucumber, red pepper, onion, garlic, parsley, and cilantro. Reserve 1/2 cup of the chopped mixture for garnish, if desired.
● Add all ingredients except for the reserved vegetables and avocado to a blender or food processor and puree until smooth. Season, to taste, with kosher salt.
● Serve chilled. Garnish with avocado and reserved vegetables.

Our first episode in Vegas was an all-nighter—we started the show with dinner and ended with a breakfast buffet. Here are the places we stopped at off the strip.

dinner

● Bahama Breeze, 375 Hughes Center Drive, Las Vegas, NV, (702) 731-3252

sweet

● Freed's Bakery, 4780 South Eastern Avenue, Las Vegas, NV, (702) 456-7762

snack

● Sunrise Café at Palms Casino Resort, 4321 West Flamingo Road, Las Vegas, NV, (702) 942-7777

breakfast

● Firelight Buffet at Sam's Town Hotel Gambling Hall, 5111 Boulder Highway, Las Vegas, NV, (702) 456-7777

As a way-upstate New Yorker, I have few friends who are familiar with California. Those who do know, often mention San Diego as a place they really like, and would revisit on a dime. And now, thanks to the Food Network, I've become a member of this group!

breakfast

The Big Kitchen is a place more memorable for the company than the food. That's saying something, because the food is really good. In fact, it was in Big Kitchen that I had the only tofu I've ever enjoyed. The breakfast was tofu ranchero, a sautéed melange of peppers, onions, mushrooms, herbs and spices, and tomatoes, with some tofu thrown in for protein. I was shocked to find myself saying, "this was delicious!" So the food is good, but meeting Judy, the owner of Big Kitchen, is worth a trip from anywhere. Judy is a walking, talking, warm and engaging, living encyclopedia of pop culture and contemporary American history. Talk about it all with Judy, after the morning rush, of course: politics, sex, drugs, rock-n-roll. No topic is taboo. She's seen it or heard it all first hand and has her opinions, too. The walls are covered with autographed pictures and souvenirs from celebrities she's known over the years. One star signed a wall in the kitchen where she used to work alongside Judy. Her name? Whoopi Goldberg.

● **The Big Kitchen, 3003 Grape Street, San Diego, CA, (619) 234-5789**

❝ In fact, it was in Big Kitchen that I had the only tofu I've ever enjoyed. ❞

recipe courtesy The Big Kitchen $40ADAY

APPT - SOUP/SAL - ENTREE - VEG/POT - DESSERT - BEV

Tofu Ranchero
SERVES 4

Tofu Ranchero

Vegetable oil, for pan

16 ounces tofu, diced

6 cups diced mixed vegetables (onions, green bell peppers, zucchini, carrots, mushrooms)

2 cups salsa

8 (6-inch) corn tortillas

1 cup Monterey Jack cheese, grated

● Place a large sauté pan coated with oil over medium-high heat and sauté tofu and vegetables until al dente, 6 to 8 minutes. Add salsa and cook until heated through. Warm corn tortillas and place 2 on each plate. Serve tofu ranchero over corn tortillas and top with grated cheese.

lunch

From the first time the segment aired on $40 a Day, people have stopped to thank me for tipping them off to Point Loma Seafoods in San Diego. This place is right on the water, where the products they sell were swimming just a few hours earlier! Not only are the seafood items  fresh, Point Loma is a marketplace and an eat-in/carry-out restaurant. If you live here, you can shop for home, dine, or do both! On the show, I enjoyed a cup of chowder and a sweet scallop sandwich. Yumm-o! The scallops are lightly fried and served with a special sauce on freshly baked bread. Simple, sweet, and delicious! Prices are great. Go on a sunny day, sit outside, and bring the kids.

● **Point Loma Seafoods, 2805 Emerson Street, San Diego, CA, (619) 223-1109**

dinner

In Old Town the Mexican food is authentic and, for the most part, affordable. Ladies making tamales and flour tortillas can be seen in many restaurant windows while you wait for open tables. We went to the Old Town Mexican Cafe for pork carnitas and mango margaritas. I especially enjoyed the drink.

● **Old Town Mexican Cafe, 2489 San Diego Ave., San Diego, CA, (619) 297-4330**

sweet

MooTime Creamery offers delicious ice cream in many rich flavors. Still, I like vanilla. This one was a little too sweet for me, but the consistency was extra creamy, dense. The vanilla was all natural and the ice cream, freshly made. Prices were fair, and I would return for another scoop or two.

Vanilla Ice Cream

● **MooTime Creamery, 1025 Orange Avenue, San Diego, CA, (619) 435-2422**

Part of the wonderful experience I had in this city can certainly be attributed to my accommodations. I stayed at the Surf and Sand Resort. Each room felt like a private bungalow. I had a fantastic view, right on the beach. The gym was filled with state-of-the-art equipment and it was always empty! The spa was lovely, the restaurant and bar, overlooking the ocean, very romantic and packed at all hours. If I ever get back to Laguna I am going back to this place. It's a slice of heaven! The city itself is warm and very art-oriented. Galleries are clustered all over town, all within walking distance, but there are free jitney buses, too. It is safe, quiet, and charming to walk the streets here. If the city is having one of its famous art walks, participate. Each gallery offers snacks and sips of wine and the art is so diverse it's as if you are taking in five different museums in one evening. You'll have a wonderful time.

breakfast

What fun! This place is on the PCH, the Pacific Coast Highway. One of the prettiest roads in the US to drive along, in my opinion. Coyote Grill has great food and a wonderful atmosphere; I had egg enchiladas and they were just right, and at the right price. (see recipe on opposite page)

● Coyote Grill, 31621 Pacific Coast Highway, Laguna Beach, CA, (949) 499-6344

Enchiladas and Eggs

1/2 pound dried Anaheim chiles

8 cups water, plus more for soaking chiles

1 & 3/4 ounces chicken base

1/2 cup plus 2 tablespoons cornstarch

1/2 cup shortening or vegetable oil

12 (8 to 10-inch) corn tortillas

1 & 3/4 cups grated Cheddar

1 & 3/4 cups grated Monterey Jack

1/2 cup sliced scallions

Black Beans, recipe follows

8 to 12 eggs, cooked as desired (scrambled, over easy, etc.)

● Remove stems from chiles and discard; place chiles in a large bowl and pour in enough boiling water to cover. Weigh down chiles with a plate to ensure that they stay submerged. Soak for at least 4 hours to overnight; discard water.

● Make the sauce: Fill a blender halfway with the soaked chiles (you may need to do this in batches, depending on the size of your blender) and cover with enough fresh water to puree chiles (about 4 cups in all); puree until smooth. Pour the puree into a stockpot, add chicken base and 3 & 1/2 more cups water. Bring the sauce to a boil. Mix together 1/2 cup cold water and the cornstarch, stirring until smooth. Add to the sauce and stir. Simmer for about 20 minutes. Strain the sauce with a chinois or fine-mesh strainer to remove the seeds.

● Preheat oven to 375°F. In a deep frying pan warm the shortening or oil over medium heat to about 350°F. Slide 1 tortilla at a time into the oil and coat with oil to make the tortillas pliable; remove after a few seconds—make sure the tortilla doesn't fry.

● Coat the bottom of a 9 by 13-inch baking dish with about 1 cup enchilada sauce. Lay a tortilla down on a work surface; fill with 1/4 cup Cheddar and Jack cheeses and 2 tablespoons sauce. Roll the tortilla and place in the baking dish. Continue with the remaining tortillas. Cover the enchiladas with sauce so that the tortillas are coated thoroughly. Reserve any leftover enchilada sauce for another use. Sprinkle the remaining cheese on top and bake until the cheese has melted, 15 to 20 minutes. Garnish with scallions. Serve the enchiladas with 2 eggs per person, cooked any style, and black beans.

Enchilada and Eggs

Black Beans:

1 & 1/2 pounds dried black beans

3 tablespoons salt

1/2 yellow onion

1 gallon water

● Boil all ingredients in a pot until beans are tender, about 2 & 1/2 hours. Remove the onion.

173

lunch

Zinc was a perfect example of the whole Laguna Beach experience for me. It was eclectic, artistic, colorful, and comfortable. The foods were amazing, really. The salads and sandwiches were luscious and in unusual combinations, but I was most tempted by a classic for me, a roasted eggplant sandwich. After lunch in the tiny, beautifully gardened terrace, I went back into the market and did some shopping for a few small home gift items and books.

● **Zinc Café & Market, 344 Ocean Avenue, Laguna Beach, CA, (949) 494-2791**

Eggplant Sandwich

❝ Zinc was a perfect example of the whole Laguna Beach experience for me. It was eclectic, artistic, colorful, and comfortable. ❞

recipe   courtesy Zinc Café & Market $40 A DAY

APPT - SOUP/SAL - ENTREE - VEG/POT - DESSERT - BEV

Eggplant Sandwich

SERVES 3

1 medium-sized eggplant
1 teaspoon olive oil, plus more for brushing
Salt and freshly ground black pepper
1 baguette
1/4 cup crumbled feta cheese
1/4 cup crumbled goat cheese
2 tablespoons chopped fresh oregano leaves
2 red bell peppers, seeded and sliced
2 green bell peppers, seeded and sliced
2 tomatoes, cored and sliced
1 red onion, sliced
1 bunch fresh cilantro leaves

● Preheat oven to 375°F. Cut eggplant into 15 slices, brush each slice with olive oil, place on cookie sheet, and sprinkle with salt. Bake for 25 minutes and let cool.
● Cut baguette into thirds and slice in half horizontally for sandwiches. Mix feta and goat cheeses together; set aside. In separate bowls place oregano, salt, pepper, and olive oil.
● Spread cheese mixture on one side of baguette and brush other side lightly with olive oil. Spread 5 pieces of eggplant on baguette; top with generous amounts of red and green peppers, tomatoes, red onion, and cilantro. Sprinkle with oregano, salt, and pepper.

sweet

This area of California is known for its huge production of dates. So, date shakes, made of blended milk, ice cream, and ground-up pitted dates are the drink here. The most famous place to shake it up is this little shack by the side of the road on a cliff. I had a Monkey Date Shake with peanut butter, bananas, cold skim milk, and lots of dates. I went wild for it! I make myself date shakes at home now and I even taught a really basic one on my cooking show. Get on out to this shack!

● **Crystal Cove Shake Shack, 7703 East Coast Highway, Newport Cove, CA, (949) 497-9666**

dinner

This is another local favorite. It's a classy little hide-away, right in plain sight. It's easy to find but has an entrance that is set back a bit and inside it's cozy, chic, and elegant. Again, it's very romantic. I really wished my boyfriend were with me. The food was very comforting. I ordered a salad for supper to go light, but man it was rich and I was grateful! It was a mix of dark greens, chicken, apple, gorgonzola cheese, and candied walnuts. For the quality and setting, prices were fantastic and that goes for the wine and cocktail lists as well. If you can, take your sweetie here for a special night.

● **The Sundried Tomato Cafe and Catering Company, 361 Forest Avenue, #103, Laguna Beach, CA, (949) 494-3312**

PALM SPRINGS

The sun, prior to taking it's place in the sky, was born and raised in Palm Springs. Man, is it hot and sunny here. Everyone seems to drive convertibles; there was even a huge, classic convertible car show while I was in town. The downtown area has fantastic shopping. Homes in the residential areas are meticulously kept and adorable. This is a utopian community of good-looking, tan, well-off people who are very laid back, except on the golf course. They take golf very seriously here, dead serious. Me, I had never picked up a club, until my trip to Palm Springs. I got a lesson from a world-class pro and I actually hit a couple of drives. It was fun to make contact that first time, —quite a rush, really. But, I don't think I could handle the stress of taking up this relaxing sport.

breakfast

This place had just opened recently when I was in town, and I'm sure it must still be going strong because the menu was so creative and the prices so reasonable. I had a black bean and poached egg dish that was hearty and satisfying. Barry, the co-owner and host, was very friendly and made my experience memorable. You'll leave here with a mouthful of smiles.

● More Than a Mouthful Cafe, 134 East Tahquitz Canyon Way, Palm Springs, CA, (760) 322-3776

lunch

The freshness of the fish and seafood at this local favorite says it all. You have the option to eat-in or carry-out prepared foods or buy your seafood raw, all at great prices. The side door of the market opens onto a large, outdoor dining area that is heavily trellised with lush green vines, making it cool and shady. I had some light, tasty fish tacos and a local ice-cold beer. It really hit the spot!

● Fisherman's Market & Grill, 235 South Indian Canyon Drive, Palm Springs, CA, (760) 327-1766

dinner

This place was in the thick of the strip, Palm Canyon Drive. It had a terrific-looking menu, a funky, modern interior design and even better, an early-bird special. I had a delicious chicken piccata with capers, butter, wine, and asparagus tips for half the regular price.

● **Kaiser Grille and Bar, 205 South Palm Canyon Drive, Palm Springs, CA, (760) 323-1003**

drink

This is a hopping bar with a typically Californian feel to it. The drink menu constantly changes, but I had a truly original offering that you should ask for, even if it's no longer on the menu. Called the Silver Salmon Martini, it was a slightly fruity vodka martini with a few gems at the bottom of the glass: salmon roe. Prices were very friendly, as was the bartender. It was the perfect end to my balmy, Palmy day.

● **Twisted Fish Company (now closed)**

recipe courtesy Twisted Fish Co. $40ADAY

APP - SOUP/SAL - ENTREE - VEG/POT - DESSERT - BEV

Silver Salmon Martini
SERVES 1

1 teaspoon sugar
1 ounce vodka
1 ounce silver rum (recommended: Bacardi)
1/2 ounce pineapple juice
1/2 ounce grape juice
1/2 ounce pink lemonade
1/2 teaspoon caviar or salmon egg roe

● Place sugar in a small saucer. Dip the rim of a glass in water and press rim into sugar to coat.
● Mix vodka, rum, pineapple juice, grape juice, and pink lemonade in a shaker. Put caviar in the glass and pour the drink over the caviar.

recipe courtesy Kaiser Grille and Bar $40ADAY

APPT - SOUP/SAL - ENTREE - VEG/POT - DESSERT - BEV

Chicken Piccata
SERVES 2

2 (8-ounce) boneless, skinless chicken breasts
Salt and freshly ground black pepper
All-purpose flour, for dredging
2 tablespoons clarified butter (melt unsalted butter slowly; skim off foam and discard; use remaining clear liquid), or olive oil
2 tablespoons dry white wine
1 cup chicken broth
2 lemons, juiced
1 tablespoon capers
1 tablespoon chopped sun-dried tomatoes
2 tablespoons cold butter
1 tablespoon chopped fresh flat-leaf parsley leaves

● Slice chicken breasts diagonally into 3 medallions each. Pound them with a meat mallet or rolling pin to 3/4-inch thickness between 2 sheets of plastic wrap. Season with salt and pepper.
● Dredge the flattened chicken medallions in flour. Heat clarified butter or olive oil in a skillet over high heat. Sauté the chicken scaloppine 2 minutes on each side; remove and keep warm. Discard oil or butter. Lower heat, then add white wine, and reduce by half, about 1 minute. Add chicken broth, lemon juice, capers, and sun-dried tomatoes. Reduce by half again and whisk in cold butter to thicken sauce; adjust seasoning. Place the chicken on a serving plate, garnish with the pan sauce and chopped parsley.

This episode, my first for the show, included many personal firsts as well: The first time I've ever driven a convertible, my first meal at a biker joint, my first "health" drink. In planning my wardrobe, I may have worn my first (and possibly last) pastel-colored item of clothing on air, a baby-blue boat-neck tee shirt. Pastels and I just don't mix well. I drove around palm tree-lined streets like Axel Foley in Beverly Hills Cop, loving the weather and my car!

breakfast

RESTAURANTE
Guelaguetza
AUTENTICA COMIDA OAXAQUEÑA

Guelaguetza was our first stop. It took me half a day to figure out how to say the name (Gay-la-gayt-zah). At this tiny hideaway, Soledad, a woman originally from Oaxaca, Mexico, made the most delicious mole sauces I have ever tasted. In different colors and flavors, the sauces varied from the traditional, spicy, dark mole with a bit of dark, bitter chocolate, to a light, verdant (green) mole, another first for me. Soledad took some short cuts for our filming, but it normally takes her days to prepare each of the sauces. Her food was magic. Given the work and craftsmanship of her meals, Soledad's service to her customers is surely a true labor of love. Next, the farmers market in Santa Monica, a great way to enjoy the California sun while continuing to eat! The stalls were bursting with color, scents, and textures, lots of fresh fruits and veggies, drinks, raw nuts and more. Samples were plentiful. Foods were mostly organic, and the prices almost wholesale.

● Guelaguetza Palms Restaurant, 11127 Palms Boulevard, Los Angeles, CA, (310) 837-1153 ● Santa Monica Farmers' Market, Arizona Avenue & 2nd Street, Santa Monica, CA, (310) 458-8712

snack

Elixir, our "snack act" in the show, is a bar that serves concoctions of herbal reme-
dies, mixed with natural flavorings, and soda water. The drinks are expensive, but

they were designed to have medicinal purposes, beyond their ability to refresh. I was "examined" at the tonic bar and prescribed a
potion for "energy, strength, and clarity of thought." It was sweet. It
had bubbles. I felt the same lack of clarity afterward, but it was a
completely unique experience. Outside, in the Zen rock garden, I
watched well-dressed young people drinking their health tonics,
while working their cell phones, and smoking cigarettes. This was an
odd juxtaposition for me, a very LA experience.

● **Elixir Tonics & Teas, 8612 Melrose Avenue, Los Angeles, CA,
(310) 657-9300**

lunch

After that, I got caught up in Neptune's Net. It rocked! I love bikers! I've waited
on many, during my waitress years in the resort of Lake George, NY, home to
Americade, one of the largest rallies held in the US. Still, Neptune's was my first

trip to an official "biker hangout." The seafood was very fresh
and prices very reasonable, but
the real reason to go is for the
vibe and the scene. If you want
to increase your cool-factor in
life, head to The Net the next
time you're driving on the PCH
(Pacific Coast Highway).

● **Neptune's Net, 42505 Pacific
Coast Highway, Malibu, CA,
(310) 457-3095**

❝ **If you want to increase your cool-factor
in life, head to The Net.** ❞

recipe	courtesy Neptune's Net	$40ADAY
APP - SOUP/SAL - ENTREE - VEG/POT - DESSERT - BEV			

Tartar Sauce
SERVES 10 TO 12

1 pint mayonnaise
2/3 cup dill pickle relish
2 tablespoons minced white onion
2 tablespoons lemon juice
2 tablespoons pickle juice

● In a medium bowl, mix all ingredients together.
Refrigerate until ready to use. Serve with fried
fish, calamari, or crab cakes.

dinner

Authentic Cafe was our dinner choice for the show. Chef Roger Hayot named his
restaurant well; he's very genuine. His menu was eclectic, layered with many
global influences. He made me a salmon with a sweet corn, coconut, and lemongrass sauce. While cooking, Roger explained that he kept his prices low, so he
could share his food with more members of his community. The food was very
Authentic, and very delicious.

● **Authentic Cafe, 7605 Beverly Boulevard, Los Angeles, CA, (323) 939-4626**

SANTA BARBARA

Santa Barbara has just about everything—great shops, gardens, art galleries and museums, endless beaches, and of course, lots of restaurants and cafes. This is the California you know from postcards. It's laid-back, gorgeous, and full of happy-looking people, young and old.

breakfast

Cold Spring Tavern has always been the only stop for food and drink in the rocky, winding San Marcos Pass. Like a movie set from a quality Western, it's dark and drafty, yet quaint and homey. More than a hundred years ago, stagecoaches lined up outside the tavern, allowing their horses to take water and feed. Today, Harley Davidson motorcycles, convertibles, and minivans fill the driveway. When we visited, I was enlightened by a chat with the owner, a centenarian. From this visit I learned about the keys to a long, full life: good food, good humor, humility, and humanity. I had a huge, delicious breakfast. The breads are homemade, the coffee strong and good.

Clam Chowder

● **Cold Spring Tavern, 5995 Stagecoach Rd., Santa Barbara, CA, (805) 967-0066**

❝ **Like a movie set from a quality Western, it's dark and drafty, yet quaint and homey.** ❞

lunch

At the Santa Barbara Shellfish Company out on the pier, you can choose your crustacean from a tank: cruel, but fresh and tasty. I had a grilled lobster Caesar salad. I took full advantage of great weather and sat outside, though the views from the charming, casual interiors are great, too. Prices are reasonable. The restaurant also has a more upscale sister establishment. I dined at both, and I actually preferred my meal here, at half the price.

● **Santa Barbara Shellfish Company, 230 Stearns Wharf, Santa Barbara, CA, (805) 966-6676**

❝ You can choose your crustacean from a tank: cruel, but fresh and tasty. ❞

Grilled Lobster

dinner

Camino Real Cafe is located in a large strip mall in Goleta, not easy to find if you're from out of town. We went because the chef Tom Garnet was a crew member's family friend and word had it that he was terrific and very talented; I hope he hasn't already moved on. I had a flat-iron steak, a new cut of meat to the gourmet scene at the time we taped this show. It was skillfully prepared and the side of spicy black beans was simple, but flavorful. The price for my steak dinner was actually comparable to my breakfast at Cold Spring Tavern. If you have friends and family at UCSB, you'll be right in the neighborhood to check out Camino Real.

● **Camino Real Cafe, 6980 Marketplace Drive, Goleta, CA, (805) 961-4777**

| recipe | MAKES ONE 10-INCH 3-LAYER CAKE | adapted from Sojourner Cafe | $40ADAY |

APPT - SOUP/SAL - ENTREE - VEG/POT - DESSERT - BEV

Chocolate Fudge Cake with Vanilla Buttercream Frosting and Chocolate Ganache Glaze

Cake:

3/4 cup canola oil, plus more for pans

3 cups firmly packed brown sugar

3 eggs

2 & 2/3 cups all-purpose flour

2 & 1/4 teaspoons baking powder

2 & 1/4 teaspoons baking soda

1 & 1/2 teaspoons salt

1 tablespoon pure vanilla extract

1 & 1/2 cups milk

1 & 1/2 cups water

1 cup plus 2 tablespoons cocoa powder

Frosting:

2 pounds (8 sticks) unsalted butter, softened

4 cups sifted confectioners' sugar

2 tablespoons pure vanilla extract

1 pinch salt

Ganache:

1 & 1/4 cups semisweet chocolate chips

2 teaspoons light corn syrup

3/4 cup heavy cream

● Make the cake: Preheat oven to 350°F. Grease three 10-inch cake pans, and line the bottoms with parchment paper or dust lightly with flour. In the bowl of an electric mixer, combine brown sugar and oil. With the mixer set on low, mix in eggs; continue mixing until light and fluffy, 3 to 4 minutes.

● In a separate bowl, sift together flour, baking powder, baking soda, and salt. In a small bowl, mix vanilla into milk. Bring 1 & 1/2 cups water to a boil; remove from heat. Add cocoa to water and whisk until smooth.

● To the egg mixture, alternately add the dry ingredients and the milk mixture, beginning and ending with dry ingredients. Turn off the mixer and scrape down the sides of the bowl after each addition. With the mixer on low, add hot cocoa. Scrape down the sides of the bowl and pour batter into prepared cake pans.

● Bake the cake for about 15 minutes or until a tester comes out clean. When cake layers have cooled, remove from pans and refrigerate until cold.

● Make the frosting: In the bowl of an electric mixer beat softened butter on low while adding confectioners' sugar. When all the sugar is mixed in, turn off the mixer and scrape down the sides of the bowl. Add vanilla and salt and let the mixer beat for 5 to 7 minutes on medium speed. Place one cake layer on a serving platter and spread with frosting. Top with a second layer and spread with frosting. Top with the third layer and spread top and sides with frosting. Refrigerate the cake for 10 to 20 minutes to set up the frosting.

● Make the ganache: Place chocolate chips and corn syrup in a heatproof bowl. In a small saucepan bring heavy cream to a full boil. Pour cream over chocolate and whisk until smooth. Pour warm ganache over the top of the cake and, with a cake spatula, smooth the top of the cake and allow ganache to spill over the sides. Refrigerate for at least 20 minutes. Serve the cake cold or allow it to come to room temperature before serving.

❝ I wanted to try everything that passed by my table: entrées, salads, pastas, and desserts. ❞

𝒮weet

Sojourner Cafe is typical of Santa Barbara, a gathering place with a wonderful mix of art, great food, and community. I went to this neighborhood cafe for a dessert, and had a triple chocolate (dark, milk, and white) cake that was heavenly. (see recipe on opposite page) I wanted to try everything that passed by my table: entrées, salads, pastas, and desserts. The menu was creative, offering vegetarian and organic foods, as well as more traditional items. Charming hand-painted details decorated the windows and the walls served as retail gallery space for the work of many local artists. I enjoyed my sojourn at Sojourner Cafe!

● Sojourner Cafe, 134 East Canon Perdido Street, Santa Barbara, CA, (805) 965-7922

Chocolate Cake

Tony Bennett left his heart in a very romantic place: The mysterious fog, rolling in off the Bay, the drama of crossing that HUGE, pink bridge in a tiny little car, the fabulous foods from the exotic tastes of Chinatown to the sweet, fresh, local seafood, and the cable cars that go up and down amazingly steep hills, just like the ups and downs of love. I'm hooked and misty-eyed, too!

breakfast

Chicken Meatball Dim Sum

> **The expertise that goes into each tiny, tasty dumpling is awesome.**

Joe Chan at The Oriental Pearl is a gracious host and this restaurant, like a pearl, is one in a million. The expertise that goes into each tiny, delicious dumpling served at The Pearl is awesome. I sampled several dishes, because they were affordable. The most impressive was a dumpling called a beggar's pouch. Made of a layer of cooked egg whites, as thin as a sheet of tracing paper, the pouch is filled with a delicately flavored, bite-size chicken meatball. The flavors I remember most: green onion, lemongrass, ginger, and garlic. When you go to this gem of a restaurant, bring a big appetite and a small budget. Joe will send you home double-happy!

● Oriental Pearl, 760 Clay Street, San Francisco, CA, (415) 673-1101

lunch

Swan Oyster Depot is an elbows-on-the-table, no-nonsense, doesn't-get-fresher-than-this joint that serves up crab and calamari, rather than chili dogs and patty melts. The Swan is no beauty in the décor department, but that's one way to keep the prices down. This duckling is beautiful to me though: hot sauce and tiny American flags decorate the fountain counter. Forget the white table cloths! Give me a clean kitchen and fresh, really good food and I'm yours! The seafood salads, cracked crab, oysters, and shrimp are all prepared in front of you. Belly up to the counter at Swan Oyster Depot as often as you can whenever you are in SF.

● **Swan Oyster Depot, 1517 Polk Street, San Francisco, CA, (415) 673-1101**

---

recipe   courtesy Swan Oyster Depot $40ADAY

APPT - SOUP/SAL - ENTREE - VEG/POT - DESSERT - BEV

Crab Louie Salad
SERVES 4

Louie Dressing:
2 cups store-bought mayonnaise
1 cup tomato ketchup
1/2 cup sweet relish
1/2 cup chopped black olives
2 hard-boiled eggs, chopped

Salad:
1 head iceberg lettuce, chopped
8 to 12 ounces fresh Dungeness crabmeat
1 avocado, peeled, pitted, and thinly sliced lengthwise
3 medium tomatoes, quartered
1/2 pound asparagus spears, cooked

● Make the dressing: Mix together mayonnaise, ketchup, relish, olives, and eggs in a medium-size bowl.
● Make the salad: Make a bed of iceberg lettuce on a large serving plate. Top with crabmeat, avocado, tomatoes, and asparagus. Drizzle with Louie dressing and serve immediately.

❝ Forget the white table cloths! Give me a clean kitchen and fresh, tasty food and I'm yours! ❞

---

recipe   courtesy Swan Oyster Depot $40ADAY

APPT - SOUP/SAL - ENTREE - VEG/POT - DESSERT - BEV

Calamari Salad
SERVES 4

Juice of 1 lemon
Salt
16 squid, cleaned and cut into rings
1/2 cup chopped white onion
1/2 cup chopped celery
3 garlic cloves, minced
2 tablespoons chopped fresh flat-leaf parsley
1/2 cup olive oil
1/4 cup red wine vinegar
Pinch dried thyme
Pinch dried basil
Pinch dried oregano

● To a large pot of boiling water, add lemon juice and enough salt to make the water taste salty. Add squid rings and cook until just cooked through but not rubbery, 1 & 1/2 to 2 minutes; drain and transfer to a serving bowl.
● Combine onion, celery, garlic, parsley, olive oil, vinegar, and herbs with cooked squid. Serve at room temperature or cool.

sweet

Petit Gateau

Citizen Cake is too cool. Pastry chef/owner Elizabeth Faulkner is a rock star. She looks like a young American cousin to Annie Lenox. This pastry shop/eatery is a museum of edible contemporary art. Her pastries are like small, delicious indie films: you are drawn in by their titles (like the Mojito pastry of mint and chocolate that she made with me) then, once you take a taste, the story unfolds and you are hooked! On $40 a Day, Elizabeth showed me how she makes that great Mojito pastry and yet, on my show budget, I could only afford a cookie. In real life, I say break your piggy bank and pay Elizabeth anything for one of the sweetest and finest tastes to ever pass your lips.

● **Citizen Cake, 399 Grove Street, San Francisco, CA, (415) 861-2228**

❝ **The pastries Elizabeth creates are like small, delicious indie films...** ❞

dinner

Coquille Saint Jacques

Le Metro Café is a funky little bistro, the kind of place one expects to find in San Francisco; it's innovative, affordable, and the food is artful yet classic. I had a Coquille Saint-Jacques and it was every bit as good as some I've had at four times the price! (see recipe on opposite page) The chef is classically trained and it shows; the wines are fine and reasonably priced, too. Better still, the rooms of this small house are filled with interesting works by local artists.

● **Le Metro Café, 311 Divisadero Street, San Francisco, CA, (415) 552-0903**

Coquilles St. Jacques

2 tablespoons butter

2 teaspoons chopped shallots

2 teaspoons chopped garlic

12 medium clams, scrubbed

18 black mussels, cleaned and de-bearded

Salt and freshly ground black pepper

1 cup white wine

3 tablespoons olive oil

6 sea scallops

12 medium shrimp

8 ounces white mushrooms, sliced

Velouté Sauce:

3 tablespoons butter

3 tablespoons all-purpose flour

Juice of 1 lemon

1 quart fumet (fish stock)

1 pint heavy cream

Salt and freshly ground black pepper

1 cup bread crumbs

4 teaspoons chopped fresh flat-leaf parsley

● Melt butter in a large skillet over low heat. Add shallots and garlic, cover tightly, and sweat until translucent and soft, about 2 to 3 minutes; do not let brown. Add clams and mussels and toss everything together. Season with salt and pepper. Add white wine and bring to a simmer, stirring and scraping the bottom of the pan with a wooden spoon to remove any browned bits that have stuck to the pan. Cover and simmer until mussels and clams start to open, about 5 minutes. Strain mussels and clams, reserving the liquid, and set aside (the cooking liquid will be used to make the velouté sauce).

● In the same large skillet, heat 2 tablespoons olive oil over high heat until oil is smoking. Season scallops and shrimp with salt and pepper. Carefully place scallops in the pan and sear until golden brown on both sides. Remove from the pan and set aside. Add shrimp to the same pan and sauté until cooked through, about 1 to 2 minutes on each side. Remove from the pan and set aside. To the same pan, add the remaining 1 tablespoon olive oil and let it get hot. Add mushrooms and sauté until they are cooked and most of their liquid is released. Season with salt and pepper. Remove mushrooms from the pan and set aside.

● Make the velouté sauce: Melt butter in a sauté pan over low heat; add flour to make a roux, stirring until evenly mixed. Let cook for a few minutes until the mixture resembles pancake batter. Place the pan you used for the shellfish over medium heat and add reserved cooking liquid, lemon juice, and fumet; cook until reduced by half. Add cream and reduce by half. Add the roux and stir until smooth and thick. Season with salt and pepper.

● Preheat the broiler. Remove mussel and clam shells. Cut scallops into quarters and remove any shells from shrimp. Add mushrooms, scallops, shrimp, mussels, and clams to the velouté sauce and stir. Fill 4 individual heatproof baking shells or bowls with the seafood velouté and sprinkle with bread crumbs and parsley. Place under a broiler until the tops become golden brown. Place each hot dish onto another plate to serve.

MONTEREY

Since I'm from the "other coast," I knew very little about California as a whole. In fact, before this trip, when I heard the name Monterey, I thought Jack cheese, of course! I just had no idea....

breakfast

First Awakenings is a great way to start any day. The food is fantastic and the menu very original, as is the décor inside. Murals and original art reflect the customer base of local artists. Sitting outside is just fun! There are huge fire pits on the patio; you feel as if you're going to a beach blanket bingo party. The restaurant has a great location on Cannery Row at the waterfront, near the amazing aquarium. Try the overstuffed, California breakfast crepes. "Yumm-o!"

● First Awakenings, 125 Oceanview Blvd., Pacific Grove, CA, (831) 372-1125

recipe courtesy First Awakenings $40ADAY

APPT - SOUP/SAL - ENTREE - VEG/POT - DESSERT - BEV

First Awakenings' Crepes
SERVES 6 (12 CREPES)

1/2 teaspoon salt
2 tablespoons vegetable oil, plus more for pan
4 eggs, beaten
3 cups milk
2 cups all-purpose flour
2 tablespoons confectioners' sugar
2 teaspoons pure vanilla extract

Breakfast Crepes

● Combine all ingredients in a large mixing bowl and mix with an electric mixer until well blended, about 60 seconds. Strain the mixture through a fine-mesh sieve to remove any lumps.
● Heat a 10-inch nonstick sauté pan over medium heat. Coat pan with a little oil and pour about 1/4 cup batter into the pan; then rotate the pan to spread the batter evenly. Cook until the top of the crepe appears dry, about 1 minute. Flip the crepe and cook on the other side for about 20 seconds. Remove from the pan to a rack and continue making crepes with remaining batter. Serve with your favorite sweet or savory filling.

❝ There are huge fire pits on the patio; you feel as if you're going to a beach blanket bingo party. ❞

lunch

The Corkscrew Café's sign, a HUGE corkscrew, gets your attention, and once you enter you realize it is much more than a café. It's also a corkscrew museum, the only one of it's kind and you soon learn that corkscrews come in all shapes and sizes; this collection dates back hundreds of years. Walter Georis and his beautiful wife, the proprietors, also have a garden, in which many ingredients that fuel their menu

are grown. Out back, they have a gallery of folk art and winding paths that off-set unusual pottery collections and statuaries. I dined on greens that I helped gather. They were sparsely dressed and piled alongside a portobello sandwich which was beefy, yet meat-free. Walter's wine was delicious, a slightly spicy yet delicate selection.

● **Corkscrew Café, 55 West Carmel Valley Road, Carmel Valley, CA, (831) 659-8888**

sweet

The Tuck Box is no bigger than a bread box. It also sits appropriately in Carmel By The Sea, which is itself a tiny community. There are no tall sign posts and the buildings are all white with thatched or tiled roofs. The primary business is art, and the galleries are diverse and amazing. The town looks like a Disney movie; I expected

any number of the Seven Dwarfs to appear at any moment. At Tuck, I had tea and the largest scone I've ever laid eyes on! The recipe is a well-guarded secret, even to The Food Network, so you'll just have to go in person to enjoy it.

● **The Tuck Box, Dolores Street between 7th and Ocean Avenues, Carmel, CA, (831) 624-6365**

❝ **The town looks like a Disney movie. I expected any number of the Seven Dwarfs to pop out at me at any moment.** ❞

dinner

Cafe Fina is the star of Fisherman's Wharf, and that's who it attracts. Its walls are covered with pictures of hundreds of celebrities who have dined here, including The Godfather of this area, Clint Eastwood. Chef and owner Dominic Mercurio made me a tasty local favorite, sand dabs with veggies and rice; his calamari salad was also fantastic. You cannot beat the view. Be on the lookout for the sea lions! And pick up a bag of his yummy flavored almonds on your way out.

● **Cafe Fina, 47 Fisherman's Wharf, Monterey, CA, (831) 372-5200**

Sandabs

recipe | SERVES 4 | adapted from Cafe Fina | S40ADAY

APPT - SOUP/SAL - ENTREE - VEG/POT - DESSERT - BEV

Pasta Fina

1 pound fresh linguine
2 to 4 tablespoons olive oil
1/2 cup white wine
3 cups clam juice
3/4 cup (1 & 1/2 sticks) butter
3 cups diced tomatoes
2 cups chopped scallions (from 2 bunches)
1 pound baby shrimp, peeled and de-veined
1 cup black olives
Salt and pepper, to taste

● Cook linguine in boiling salted water until al dente. Drain and toss with 2 to 4 tablespoons olive oil to help prevent pasta from sticking together; set aside.
● In a large sauté pan, combine wine and clam juice and cook over high heat until reduced to 1/4 the original volume of liquid. Add butter, tomatoes, scallions, baby shrimp, and black olives. Continue cooking over high heat, stirring occasionally, until butter is melted. When butter has melted, cook for 5 more minutes. Season with salt and pepper, to taste. Add the pasta to the mixture and toss to heat through.

I love wine. My first word in life was neither mama or dada, it was vino! I used to drink my grandpa's wine (diluted with lots of water) in my bottle. I was a quiet, rosy-cheeked kid. Now, you may be saying, "Oh, that's what happened to her." Things don't change. When I heard we were going to do a show in wine country, I said "Salute! Pour me some vino, Bello!"

tasting

So, go back and begin at the middle of my day's visit: I went to V. Sattui Winery in Napa Valley where I had a tour and wine tasting, and sampled many cheeses offered in their gourmet food marketplace. V. Sattui Winery looks like a Mediterranean estate that's been standing for hundreds of years, but it was built fairly recently in the mid '80s. (We Americans are masterful at knock-offs). Though the "castle" went up in 1984, the V. Sattui family has been producing wines for generations with great pride. I found their wines luscious, worth a trip across the country. Good thing, too, because that's how far one would have to travel to buy them. Many are limited in production, not widely distributed, and sold only at the winery. I purchased a four-pack to bring home as a one-of- a-kind gift for my family and friends.

● V. Sattui Winery, 1111 White Lane, St. Helena, CA, (707) 963-7774

tasting

I also stopped by Rutherford Hill for a tasting. What a looker! This beautiful tasting room has a warm tone, with clean, modern lines. I also remember the view as my favorite in the Napa Valley; it surveyed all of the rolling hills covered with olive trees and grape-laden vineyards. Here, I gave myself a gift of one of their wines.

● **Rutherford Hill Winery,
200 Rutherford Hill Road,
Rutherford, Napa Valley,
CA, (707) 963-1871**

❝ **I remember the view from their perch
as my favorite in Napa Valley.** ❞

breakfast

Breakfast actually would have come in way under budget if I had bought what I truly wanted at this café, crusty bread and strong coffee. Basque Boulangerie has some of the crustiest, tastiest breads I've ever had. Unfortunately, a crust of bread does not make for fabulous food television. So, we shot their recommendation instead, a cream-filled breakfast Napoleon of sorts, their Beehive Cake, a honey cake, layered with nuts and custard. It was a little too sweet to be a breakfast choice for me, but it was delicious! Still, I highly recommend all the breads, with a nice, hot beverage for dunking!

● **Basque Boulangerie Café, 460 First Street East, Sonoma, CA, (707) 935-7687**

lunch

Lunch, here in the countryside of California, actually made me think of my Cajun-born daddy (he's from Louisiana and makes a mean gumbo!). This restaurant, named for a Louisiana hound dog, has one of my favorite mixes: a combination of fine dining and easy atmosphere. I went for lunch when it's the same tasty food as at dinner, but in smaller portions and at budget-friendly prices. The menu offered lots of half-orders, specials, and salads. I had

Salmon Caesar Salad

salmon, grilled on charred hardwood, and served on a Caesar salad, of sorts. The dressing had a Southern citrus-like twist. Delish! I also had a cup of Rooster Gumbo. It took the chef two days to make his gumbo, just as long as it takes my Cajun daddy to make his!

● **Catahoula Restaurant (now closed)**

dinner

Della Santina's is a tiny, family-run, home-style restaurant in Sonoma. Charming and warm, eating here feels as if I were eating at home with

Della Santina's
TRATTORIA • ROSTICCERIA • PASTICCERIA

my little Sicilian mama. This is Italian secret-recipe cooking at it's best: even if you had the recipe, you wouldn't be able to recreate what they make at Della Santina's. I love the potato gnocchi with tomato-basil sauce. The corkage fee is small if you bring your own wine from any local winery. (see recipe on opposite page)

● **Della Santina's, 133 Napa Street East, Sonoma, CA, (707) 935-0576**

❝ Charming and warm, eating here feels as if I were eating at home with my little Sicilian mama. ❞

Gnocchi Pomodoro

Gnocchi Pomodoro

Gnocchi:

6 large baking potatoes, such as russets

2 egg yolks

1/2 cup (1 stick) butter, melted

2 teaspoons salt

Pinch white pepper

Pinch freshly grated nutmeg

2 cups all-purpose flour, plus more for dusting

Pomodoro Sauce:

1 (28-ounce) can whole Italian tomatoes

2 tablespoons olive oil

1 tablespoon chopped garlic

Salt and freshly ground black pepper

Crushed chile flakes

6 to 8 large fresh basil leaves, chopped

1/2 cup heavy cream

Grated Parmesan, for serving

● Start the gnocchi: Preheat oven to 300°F. Prick potato skins in several places with a fork and arrange on a baking sheet. Bake potatoes until tender, 1 to 1 & 1/2 hours. When potatoes are cool enough to handle, scoop the pulp from each potato and place in a mixing bowl, discarding skins. Mash potatoes to a fine consistency. Cool slightly before adding to the rest of the ingredients.

● Combine egg yolks, melted butter, salt, pepper, and nutmeg in a bowl. Add the egg mixture to the potatoes and stir to combine. Add flour, mixing in 1 cup at a time, and stir until smooth.

● Scoop out a small amount of dough and roll into a finger-size cylinder on a floured board. Cut with a knife into bite-size pieces. Use your thumb to press each piece over the back-side of the tines of a fork, making a concave shape with the indentations from the fork on the outside. Repeat with remaining dough. Place gnocchi in a pan and freeze until hard enough to handle, about 5 minutes, and then transfer to portion-size bags and store in the freezer until ready to cook.

● Meanwhile, make the sauce: Cut each canned tomato in half and remove the seeds. Chop tomatoes into small pieces and reserve both the juice from the cut tomatoes and the juice in the can. Heat olive oil in a saucepan over medium-high heat and sauté garlic for 1 minute. Add tomatoes, salt and pepper to taste, and chile flakes and bring to a simmer for 5 minutes. If necessary, add some of the reserved tomato juices. Stir in the basil and the cream and remove from heat. You can re-heat the sauce for a few minutes over medium-low heat while gnocchi are cooking.

● Bring a large pot of water to a boil and add a pinch of salt. Drop gnocchi into boiling water, 3 or 4 at a time, so that the water doesn't stop boiling. The gnocchi is ready when it floats to the top, about 2 minutes. Drain gnocchi, transfer to a serving bowl, and top with sauce. Add freshly grated Parmesan and serve immediately.

I've always wanted to travel to Oregon. Hazelnuts, huckleberries, and delicious wines were a draw for me. Even though the weather was cold and grey, the trip from start to finish was great.

breakfast

The food and drink were a real cut-above the usual, and Multnomah Falls Lodge was a warm, cozy, and beautiful retreat, though I must have mispronounced "Multnomah" about 14 times during this shoot. Wandering the paths and bridges behind the lodge had me chilled to the bone. The Lodge's hot, steaming coffee and the huckleberry pancakes were just what the doctor ordered!

● **Multnomah Falls Lodge, 50000 Historic Columbia River Highway, Bridal Veil, OR, (503) 695-2376**

Huckleberry Pancakes

❝ The food and drink were a real cut-above the usual, and Multnomah Falls Lodge was a warm, cozy, and beautiful retreat. ❞

recipe	SERVES 4	courtesy Multnomah Falls Lodge	$40ADAY

APPT - SOUP/SAL - ENTREE - VEG/POT - DESSERT - BEV

Huckleberry Pancakes

MAKES 10 PANCAKES

2 cups all-purpose flour
1 tablespoon baking powder
1/2 teaspoon salt
1/4 cup sugar
2 eggs
2 tablespoons vegetable oil, plus more for griddle
1 & 1/2 cups milk
5 ounces huckleberries*, fresh or frozen, plus extra for serving
Whipped butter, for serving
Maple syrup, for serving

● Mix flour, baking powder, salt, and sugar in a bowl. Stir in eggs, oil, and milk just until combined; do not over-mix.

● Lightly oil a griddle and heat over medium-low heat. Pour four 1/4-cup ladles full of batter on the griddle. Add 1/2 ounce huckleberries to each pancake. Cook 2 minutes on 1 side, dabbing the batter over the berries on top to prevent them from sticking when flipped. Flip pancakes and then cook another 2 minutes on the other side.
● Place the pancakes on a large plate and serve with extra huckleberries, whipped butter, and hot maple syrup.

*Note: If huckleberries are hard to find, use blueberries instead.

lunch

Bush Garden is a great place for sushi! So much fun! If you want to sit at the bar, get there early for lunch. There are also low, sleek tables but, hang on! You don't have to sit on your legs. Under each table, there is a large, square hole in which you can dangle your legs while maintaining the illusion that you are very flexible. I had lunch specials of nigiri sushi and California rolls, tasty fish and rice at a tasty price, in a city that is known for good seafood.

● **Bush Garden Japanese Restaurant, 900 SW Morrison Street, Portland, OR, (503) 226-7181**

recipe	SERVES 6	courtesy Bush Garden

APPT - SOUP/SAL - ENTREE - VEG/POT - DESSERT - BEV

California Rolls

3 & 1/3 cups rice

5 & 1/3 tablespoons sushi vinegar*, or 5 & 1/3 tablespoons rice wine vinegar plus 5 tablespoons sugar and 3 tablespoons salt

10 sheets nori seaweed, halved

1/2 pound imitation crabmeat, cut into long, thin pieces

1/4 cup mayonnaise

1 cucumber, peeled, seeded, and julienned

1 avocado, peeled, pitted, and cut into long, thin pieces

Sesame seeds, for garnish

● Cook the rice: Wash rice until the water rinses clear. Drain rice in a colander and let it stand for 30 minutes. Place rice in a pot or rice cooker and add 4 cups water (or follow the instructions on rice cooker). Bring the water to a boil. Reduce the heat to a simmer and cover the pot. Cook for 15 minutes. Remove the cover, place a damp towel over the rice, and let cool for 10 minutes.

● Make the California rolls: Cover a makisu (sushi rolling mat) with plastic wrap. Place half a sheet of nori over the plastic on the mat. Spread a handful of rice evenly over nori. Toss imitation crabmeat with mayonnaise in a small bowl. Place some imitation crabmeat along the center of the rice. Add some cucumber and avocado along the center of the rice. Using the mat and plastic wrap, roll nori around the filling and press lightly to seal. Remove the mat and plastic wrap and sprinkle the roll with sesame seeds. With a sharp knife dipped in very hot water, cut the sushi roll into bite-size pieces. Repeat with the remaining ingredients.

*Note: If you can't find sushi vinegar you can make it by pouring rice wine vinegar, sugar, and salt into a saucepan over low heat; stir until dissolved. For sweeter vinegar, add more sugar. Pour sushi vinegar over cooked rice; mix gently. Let cool to room temperature.

California Rolls

drink

McMenamin's Brewery—and art galleries, retail shops, inn and restaurant—reminded me of the Beatle's Sergeant Pepper's album. I felt as if I were walking through a tripped-out cartoon of the world at large. What a wonderful, imaginative place to spend a day or more. There are small restaurants and pubs outside the main complex, but the inn and brewery are a must if you travel to Oregon.

● **McMenamins Edgefield, 2126 SW Halsey St., Troutdale, OR, (503) 669-8610**

dinner

Higgins is one of the top five restaurants we've showcased on $40 a Day, or on any other Food Network show, I would bet. While I was in the dining room, two local vendors delivered tiny batches of organically grown delicacies from their gardens. The menu here changes daily, and features whatever is fresh, local, and in season at a fair price. Eating with chef Higgins is a pleasure because he takes joy, not only in cooking, but also in sharing. His sense of pride in his community and his dedication to his friends and neighbors motivates him to keep prices affordable. We had salmon with local produce. It was fabulous. The restaurant is relaxed, bright, calming. The evening I spent with Greg Higgins and his food made for one of the best dining experiences I've ever had in years of taping great food and travel. (see recipe on opposite page)

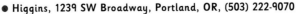
Chinook Salmon

● **Higgins, 1239 SW Broadway, Portland, OR, (503) 222-9070**

Horseradish-Crusted Chinook Salmon with Braised Greens and Roasted New Potatoes

Vegetable oil, for pans

Salt and freshly ground black pepper

8 new potatoes, halved

2 tablespoons prepared horseradish

1 cup chopped fresh flat-leaf parsley

1/2 teaspoon grated lemon zest

2 tablespoons whole-grain mustard

3 tablespoons minced garlic

1 cup panko (Japanese-style) bread crumbs (found in Asian food markets)

8 tablespoons extra-virgin olive oil

4 (2-inch-by-2-inch-by-1-inch) Chinook salmon fillets

2 tablespoons canola oil

1 cup fish stock or clam juice

8 cups mixed braising greens (chard, kale, mustard greens, endive), coarsely chopped

Juice of 1 lemon

● Preheat oven to 425°F. Coat a baking sheet with oil and sprinkle it with salt and pepper. Place potatoes, cut side down, on the baking sheet and place in the oven. Roast until just golden brown and just tender, 20 to 25 minutes. Remove potatoes from the oven and keep warm.

● Mix horseradish, parsley, lemon zest, mustard, and 2 tablespoons of the garlic in a small bowl. Add bread crumbs and toss gently to combine. Drizzle 6 tablespoons olive oil over the crumb mixture and stir gently, taking care not to break up the crumbs or make the mixture too heavy. Season to taste with salt and pepper.

● Grease an 8-inch square baking pan with vegetable oil. Season salmon fillets with salt and pepper. Heat canola oil in a large sauté pan over medium-high heat. When oil just begins to smoke, sear the salmon squares, skin side up, 2 pieces at a time, for 2 to 3 minutes. Remove to prepared pan, seared side up; repeat the process with the remaining salmon. Sprinkle the bread crumb mixture over the top of the fish, creating an even layer that's 1/8 to 1/4 inch thick. Place in the oven and roast salmon until the crust is golden brown and fish is just firm, 5 to 7 minutes.

● While salmon is baking, bring fish stock, the remaining 2 tablespoons olive oil, and the remaining tablespoon garlic to a boil in a nonreactive (anything but aluminum or cast iron) saucepan. Add greens, cover, and cook until greens are wilted, 2 to 3 minutes. Add lemon juice and season to taste with salt and pepper. Arrange the greens in the center of 4 shallow bowls; surround with roasted potatoes and braising liquid. Top each with a roasted salmon fillet.

How do I love Seattle? Let me count the ways: Sleepless in Seattle (the movie), Frasier, Starbucks, grunge rock, Experience Music Project, the Needle, Pike's Market, The Sonics, and on and on.

breakfast

For me, coffee is a vice. My blood has an 80-20 count, caffeine to platelets. Seattle smells like coffee, everywhere. You can't travel three city blocks here without passing five counters, shops and/or carts, all selling coffee. Yeah! In our show, Caffe Ladro (Caffe Thief) was our pick for a Seattle coffee experience. Nice choice! Ladro has a small, specialty shop feel to it, seems accessible, with prices a little lower than

Starbucks. I'm still a Starbucks fan, too, but Starbucks is now a huge, public company, with a store even in my remote hometown. When you're in Seattle, your challenge becomes finding a coffee house that's not part of a chain. Ladro has a few locations in the city and has a very creative menu. On weekends, try the espresso chip pound cake. (see recipe on opposite page)

● **Caffe Ladro, 7011 California Avenue, Seattle, WA, (206) 938-8021**

Espresso Chip Pound Cake

Espresso Pound Cake

1 pound (4 sticks) butter, plus more for pan

3/4 cup sugar

2 cups firmly packed brown sugar

5 eggs

1 tablespoon pure vanilla extract

2 tablespoons sour cream

3/4 cup buttermilk

1 cup brewed espresso

4 cups all-purpose flour, plus more for pan

1 tablespoon baking powder

1/2 tablespoon salt

2 cups semisweet chocolate chips (12 ounces)

Confectioners' sugar, for garnish

● Preheat oven to 350°F. Grease and flour a Bundt cake pan. Cream butter, sugar, and brown sugar together with an electric mixer. Start on a slow speed until blended, then turn it up to the highest speed and mix until light and fluffy, 3 to 4 minutes. Add eggs and vanilla and mix on medium speed just until eggs are fully broken up and combined; do not overmix. Add sour cream, buttermilk, and espresso, and mix until combined; if you are using hot espresso, pour it slowly into the mixture so that it does not cook the eggs.

● In a separate bowl, sift flour, baking powder, and salt together. Add the dry ingredients to the wet mixture, mix until combined. Fold in the chocolate chips.

● Scoop the cake batter into the prepared pan. Place the pan on a cookie sheet in the oven (this will prevent spills from falling into the oven and burning) and bake until a knife inserted into the cake comes out clean, 1 hour and 15 minutes to 1 hour and 45 minutes. Tent with aluminum foil after 40 minutes of cooking to prevent cake from browning too much.

● Let the cake cool to room temperature, then invert it onto a platter. Garnish with confectioners' sugar.

recipe	SERVES 4	courtesy Agua Verde	$40ADAY

APPT - SOUP/SAL - **ENTREE** - VEG/POT - DESSERT - BEV

Halibut Tacos

Halibut Tacos:
Vegetable-oil cooking spray
1 pound halibut fillets
Lemon pepper seasoning
12 (6-inch) corn tortillas, warmed
1 cup chopped cabbage
1/2 cup Creamy Avocado Sauce (recipe follows)

● Spray a grill with vegetable-oil cooking spray and preheat the grill. Season halibut with lemon pepper. Place halibut, skin side down, on the hot grill and cook for about 15 minutes, turning once. Fillets should be flaky and white throughout, but be careful not to overcook. Place 1/4 of the halibut over 3 warm tortillas. Add 1/4 cup cabbage and top with 2 tablespoons creamy avocado sauce. Roll up tortillas, if desired. Repeat the process 3 more times.

Creamy Avocado Sauce:
1 avocado
2 scallions, chopped
1 to 2 garlic cloves, chopped
1 cup sour cream
2 cups mayonnaise
1 teaspoon green habañero sauce
1 teaspoon apple cider vinegar
1 teaspoon lemon pepper

● Mix all of the ingredients together in a medium-size bowl. Stir or gently mash until the avocado is no longer chunky and the sauce is smooth and creamy.

Halibut Taco

lunch

For lunch, we went to a college student hangout, also very popular with locals of every age: Agua Verde. This colorful small restaurant is cool because you can kayak in and out of it, if you like! Bright and smartly decorated, it has great views, very reasonable prices, and fresh, appealing food. Most people think Mexican food is easy to make and hard to screw up. Wrong. Mexican food is also not the fried, refried, greasy, salty fast foods usually offered up as the-real-deal. Here, I enjoyed delicious grilled halibut soft tacos, high in protein, low in fat, spicy, but not at all hot. For good, affordable, authentic Mexican anything, when in Seattle, try Agua Verde.

● **Agua Verde, 1303 NE Boat Street, Seattle, WA, (206) 545-8570**

drink

"Looped" is the term that best describes what I became in the next act of the Seattle show. I visited the Red Hook Brewery, took a tour and enjoyed a tasting. I think I liked the Red Hook Chinook the best. The food looked great, too, and I really could have used some! Try the tour and the sampler and break your budget to work in a meal here as well.

● **Red Hook Brewery (now closed at this location)**

dinner

Bick's Broadview Grill is more "off the beaten path" than we all had expected. But this was one occasion when the food was so good, and so reasonably priced, that it was totally worth the effort of finding it, and for sure, I will return. One of the few totally vegetarian meals we've done on the show, this place will please meat-eaters and meat-free-ers alike. I had a ginger and lemon grass-stuffed portobello mushroom and a lovely glass of wine. This joint was really jumping at happy hour!

● **Bick's Broadview Grill, 10555 Greenwood Avenue North, Seattle, WA, (206) 367-8481**

The B in B.C. doesn't stand for British, it stands for BIG! Big mountains, big totem poles, big snowfalls—the great outdoors surrounding a big city. When we traveled here, it was very cold and snowy, yet breathtakingly beautiful. Magical. Being here, I felt as if I were in a scene from a film noir. Biplanes took off and landed every few minutes, gliding through the mist rising off the water. Very Bogart. This city intrigues me. My time here was too short. I hope to return, soon.

breakfast

Sweet Cherubim was a health foods market we stopped at for a parantha and a spirulina drink. The vegetable-stuffed flat bread (parantha) was tasty enough, though I'd rather have stopped at any number of falafel joints downtown instead. But, this spirulina algae drink, yuck! It had lots of berries, so I swallowed them and tried to extol some of its virtues on camera, but I really don't care for chewy drinks. I think I would rather take my chances and continue to eat meats, cheeses, and to drink fine wines than to have to eat sufficient amounts of so-called "health foods." Maybe they are an acquired taste, and some of it must be good. In my family, however, meat, fish, eggs, and cheese are all health foods. And I'll take a nice glass of wine over spirulina any day.

● **Sweet Cherubim Organic and Natural Food Store, 1105 Commercial Drive, Vancouver, BC, Canada, (604) 253-0969**

lunch

Sha-Lin Noodle House ROCKS! I had such fun here! They actually tried to teach me to pull my own noodles! Like a game of cat's cradle gone horribly wrong, my noodles met a sad end. Luckily, the pros at Sha-Lin have been pulling noodles for generations. They can turn a pile of flour, water, and vegetable oil into angel-hair pasta in seconds, no machinery involved, just the ten digits God gave us. Amazing! The noodles that built the Sha-Lin house are

Dragging Noodles Soup

pulled in front of your eyes, behind a clear plastic room divider, in full view of the dining area. The fresh noodles are piled into bowls with crisp, bright, chopped vegetables and your choice of meat, seafood, or tofu, then steeped with very hot broth. Plates are used to cover the bowls and trap the steamy heat. A few minutes later, you have a light, delicious, delicate soup. No two bowls are ever alike. Slurping is encouraged. Enjoy!

● **Sha-Lin Noodle House, 548 West Broadway, Vancouver, BC, Canada, (604) 873-1816**

recipe | SERVES 5 | courtesy P. I. of Culinary Arts | $40ADAY

APPT - SOUP/SAL - ENTREE - VEG/POT - DESSERT - BEV

Sautéed Salmon with Sweet Potato, Papaya Rougaille and Israeli Couscous

Papaya Rougaille:

1/2 red onion, finely chopped

1/2-inch disk fresh ginger, finely chopped

1 & 1/2 ripe tomatoes, seeded and chopped

1/2 papaya, or 1/4 cantaloupe and 6 strawberries, finely chopped

1 clove garlic, minced

1/2 bunch green onions (scallions), finely chopped

1/2 lemon or lime, juiced

1/2 tablespoon red wine vinegar

1/8 cup olive oil

Salt and pepper

Couscous:

Salt

1/2 pinch Spanish saffron

8 & 1/2 ounces Israeli couscous

1 large sweet potato, diced and cooked in salted water

1/2 zucchini, diced and cooked in salted water

1/2 large roasted red pepper, peeled, seeded and cut into small dice

1 & 1/2 ounces butter

3 shiitake mushrooms

1 clove garlic, chopped

1/2 small onion, chopped

1/2 teaspoon cumin powder

Salmon:

5 (5 & 1/4-ounce) salmon fillets

Salt and freshly ground black pepper

1/8 cup olive oil

Fried spaghetti, optional, for garnish

● To make the rougaille: Combine the onions, ginger, tomatoes, papaya, garlic, and green onions in a bowl. Add lemon or lime juice, red wine vinegar, and olive oil. Season with salt and pepper, to taste. Make the rougaille up 2 to 3 hours before serving, and let stand, covered, at room temperature.

● Preheat the oven to 350°F.

● To make the couscous: Fill a saucepan about 3/4-full with water, a little salt, and a little saffron for color. Bring to a boil, add the couscous, and cook for about 2 minutes. Drain couscous and run under cold water to stop the cooking. Add the sweet potato, zucchini, and red pepper to the couscous and toss to combine.

● Heat butter in a small pan over medium heat. Add mushrooms, garlic, onion, and cumin and sauté until mushrooms are tender. When mushrooms are soft, add the mixture to the couscous. Place the couscous in a baking dish and keep warm in the oven.

● Season salmon with salt and pepper. Heat olive oil in a large skillet over medium-high heat. Add salmon and sauté for about 1 minute per side for medium-rare. Serve the salmon on a bed of couscous. Heap the rougaille over salmon. Garnish with lengths fried spaghetti, if desired, so that they are reaching up from the salmon.

dinner

The Pacific Institute of Culinary Arts, like most culinary schools, is a wonderful place for budget travelers with gourmet tastes. Here future chefs and chefettes, under the watchful eye of master chefs, slave away, and produce splendid, artful meals for a fraction of their true value. The menu changes daily. I had Pacific Northwest salmon with papaya and sweet potato. (see recipe on opposite page) You may do even better!

Salmon Couscous

● **Pacific Institute of Culinary Arts, 1505 West 2nd Avenue, Vancouver, BC, Canada, (604) 734-4488**

sweet

Death By Chocolate—what a way to go! Delightful, devilish treats await you here. They made me some complicated concoction with three different chocolates. I thought why all the fuss? I don't even care for sweets. Then, I took a taste! Yummo! Turns out, I love sweets—especially these chocolate sweets, in all varieties.

● **Death by Chocolate, 1598 West Broadway, Vancouver, BC, Canada, (604) 730-2462**

haw.aii

OAHU
MAUI
BIG ISLAND

OAHU

I keep meaning to ask if the name Oahu means anything. It sounds like "Whoa-Hoo!" like, "Yippie!" ya know, an exclamation of joy. Anyway, O-AHU! Oahu is where they keep Waikiki Beach, so it's the most commercial of the islands. However, there's a reason that "touristy" places are popular with tourists. They're beautiful! Waikiki beach is fun, lively, and really pretty. There are huge catamarans that sail at all hours, surf lessons (I took one and got up!), and of course sun-bathing, with a beach bar never more than fifty feet away. Take the paper parasols home with you!

breakfast

Visiting this restaurant for breakfast is like being invited to a really nice wedding reception at dawn. The breakfast buffet is as much a feast for the eyes as it is for the stomach. There are endless arrays of tropical fruits, all colorful and perfectly ripe. There are eggs, meats, sweets, and my favorite item, Haupia macadamia nut bread pudding. Outrageously delicious! The restaurant's entire front wall opens on to the beach, so go early to get a good seat. The price of the buffet was so reasonable, I felt guilty.

● Shorebird Restaurant & Beach Bar, Outrigger Reef Hotel, 2169 Kalia Road, Honolulu, HI, (808) 922-2887

ShoreBird
RESTAURANT & BEACH BAR

recipe SERVES 12 TO 15   adapted from The Shorebird $40ADAY

APPT - SOUP/SAL - ENTREE - VEG/POT - DESSERT - BEV

Haupia Macadamia Nut Bread Pudding

Macadamia Bread Pudding

15 croissants, preferably day-old
5 eggs
2 (14-ounce) cans sweetened condensed milk
3 cups coconut milk
1 cup sugar
1 cup shredded coconut
1 cup chopped macadamia nuts

● Preheat oven to 300°F. Cut croissants into 1-inch cubes and press into a 9 & 1/2 by 13 & 1/2-inch baking dish. With an electric hand-mixer, mix eggs, evaporated milk, coconut milk, sugar, and water until it has a custardlike texture. Pour custard mixture over bread cubes. Top with shredded coconut and macadamia nuts. Bake until custard is just set, 1 hour and 15 minutes to 1 & 1/2 hours.

North Shore Country
OKAZU & BENTO

Hale'iwa, Hawai'i

lunch

A trip to the North Shore is a must. You have to check out the
surfers—the scene is out of control, totally insane. You'll quickly see what I mean: walls of ferociously churning water and tiny, seemingly frail
bodies cutting in and out of them—CRAZY! I went to this really cool take-out shop
and got a HUGE feast of a bento box with all kinds of sushi, sashimi, and
Japanese treats. If this shop is gone, there are others to try; bento boxes make a
perfect, healthy picnic food to take over to the beach. Note: SPAM (the canned
meat) is HUGE in Hawaii and SPAM sushi rolls are everywhere, even in the gas
station markets. You have to try one. It's an island rite of passage.

● **North Shore Country Okazu & Bento, Hale'iwa Shopping Plaza, 66-197
Kamehameha Highway, Hale'iwa, HI 96712, (808) 637-0055**

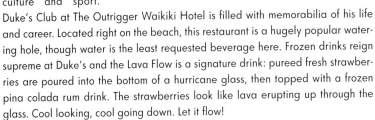

Lava Flow
SERVES 1

1 ounce coconut syrup

2 ounces pineapple juice

1 & 1/2 ounces rum

Splash vanilla ice milk (or ice cream)

1/2 cup ice

1 & 1/2 ounces strawberry purée

● Combine all ingredients except strawberry purée in a blender. Blend and pour into a cocktail glass and garnish with strawberry purée.

Lava Flow

drink

Duke was the king of surf in Hawaii. I can't remember how to spell his last name, but I do remember he was a handsome man who ruled when it came to long-board culture and sport. Duke's Club at The Outrigger Waikiki Hotel is filled with memorabilia of his life and career. Located right on the beach, this restaurant is a hugely popular watering hole, though water is the least requested beverage here. Frozen drinks reign supreme at Duke's and the Lava Flow is a signature drink: pureed fresh strawberries are poured into the bottom of a hurricane glass, then topped with a frozen pina colada rum drink. The strawberries look like lava erupting up through the glass. Cool looking, cool going down. Let it flow!

● **Duke's Canoe Club Waikiki, 2335 Kalakaua Avenue, #116, Honolulu, HI, (808) 922-2268**

Surf Turf Combo

dinner

What a blast-from-the-past! I felt I was in a scene from Dr. No or some other late '60s spy flick! This place is a beautiful collection of all things cool from that era, including columns, art, lighting, and beautiful furnishings from many of the greatest hotels of Waikiki. The Marina (Mariana) is a fabulous place to go and feel fabulous! You wander down winding gangplanks into huge, but hidden, dining areas. Cocktails are classics, the live music very supper-club in repertoire, and the continental cuisine, a throwback, too. There's steak, seafood, and chops, simply prepared and simply delicious.

● **La Mariana Sailing Club, 50 Sand Island Rd., Honolulu, HI, (808) 848-2800**

Maui—WOWIE! Love, love, love, is all I have to say about Maui, from Lahaina to Paia. In real life, my mom's favorite restaurant in the U.S. is Longhi's Italian restaurant in Lahaina. It can be pricey, for our show anyway, but man is the food good! If you are going to Maui, save up an extra $40 per person, and go to Longhi's in Lahaina.

breakfast

Charley is a dog, a really big Great Dane. He's the namesake of this great joint which is a favorite of local Willie Nelson. There's music at night, and good food and drink, at all hours. I had a HUGE pancake breakfast. Pancakes are big in the

islands. I had tons of macadamia nuts on this one. Yummy. Everything here is good and whether you are a biker, a hiker, or a family with little tikes, you'll fit right in at Charley's. If you get really lucky, you might even catch Willy playing in the bar at night!

● Charley's Restaurant, 142 Hana Highway, Maui, HI, (808) 579-9453

lunch

This was by far the hardest place we've ever had to find for
the show. Lucky for Jennifer and for all of us, it was totally
worth the trouble. Jennifer's has no sign. I had to wander aimlessly, asking dogs
and children for directions. FINALLY, I came across the landmark, "the satellite
dish" that everyone had told me to look for. It turns out that Saigon Café has the
best Vietnamese food I've ever had, anywhere on the planet! Every favorite deli-
cacy can be found on the HUGE menu. I had a hard time deciding. I went with
chicken, vegetable, and herb wraps, which you prepare at the table by rolling the
delicate wraps with mint, basil, grilled chicken, and veggies. Simple, clean flavors
highlight this beautiful, sometimes misunderstood, cuisine. Call ahead, get directions, and leave early for your meal here, but do not miss it!

● **A Saigon Café, 1792 Main Street, Wailuku, HI, (808) 243-9560**

drink

I don't get the name, still. When I asked the owner why he called it "later" garage, he said he just thinks the word is fun. Okay. Well, it is a garage, painted brightly, with a varied menu of cocktails and fun foods. I had a ginger mañanatini, which was a little strong for me. I also had a quesadilla, of sorts, made of corn rather than flour which I prefer. The salsa was great and the fish dishes looked especially good. I would return, but I would have a different dish. The owner was incredibly nice to his guests.

● Mañana Garage, 33 Lono Avenue, Maui, HI 95732, (808) 873-0220

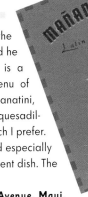

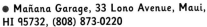

Ginger Mañanatini

❝ Well, it is a garage, painted brightly, with a varied menu of cocktails and fun foods. ❞

Above and opposite page: scenes from the Old Lahaina Luau

dinner

Karaoke and sushi, two great reasons to love life! I took up karaoke on a super-dare and I consider sushi a real go-to cuisine for me whenever I travel. I enjoyed some really good unagi, barbecued eel here. I had a miserable performance at karaoke, but I did it! This place is great! Go have fun, sushi, a couple of sakes, and a good solo!

● **Sansei Seafood Restaurant and Sushi Bar, 115 Bay Drive, Kapalua, HI 96761, (808) 669-6286**

Lunagi Roll

BIG ISLAND

The Big Island of Hawaii was one surprise after another for me. There's a huge Hawaiian cowboy culture—who knew? I took a wonderful horseback ride all through the plantation fields. On the ride I learned about many aspects of Hawaiian cowboy-life and I learned about the slack guitar played by Hawaiian cowboys. Slack guitar is out-of-tune guitar, played that way on purpose! Cowboys from the main land who came here to work the pineapple and coffee plantations brought guitars with them, but these main-land guys refused to teach the locals how to play this sit-around-the-campfire thing. So, the local guys and gals said, "Oh, well, be that way," and they went on to teach themselves how to play the instrument, their way. Tuning the instrument had to be reinvented as well, and so, "slack guitar" was born and it became a whole new musical language played on this classic instrument.

breakfast

What's a Maha? Maha is a person, a big, lovely person who can really cook! To say she is a fixture in her community is true enough, but truer still, Maha is a fixture in her own kitchen! Maha cooks in a small trailer outside her own restaurant and she is literally a fixture in that she can't get out of her kitchen when she is working; the service counter and her cooking equipment fence her in. Crazy as it

> **❝ Enjoy your meal and go out to thank Maha in person. Give her a kiss from me, too. ❞**

Poi Pancakes

looks, the system works and Maha's food is the proof of that! I had her poi pancakes. Poi, ground taro root, is terrible stuff, at least to me. Tasteless and with an odd texture, you can't convince me that anyone—other than the Islanders who are raised with it—actually likes eating it. Given the challenge of the main ingredient and that poi is a staple in the Hawaiian diet, I decided to see what Maha could do with it. You would not believe how delicious her poi pancakes are! In Maha's batter, the texture of the poi became a plus. The cakes were topped with nuts and coconut syrup—so good, sweet, creamy, and buttery I could have cried! Have the pure Kona coffee, as well. Enjoy your meal and go out to thank Maha in person. Give her a kiss from me, too.

● Maha's Cafe, 651148 Mamalahoa Highway, Kamuela, HI, (808) 885-0693

---

recipe *courtesy Maha's Cafe* $40ADAY

APPT - SOUP/SAL - **ENTREE** - VEG/POT - DESSERT - BEV

Poi Pancakes
SERVES 6

2 eggs
1/4 cup (1/2 stick) butter, melted
1 cup milk
1 & 1/4 cups all-purpose flour, sifted
1 tablespoon sugar
4 teaspoons baking powder
3/4 teaspoon salt
1/4 to 1/2 cup frozen poi, coarsely crumbled
Coconut syrup, such as Hawaii's Own Coconut Syrup

● Beat eggs in a bowl and set aside. Melt butter in a saucepan over medium-low with milk. Let cool slightly; add to egg mixture. In a separate bowl, sift all the dry ingredients together. Add eggs to dry mixture, stirring just to moisten; do not overmix.
● Just before you pour the pancakes, crumble defrosted poi into the mix. This will result in little "pudding pockets" in the cake. Heat the griddle, then spoon mixture onto griddle, and cook until bubbles form around the edges. Flip the cakes and cook until the bottom is slightly browned, about 25 seconds more. Top with coconut syrup.

lunch

This little joint hops and rocks! It was packed, just like Mel's drive-in. All the salads and sandwiches and especially their famous sweet cake-like donuts looked great! All the locals eating here seemed really happy, too. I had a beef teriyaki plate, a popular staple. It was really tasty, satisfying, and inexpensive. Check out the Tex.

● **Tex Drive In, 45-690 Pakalana Street, Honokaa, HI, (808) 775-0598**

---

recipe courtesy Tex Drive In $40ADAY

APPT - SOUP/SAL - **ENTREE** - VEG/POT - DESSERT - BEV

Teriyaki Beef
SERVES 4 TO 6

3/4 cup low-sodium soy sauce

1/4 cup water

1 teaspoon grated fresh ginger

1 teaspoon minced garlic

2 to 3 tablespoons oil or butter

1 to 1 & 1/2 pounds roast beef, sliced thin

● Mix soy sauce, water, ginger, and garlic together. Marinate beef slices in sauce for at least 1 hour.
● Heat oil or butter in a skillet and fry beef until tender, about 4 minutes per side.

---

recipe courtesy Huggo's on the Rocks $40ADAY

APPT - SOUP/SAL - ENTREE - VEG/POT - **DESSERT** - BEV

Mud Pie
MAKES ONE 10-INCH PIE

35 chocolate sandwich cookies (recommended: Oreos)

1/2 cup (1 stick) butter, melted

1 gallon coffee ice cream (amount varies depending on size of the bowl)

2 cups store-bought chocolate fudge sauce, plus more for serving

Whipped cream, for serving

● Grind cookies into crumbs in a food processor. Add melted butter to crumbs to make a formable consistency. Press into a 10-inch pie pan leaving a slight mound in the center and pressing the crust all the way up the edge. Freeze the crust for several hours. Meanwhile, pack ice cream into a mixing bowl the same diameter as the pie pan. Freeze the ice cream in the bowl for several hours.
● Invert ice cream bowl onto crust and work ice cream out of the bowl with a rubber spatula. Pour fudge sauce on top of the mud pie. Cover with plastic wrap and freeze again.
● Cut into slices to serve. Decorate with whipped cream and chocolate sauce.

sweet

Not many times have I faced food bigger than my stomach, but Huggo's shut me down! I had a mud pie here that was huge! Imagine a big piece of pie, then multiply that slice times 10, and you'll be close to the size I was given to eat. It must have contained a pint and a half of ice cream. Lucky for me, I am not shy, so I had no problem asking a cool girl named Susan to help me eat it. We hulaed together with some dancers on stage, which turned out to be a real bonding experience. Huggo's has tiki torches, a fancy sister restaurant, and it overflows with good-looking people having a really good time. It seemed to be "the spot" in Kailua-Kona.

● **Huggo's on the Rocks, 75-5828 Kahakai Road, Kailua-Kona, HI, (808) 329-1493**

Mud Pie

dinner

Bamboo is attached to a wonderful art gallery, so you can order, shop, and eat. Cool! I had chicken-filled potsticker dumplings that were delicious, nutritious, and best of all, cheap.

● **Bamboo Restaurant, Hakoni Pule Highway 270, Hawi, HI, (808) 889-5555**

bamboo
Restaurant & Gallery

Fine Island Cuisine

P.O. Box 1463
Kapaau, HI 96755
(808) 889-5555
Fax: 889-6152
www.thebamboorestaurant.com
bamrest@interpac.net

recipe	SERVES 4 TO 6	courtesy Bamboo Restaurant

APPT - SOUP/SAL - **ENTREE** - VEG/POT - DESSERT - BEV

Chicken Pot Stickers

Chicken Potstickers

1 tablespoon vegetable oil

1 pound ground chicken

2 tablespoons minced garlic

2 tablespoons minced fresh ginger

2 tablespoons minced shallots

1 cup chunky peanut butter

1/4 cup firmly packed brown sugar

2 tablespoons Thai hot chili paste

2 tablespoons chopped fresh basil leaves

2 tablespoons chopped fresh cilantro leaves

30 wonton wrappers

Chili-Mint Dipping Sauce (recipe follows)

● Make the filling: In a hot skillet, add the oil and heat. When the oil is hot, add the ground chicken, garlic, ginger, and shallots and sauté until the chicken is thoroughly cooked. Drain off the excess fat and mix chicken in a bowl with peanut butter, brown sugar, chili paste, basil, and cilantro. Chill the mixture.

● Make the pot stickers: Place a small amount of filling in the center of a wonton wrapper. Bring the edges up around the filling or simply fold into triangles, using a dab of water to "glue" the edges together.

● In a pot fitted with a steamer basket, bring 1 to 2 inches of water to a boil. Steam the pot stickers in the steamer basket until the wrappers are translucent, 8 to 10 minutes; serve with chili-mint dipping sauce.

Chili-Mint Dipping Sauce:

1 (7-ounce) bottle Thai sweet chili sauce

1/4 cup rice vinegar

1/2 cup sugar

1/4 cup chopped fresh cilantro leaves

1/4 cup chopped fresh mint leaves

1 teaspoon sesame oil

● Puree ingredients in a food processor for 1 minute. Serve at room temperature.

europe

AMSTERDAM
BRUSSELS
PARIS
FLORENCE
TUSCANY
ROME

AMSTERDAM

Bridges, bicycles, small dogs, pancakes, and the haunting presence of Van Gogh and Anne Frank make up the patchwork of my memories of Amsterdam. We stayed in a small inn, The Bridge Hotel. It was a steep walk up to my floor, an even steeper climb for the crew with 40-kilo case loads of equipment to haul. The rooms were unique flats with large, pane-glass doors and windows that opened onto breathtaking views, made more spectacular by night, of bridges dotted with round, bright lights over the waterways. All in all, my room especially, was worth the climb. This city is infamous for its red-light district and pot den/coffee houses. As a young woman not interested in either, I wondered how I would fit in. It turned out to be no problem at all. A word of warning to the wise, however; the Dutch love their dogs, and with no curbing laws, there is plenty of dog poop to show for it. A member of our crew stepped in street candy eleven times in three days. You're forewarned.

breakfast

I like bars. There is something relaxing about an environment of small tables where one can casually eat, rest, and drink without having to deal with a hostess and three or four servers. At De Prins, you come as you are, sit where you like, and eat what they're making. The bar has a huge selection of beers, ales, wines, ports, and spirits at not-for-tourist prices. Sandwiches are simple and satisfying, and made on farm bread with traditional fixings. This is an elbows-on-the-table place, one of many, one of the best.

● **Café De Prins,
Prinsengracht 124,
Amsterdam, Netherlands,
(011) 31-20-6249382**

❝ Go hungry to The Pancake Bakery with friends so you can order several types of pancakes to share. ❞

lunch

Next to the bloom of a tulip, I believe the most adored earthly delight in Amsterdam is a well-made pancake. The Pancake Bakery is near both the Anne Frank House and The Van Gogh Museum: Make it a point to stop here. Sit near the open kitchen where the pancakes are made, if you can; it's quite a show. Jeroem made my pancake for me. Before I tell you how mine was made, you have to forget about flap jacks and maple syrup made the traditional way. Pancakes in Amsterdam are about ten inches in diameter and can be savory or sweet. They are eaten for breakfast, lunch, or supper and one is a serving; there is no stacking. Some favorite combinations are mushroom and cheese, apples and calvados brandy, ham and onion. Toppings are as varied as the fillings and no topping at all is quite all right, too. Jeroem grasped a coiled hose that hung from above the stove and sprayed a huge, flat cast-iron griddle with a stream of vegetable oil. He pre-heated the griddle over moderate heat, then poured the pancake batter onto the griddle and spread it out some nine inches or so. He scattered very thinly sliced mushrooms, chopped ham, and gruyere cheese across the pancake. His Popeye-esque arms bulged as he lifted the heavy skillet for the first of hundreds of times in this day and flipped the cake. My advice: Go hungry to The Pancake Bakery with friends or ingratiate yourself to a group of strangers so you can order several types of pancakes to share. No one should try just one.

● **The Pancake Bakery, Prinsengracht 191, Amsterdam, Netherlands, (011) 31-20-6251333**

dinner

Because of past colonial history, there are numerous Indonesian restaurants in Amsterdam. One of the largest and finest is Indrapura. Very near the largest flower market I have ever seen or imagined, I happened upon a cool American, Nancy. She brought me to Indrapura and we shared this huge feast of little dishes, like Indo-tapas or an Indonesian version of Korean barbecue: spiced meat, pickled and fresh vegetables, and rice were among the offerings. These small, mixed menus make for generous meals and are very low in price so take an eating buddy and enjoy!

● Restaurant Indrapura, Rembrandtplein 42, Amsterdam, Netherlands, (011) 31-20-6237329

Pudding

sweet

This was an old factory in an industrial area that has been converted into a hip, huge, happening place. Had I the time and my $40 still in my pocket, I would have eaten at least one meal here. There was an amazing bar jammed with people, an oasis in the middle of this cold metal and brick building. There were also billiard tables, conversation areas, and a 200-seat, white tablecloth dining room all occupying the same loft-like space. I had a dessert of semolina pudding and red currant sauce. (see recipe on opposite page) I wish I could have stayed for more!

● Café-Restaurant Amsterdam, Watertorenplein 6, Amsterdam, Netherlands, (011) 31-20-6822666

APPT - SOUP/SAL - ENTREE - VEG/POT - DESSERT - BEV

Semolina Pudding with Red Currant Sauce

Semolina Pudding:
Vegetable-oil cooking spray
1 quart milk
1/2 cup sugar
3 & 1/2 tablespoons butter
3 ounces semolina

Red Currant Sauce:
12 & 1/4 ounces fresh red currants
1/2 cup water
1/4 cup sugar
Juice of 1 lemon

● Make the pudding: Rinse 8 (4-ounce) heatproof cups with cold water, dry them, and spray with vegetable-oil cooking spray.
● Combine the milk, sugar, and butter in a saucepan and bring to a boil. Add semolina, and cook, stirring constantly, until the mixture thickens about 5 minutes. Spoon the pudding into prepared cups and allow to cool to room temperature. Cover with plastic wrap and place in the refrigerator until cold, about 2 hours.
● Make the sauce: In a medium saucepan, bring currants, water, sugar, and lemon juice to a boil. Cook until the sugar is dissolved and the currants are very soft, about 10 minutes. Allow the current mixture to cool somewhat. Puree the mixture in a blender. Strain through a sieve, pressing with a ladle to extract all of the liquid and create a smooth sauce. Cool to room temperature. Cover and place in the refrigerator until cold, about 2 hours.
● When ready to serve run a paring knife between the edge of each ramekin and the pudding. Unmold onto dessert plates and drizzle with the sauce.

Here I met a crazy, wonderful woman named Elke, who spoke twelve languages fluently, and was my age! Once I got over feeling really dumb, we had lots of laughs together. Both Flemish and French are spoken here, so I really relied on Elke's help to get by. The city was grey and cold, but the palaces and plazas gilded in gold seemed haloed as they reflected streams of light that escaped the layers of clouds. In this way, Brussels was mesmerizing to me. I remember beautiful lace in shop after shop, the smell of waffles in the air from morning to night, and the Mannekin Pis, the famed statuary of a small boy relieving himself, which, at the time, was dressed in an Elvis costume, leaving me "All Shook Up."

breakfast

Famous, exceptional Dandoy is a bustling stop frequented by all savvy, returning visitors to Brussels because they know it's always good. There are two levels of seating available inside as well as a walk-up window serving passersby. I went to the street window and ordered a Liege waffle made with special pearls of sugar, about the size of tapioca, baked into the waffle batter. Sweet, crisp, hot and steaming, my waffle was true comfort food aux Bruxelles and I savored every bite.
● Biscuiterie Dandoy, Rue Charles Buls 14, Brussels, Belgium, (011) 32-2-512-65-88

lunch

The name means our daily bread and that's what you'll find: artisan breads to die for. The privately owned restaurant group includes a Le Pain Quotidien in Soho (NYC) which I frequent to this day. No matter which Le Pain Quotidien you dine in, you'll enjoy many of the same special, down-to-earth elements: communal tables, bowls of sweet butter, and delicious fruit preserves and praline spreads on the tables for anyone's use. Bread is reason enough and meal enough to enjoy; in Brussels I enjoyed their specialty, an open-faced sandwich or tartine. Mine was made with eggplant, goat cheese, and greens, all of which complimented the crusty, chewy, farm-house-style bread it was arranged on. Yumm-o.

● Le Pain Quotidien, Rue des Sablones 11, Brussels, Belgium, (011) 32-2-513-51-54

| recipe | SERVES 1 | courtesy Le Pain Quotidien | $40ADAY |

APPT - SOUP/SAL - ENTREE - VEG/POT - DESSERT - BEV

Grilled Eggplant and Tomato Tartine

2 or 3 slices eggplant, marinated in extra-virgin olive oil, garlic, and seasonings, and grilled

1 slice wheat bread

4 slices tomato

Grated Parmesan

1/2 cucumber, sliced

2 lemons, quartered

Chopped parsley leaves, for garnish

Eggplant Tartine

● Place the eggplant slices on the bread to cover it. Top with the tomato slices, arranged side by side. Cut the tartine in 4 equal triangles and transfer to a serving plate. Sprinkle with Parmesan. Garnish with the sliced cucumber, lemons, and parsley. Serve.

sweet

You can't go to Brussels without sampling waffles, mussels (when in season), fine ales and beers, Waterzooie (see next page, I had it for dinner), real fries not invented by the French—ask any Belgian and please, dip them in homemade mayonnaise not ketchup—and last but never least, Belgian chocolate. At Manon you can watch the complicated art of making the world's best-loved confection within the shop of its finest producers. Every variation in color, crème and sugar content is formulated here and then all the natural fillings, lush and decadent, are infused with flavorings of nuts, fruits, citrus, and botanicals. For about $10 US, I had a tour of Manon, watched the production of chocolates of many varieties, enjoyed a few laughs (and many chocolates!), then I left with a generous box of Belgian chocolates to take home. This was not special treatment. I joined a tour of ten or so tourists from around the globe. A good experience overall.

● Le Chocolatier Manon, Rue Tilmont 64, Brussels, Belgium, (011) 32-2-425-26-32

❝ At Manon you can watch the complicated art of making the world's best-loved confection within the shop of its finest producers. ❞

dinner

Don't try to say it, or even the street it is on, just give a slip of paper with the name and address on it to your cab driver. The name refers to a type of fish, similar to a flounder, with a sharp razorback. The restaurant is operated by a celebrity chef and restaurant critic, the Emeril of Brussels. The food is authentic Belgian fare and the ales and beers are served Belgian style, in different glasses, each uniquely shaped to reflect the characteristics of a particular beer or ale. Daniel Van Avermaet, our celebrity-foodie, made me Waterzooie, the national dish. Waterzooie can be prepared with seafood or poultry or a combination of the two. It is a "stoup"—part stew, part soup. Daniel topped off my mélange of poultry and root vegetables in broth by adding cream and the tart surprise of lemon juice. I enjoyed my waterzooie with a chilled, thin-lipped goblet filled with a crisp, bitter

Belgian Abby ale. Behind the scenes, our car was vandalized while we were taping. Windows were smashed and equipment stolen, but nothing detracted from the simple joy of our satisfying meal.

● **Au Stekerlapatte, Rue des Prêtres 4, Brussels, Belgium, (011) 32-2-512-86-81**

recipe	SERVES 4	adapted from Au Stekerlapatte	$40ADAY

APPT - SOUP/SAL - **ENTREE** - VEG/POT - DESSERT - BEV

Chicken Waterzooi

3 & 1/2 to 4 pounds chicken pieces (including bones)
4 large carrots
3 celery stalks
4 shallots or small onions
2 to 3 sprigs fresh parsley
1 sprig fresh thyme
1 bay leaf
Salt and freshly ground black pepper
2 leeks, cleaned
400 grams mushrooms (about 14 ounces)
4 egg yolks
1 cup heavy cream
1 lemon, juiced
2 tablespoons butter
Pinch nutmeg
Boiled potatoes or steamed white rice, for serving

❝ I enjoyed my waterzooie with a chilled, thin-lipped goblet filled with a crisp, bitter Belgian Abby ale. ❞

Chicken Waterzooi

● Make the stock: Place chicken in a large pot and add enough water just to cover. Cut 2 carrots, 2 celery stalks, and 1 shallot, into approximately 1-inch pieces and add to the pot. Add parsley, thyme, and bay leaf and bring to a boil. Reduce heat to maintain a simmer and poach until chicken is fully cooked, about 25 minutes. Add salt and pepper, to taste.

● Cut the remaining carrots, celery, and shallots into thin 1-inch sticks and place them in a saucepan with water to cover. Cut the leeks into 1-inch sticks and add to pan. Slice the mushrooms, season with salt and add to pan. Bring to a boil reduce heat to a simmer and cook until vegetables are tender.

● Remove chicken from pot (there should be no pink color under the skin) and strain stock through a fine sieve into another pot; discard vegetables. Remove skin from chicken. Return chicken and vegetables to the stock. Mix the egg yolks with the cream and add to the stock. Warm until heated through. Add the lemon juice and butter. Season with salt, pepper, and nutmeg, to taste.

● Serve in soup bowls with boiled potatoes or white steamed rice.

April in Paris...check another one off the life-list! The city was jaw-droppingly, awe-strikingly beautiful—ooo-la-la! However, I feel com-

pelled to be completely frank about the French in general. Bureaucracy rules and there are easier places to film and be understood. Though we carried stacks of required permits, we were shut down from shooting numerous times each day, our car was towed twice—even though we had parked as instructed—and no matter how we attempted to communicate, we were never understood. One more hint: April in Paris can be cold, très froid. Pack a parka! On the plus side, I had dreamt, as most girls have, of the day I would see gay Paris! I swooned over notions of crossing the ocean to land and bask in the warm, glowing presence of the most romantic city in the world, the city of lights—ah, how magnifique it must be, April in Paris! While not warm, it did glow. The sights of Paris are more spectacular than I could have ever imagined—and I have quite a vivid imagination. And not everyone is rude. Most of the people we worked with directly were charming, kind, and generous.

breakfast

I met a terrific American girl in Paris named Kristina. She was classy, charming, and spoke such meticulous French that I got a behind-the-scenes tour of an institution, Strohrer. Each pastry at this shop is made with generations of tradition, discipline, and eye for detail, down to tiny, chocolate signposts stuck into each pastry which read the Strohrer name in beautiful cursive script. Here, I had a Baba au Rhum. Oo, Baba-la-la! Nice!

● Stohrer, 51 rue Montorgueil, Paris, France, (011) 33-1-42-33-38-20

> **I spread my feast on a cool, crisp lawn in front of the Tower and this became one of the most memorable meals and afternoons of my life: truly magnifique!**

picnic

My favorite meal in Paris was a self-made petite picnic that I made for myself at Raspail market, one of the smaller Parisian markets located near the Eiffel Tower where I had envisioned my picnic spot. My lunch: fresh goat cheese discs coated in herbs, seeds, and peppercorn; olives in a citrus-scented brine; a fresh orange and pear, a small cluster of grapes; a hunk of farm bread, and a whole bottle of soft, luscious Burgundy wine. The total cost was about $12 US, including my wine. I spread my feast on a cool, crisp lawn in front of the Tower and this became one of the most memorable meals and afternoons of my life: truly magnifique!

● Raspail Market, Boulevard Raspail between Rue du Cherche Midi and Rue de Rennes

lunch

Paris is made up of 96 districts and in each there are probably 96 cafes to devour delicious, classic French cooking. Some cafés cost very little, others will knock your eyes out, but in my experience, it's almost impossible to find any "bad" or sloppily prepared food because Parisians, who love their cuisine and celebrate food in every way, are also customers. Prices, considering the relatively high quality of meals, are low. At Au Gourmet de l'Ile I enjoyed a prix-fixe luncheon of three courses for just about $10 US. The chef's specialty of the day was a pork loin dish called charbonne. Prix fixe is fabulous in that you are offered two or three choic-

Charbonne

es in three courses of the finest, freshest ingredients du jour for one set price. This lovely, small, and cozy restaurant is the perfect place to try fine food at prix fixe.

● **Au Gourmet de L'Ile, 42 rue St-Louis-en-l'Ile, Paris, France, (011) 33-1-43-26-79-27**

recipe	SERVES 8	courtesy Au Gourmet de L'Ile	$40ADAY

APPT - SOUP/SAL - ENTREE - VEG/POT - DESSERT - BEV

Charbonne

2 tablespoons butter

1 garlic clove, chopped

2 pounds boneless pork shoulder, cut into 1 inch cubes

1 large onion, diced

1/4 cup all-purpose flour

Salt and freshly ground black pepper

1/2 teaspoon dried sage

1/2 teaspoon dried rosemary

1/2 teaspoon ground cumin

1/2 teaspoon dried tarragon

2 bay leaves

2 quarts red wine

1 cup water

10 ounces bacon, cut into small pieces

Boiled potatoes, for serving

Croutons, for serving

● In a large saucepan, over medium-high heat, melt the butter, add the garlic, and brown the pork on all sides. Add onion and cook until softened. Sprinkle the flour over and stir to cook it for about 1 minute. Add the salt, pepper, sage, rosemary, cumin, tarragon, and bay leaves. Cover with the wine and water. Gently simmer over low heat for 30 minutes.

● Meanwhile, in a skillet, sauté bacon until the fat is rendered and bacon is golden brown. Transfer the bacon to a paper towel lined plate and drain.

● After pork mixture has cooked for 30 minutes, add bacon. Simmer for 30 more minutes. Serve with potatoes and croutons.

Boeuf Bourguignon

3 pounds lean boneless stewing beef, cut into 2-inch pieces

2 cups red wine

3 tablespoons all-purpose flour

1 piece lean smoked bacon, chopped

3 tablespoons butter

4 carrots, peeled and sliced

4 onions, peeled and sliced

1 tablespoon chopped garlic

2 cups veal stock

2 bay leaves

3 sprigs fresh thyme

3 sprigs fresh flat-leaf parsley

1 pound white button mushrooms, cleaned

Salt and freshly ground black pepper

Boiled potatoes, for serving

● In a covered container or resealable plastic bag combine the beef with the wine and marinate in the refrigerator overnight.

● Remove meat and pat dry; reserve wine. Place flour in a large resealable plastic bag and toss meat in flour; remove to a plate, shaking off any excess flour. In a large casserole over high heat, cook the bacon until the fat is rendered. Melt the butter in the bacon fat. Add beef and brown it on all sides. Transfer the meat to a plate. To the casserole add the carrots, onions, and garlic and cook until onions are translucent, about 5 minutes. Add beef back to the pot with the reserved wine, veal stock, bay leaves, thyme, and parsley. Cover and cook over low heat until meat is very tender, 2 hours.

● Add mushrooms and cook for another 15 minutes. Season to taste with salt and pepper. Serve with boiled potatoes.

❝ It is famous for having great food at cheap prices, but also for having one of the oldest toilets in Paris. ❞

Beef Bourguignon

dinner

I really loved this joint, and I do mean joint. It is famous for having great food at cheap prices, but also for having one of the oldest toilets in Paris. They use the term loosely—really old toilets are just stone holes in the ground with running water. If you are female, make sure you're feeling strong in the legs if you need to use the restroom! The food and wines at Polidor were affordable and the atmosphere, fun and lively at all hours; people were still streaming in to dine at midnight. I had Boeuf Bourguignon, 'cause you can't have enough Burgundy here. Yum and yum.

● Cremerie Restaurant Polidor, 41 rue Monsieur-le-Prince, Paris, France, (011) 33-1-43-26-95-34

europe FLORENCE

firenze is always on fire (as is my wallet when I am in town)! My favorite shopping and hands-down some of my favorite dining in Italy are in Florence. On my last trip, I bought all of my holiday gifts for family and friends and every dress, coat, and shoe I could squeeze into my suitcase. Check out all the sights, Michelangelo's David, the Duomo, and the Uffizi. Or, spend your days out in the Tuscan countryside, exploring one tiny, walled city and/or vineyard to the next. At night, come home to nest and eat at any of the following favorites: Trattoria Garga, 48 Via del Moro. I did not tape here for the show—just couldn't fit it all in. However, I come here at least twice per visit to the city. It's several small wandering rooms and the artwork painted by the owner and his wife are as loud, crazy, eclectic, and fantastic as the restaurant. Have the pasta Magnifico as an appetizer with someone you really like to kiss, because that's what this dish makes you want to do.

lunch

Italians aren't big on breakfast; lunch is the main meal. If you want a really fantastic Bistecca Fiorentina, go and find this place. If you are not familiar, Bistecca Fiorentina is a steak, cut from the back of a cow and both the cut and its preparation are particular to this city. The meat is very tender, as it surrounds heavy bones and is moderately marbled. It is cooked on huge, heavy metal grates over open fires fueled by hardwoods and charcoal. The cook who prepared my bistecca Fiorentina placed his cooking grate on an angle over an open fire that he had built on his flat-top stove. The angle of the grate allowed the fat to drip away from the meat. When the fat hit the fire, the flame-ups caused a charring at the fatty edges of the meat that was unbelievably tasty. The meat was allowed to rest for ten minutes, after which time I devoured the most wonderful steak I have ever had in my life.

● **Trattoria Sostanza, Via Porcellana 25/R, Florence, Italy, (011) 39-55-212-691**

recipe courtesy Trattoria Sostanza $40ADAY

APPT - SOUP/SAL - **ENTREE** - VEG/POT - DESSERT - BEV

Bistecca Fiorentina
SERVES 4

1 & 3/4 pounds beef cut from loin with fillet and bone steak

Salt and freshly ground black pepper

Bistecca Fiorentina

● Prepare a charcoal grill so that the charcoal is well lit and red hot without flames. When it is very hot, grill the meat 5 to 6 minutes without turning and without piercing it in any way. Turn the steak over using a spatula and season with salt and pepper. At the end, the meat should be very well done on the outside and tasty and tender on the inside.

snack

Do one thing and do it well is a lesson Florentines learned long ago! Il forno means from the oven and that's what you get here: bread and pizzas from the oven. Stop in for a slice or wedge of fantastic bread, focaccia or pizza. It's legendary, for a reason. I had a type of bread impossible to spell or pronounce: schiacciatta, I think. Look for the scariest name to say and point to it. A Florentine specialty, you gotta have it!

● **Il Forno Sartoni, Via del Cerchi 34, Florence, Italy, (011) 39-55-212-570**

Schiacciatta

dinner

This is one of my favorite restaurants in the world, period. The owner's name is Torello, which means the bull, but to me he's more like a big, smart, lovable teddy bear. Huge crowds gather in the street each night just before opening at Il Latini. Torello has wine and cheese passed among those standing on line outside. It really takes the edge off waiting. Everything on the menu comes from Torello's farms and vineyards. To start, you will be given a huge platter of prosciutto, the hams that hang from every inch of his ceiling. Next, pour yourself some of Torello's wine, which is really quite fine and a bargain. The wine is measured with a stick held up to the side of the jug. To calculate how much wine you have consumed, they align the stick against the level of wine in the jug, and they read the measure on the stick. Pretty cool. Next, have the soup trio: ribollita, famous in Tuscany, bread soup with vegetables; papa al pomodoro, bread and tomato soup; and the pasta e fagioli, macaroni and bean soup (several typical recipes follow). On the show, I stop here. In real life, I go on to have some rosemary grilled mixed meats and some fresh strawberries, all from Torello's farms. Prices are very friendly because of the massive volume of business and because Torello is his own purveyor. The last time I went to Il Latini, just a few months ago, there were five tables occupied with parties who come in because of the $40 a Day episode they had seen. That made me feel very happy and Torello must have been happy, too. He gave me a fantastic bottle of wine, not of his own making. When you go to Il Latini, look around, I bet I'll see you there!

● **Ristorante Il Latini, Via Palchetti 6/R, Palazzo Rucellai, Florence, Italy, (011) 39-55-210-916**

> **❝ To calculate how much wine you have consumed, they align the stick against the level of wine in the jug, and they read the measure on the stick. Pretty cool. ❞**

recipe *courtesy Ristorante Il Latini* $40ADAY

APP - SOUP/SAL - ENTREE - VEG/POT - DESSERT - BEV

Tomato Bread Soup

SERVES 4

2 tablespoons extra-virgin olive oil, plus more for serving

2 garlic cloves

1 pound ripe tomatoes, peeled and diced

6 fresh basil leaves, chopped, plus more for serving

Salt and freshly ground black pepper

1 quart chicken or beef stock

3 thin slices stale homemade or stale store-bought Italian bread

● Heat oil in a large skillet over medium heat. Cut garlic cloves in half and brown them in the oil. As soon as garlic starts to turn color, add tomatoes, basil, and salt and pepper to taste. Cook for 15 minutes. Meanwhile bring stock to a boil in a saucepan.

● Add boiling stock to the skillet. When stock returns to a boil, add bread and continue cooking for 15 more minutes, stirring frequently. Remove from heat and cover. After 1 hour, stir rigorously until the bread completely disintegrates. Serve hot or lukewarm, adding a touch of extra-virgin olive oil and fresh basil leaves. Do not serve with cheese.

Bean Soup with Rice

1 & 3/4 pounds dried white beans*

3 tablespoons extra-virgin olive oil

1 onion, finely chopped

2 garlic cloves, finely chopped

1 small celery stalk, finely chopped

1 bunch fresh flat-leaf parsley, leaves removed and finely chopped

1 bunch fresh basil, leaves removed and finely chopped

1 small hot chile pepper, finely chopped

2 ounces bacon, finely diced

1 pound ripe tomatoes, seeded and diced

Salt and freshly ground black pepper

1 cup rice, cooked

● Soak dried beans in water overnight or cover the beans with cold water, bring to a boil and remove from the heat. Cover and let sit for 1 hour. Drain. Place the beans in a saucepot and cover with cold water. Bring to a boil and cook until tender, about 1 hour.

● Heat olive oil in a large skillet over medium-high heat. Add the onion, garlic, celery, parsley, basil, chile, and bacon and cook until all is a light golden color. Stir in tomatoes and season with salt and pepper, to taste; continue cooking for 15 to 20 minutes. Press vegetables through a sieve into the pot with the beans. Stir well and continue cooking for 10 more minutes. Add rice. Serve hot or lukewarm.

*Note: The original recipe called for fresh white beans, shelled, but we found these hard to find. Dried white beans are a good substitute.

recipe	SERVES 4 TO 6	courtesy Ristorante Il Latini	$40ADAY

APPT - SOUP/SAL - ENTREE - VEG/POT - DESSERT - BEV

Ribollita

Ribollita

1 pound dried white beans

4 quarts plus 1 cup water

1/2 cup extra-virgin olive oil, plus more for serving

1 garlic clove

2 onions, 1 chopped, 1 thinly sliced

2 tablespoons tomato puree

1 carrot, finely chopped

1 celery stalk, finely chopped

1/2 Savoy cabbage, washed and cut into strips

1 red cabbage, washed and cut into strips

1 bunch Swiss chard, washed and cut into strips

2 Kennebec (or all-purpose) potatoes, peeled and thinly sliced

Salt and freshly ground black pepper

4 to 6 thin slices stale homemade or stale store-bought Italian bread

Red onion, thinly sliced, for serving

● Soak beans overnight in 2 quarts water; drain. Cover with another 2 quarts water bring to a boil, reduce heat, and simmer beans until tender, 45 minutes to 1 hour. Rub 3/4 of the beans through a sieve and put the bean puree back into the cooking water. Set aside the remaining whole beans.

● Heat olive oil in a large skillet over medium heat. Add the garlic and onion and sauté until soft. Add 2 tablespoons tomato puree diluted with 1 cup lukewarm water. Add the chopped carrot and celery, cabbages, chard, and potatoes. Season with salt and pepper, cook for a few minutes, then add pureed beans. Continue cooking over low heat for 1 hour. When the vegetables are well done, add the sliced bread and the reserved whole beans. Mix well, pour into a soup tureen, and serve with a touch of extra-virgin olive oil; pass the thinly sliced onion separately.

sweet

On the show, I go here for a dessert sampler which was fantastic. In real life, I don't care for sweets very much, but I go to Acqua Al 2 all the time for the best bargain in Florence, the pasta sampler. Stefano, the chef and owner, is amazing with pasta. He makes sauces out of every vegetable and herb possible. Whether you go for pasta or dessert, go. Look for the plate I signed for Stefano, up on the wall between the two dining rooms. Again, I'll see you here, too. I stop in on every trip I make to Florence. Hey! I just realized, I have no more secret hideaways left! I better get on that....

● **Acqua Al 2, Via della Vigna Vecchia 40/R, Florence, Italy, (011) 39-55-284-170**

---

recipe courtesy Acqua Al 2 $40ADAY

APPT - SOUP/SAL - ENTREE - VEG/POT - **DESSERT** - BEV

> ❝ I go to Acqua Al 2 all the time for the best bargain in Florence, the pasta sampler. ❞

Tiramisu
SERVES 4

5 eggs, separated
5 tablespoons sugar
17 & 1/2 ounces mascarpone cheese
30 ladyfingers
2 cups brewed espresso coffee
2 tablespoons instant coffee powder

● Whip egg whites with an electric hand-mixer until they form stiff peaks; set aside. Whip egg yolks with sugar until they reach a pale yellow color, 3 to 4 minutes. Whip in mascarpone cheese and continue whipping, 5 minutes.

Tiramisu

● Fold egg whites into mascarpone cream and mix. Pour 1/4 of the mascarpone cream into a large glass bowl or small individual bowls. Dip ladyfingers in the espresso 1 at a time and arrange them in 1 layer over the mascarpone. Repeat layers 2 more times. Finish with a mascarpone cream layer and sprinkle with coffee powder.

*Raw Egg Warning: The American Egg Board states: "There have been warnings against consuming raw or lightly cooked eggs on the grounds that the egg may be contaminated with Salmonella, a bacteria responsible for a type of foodborne illness. Healthy people need to remember that there is a very small risk and treat eggs and other raw animal foods accordingly. Use only properly refrigerated, clean, sound-shelled, fresh, grade AA or A eggs. Avoid mixing yolks and whites with the shell..."

You know that Billy Joel song with the line "Vienna waits for you" in it? Well, if he had written it for me, the line would've been "Siena waits for you." My favorite duomo (cathedral) in Italy is in Siena. It's on my list of the Seven Wonders of My World. Made of red, white, and black marble, the duomo's floors are covered with intricate murals formed from these pieces of colored marble. The walls and towers are all black and white striped marble. Every inch of this massive structure, inside and out, is adorned with mosaics, bright murals, and sculptures. It will change your life to see this place in person. It did mine. Oh, and every night that I am home, I feel as if I were dining in Siena. All of my dishes come from a tiny shop across from the duomo and their pattern was taken from designs on the duomo floor. When will you realize, Siena waits for you? P.S. In the center of this walled city is a plaza, a campo. Annually in this campo, they run a massive, bare-backed horse race (the Palio) with riders representing each district of the city. It can be a brutal, but fascinating event. If you are a risk taker, you might want to plan a visit around the Palio. The tower overlooking the campo is very creepy and cool. It is the tallest I've seen. At dusk, birds and bats swoop in and out of the bell tower. Across from the tower is an enoteca (wine and spirits bar) that is a particular favorite of mine. Located on the second floor, it has a small suspended terrace with the bar facing the campo. When you look across the campo at the people sitting at this bar, it looks as though the patrons are suspended in air, while enjoying their wine and cocktails.

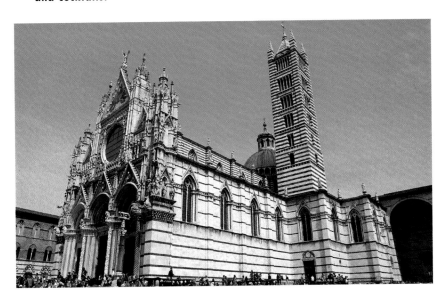

"One of my favorite excursions is to Monteriggioni, a tiny, walled city of just nine buildings and a small piazza. In the center of the piazza is a small well, Il Pozzo, the well that Dante wrote about in the Divine Comedy."

lunch

By day, from Florence or Siena, you'll want a car so you can go motor-off into Tuscany to eat, drink, and be merry. The morning we taped here I grabbed a quick cappuccino and hit the road. One of my favorite excursions is to Monteriggioni, a tiny, walled city of just nine buildings and a small piazza. In the center of the piazza is a small well, Il Pozzo, the well that Dante wrote about in the Divine Comedy. Dante's well—that's big, right? To me, what's bigger is the epic of Il Pozzo, the restaurant. Decades ago, Lucia and her husband started Ristorante Il Pozzo in some converted horse stables in this tiny, historic place. Lucia's food became so famous that movie stars and politicians, from Richard Gere to the Kennedys, came to dine here. For Lucia, the success of her business was bittersweet, she explained, while making my pappardelle pasta and wild boar sauce. Her husband left her for a waitress in their restaurant many years ago, but he didn't go far. They all continued to live in this very small community and Lucia and her husband went on running the business together, while sharing custody of their children, too. Talk about drama! Years later, Lucia's passion is still evident in every bite of some of the most exquisite food I have ever eaten. I continue to go back to this place, my well in Tuscany, as often as I can.

● **Ristorante Il Pozzo, Piazza Roma 20, Siena, Italy, (011) 39-577-304-127**

recipe	SERVES 2	courtesy Ristorante Il Pozzo	$40ADAY

APPT - SOUP/SAL - **ENTREE** - VEG/POT - DESSERT - BEV

Pappardelle al Cinghiale

Pappardelle al Cingahiale

Pappardelle:

4 eggs, lightly beaten

2 & 3/4 cups all-purpose flour

Wild Boar Sauce:

2 onions, chopped

1 sprig rosemary

1 celery stalk, chopped

Olive oil

10 & 1/2 ounces canned tomatoes, chopped

14 ounces wild boar meat, minced (or pork shoulder)

1/4 teaspoon freshly grated nutmeg

● Make the pasta: Mound the flour on a clean work surface; make a well in the center. Pour eggs into the well and with your hands mix flour and eggs together until a dough is formed.

Knead the dough until it springs back when pushed with your finger, about 10 minutes. Cover and let rest for 30 minutes. Roll the pasta to very thin sheets with a pasta machine or a rolling pin (about # 5 on a pasta machine). Cut into 3/4-inch-wide ribbons. Cook until al dente in boiling, salted water, 2 to 3 minutes. Drain.

● While the pasta dough is resting, make the sauce: Sauté onions, rosemary, and celery in olive oil until soft and starting to color. Add tomatoes, wild boar or pork shoulder, and grated nutmeg. Cook until the boar meat is cooked through and the mixture reduces to a sauce consistency, 10 to 15 minutes. Add the pasta to the sauce. Toss until the pasta is well coated and serve.

snack

I love Chianti, the wine and the region in which it is produced. When shopping for a chianti, buy those with the black rooster symbol stamped on a label around the neck of the bottle. The symbol indicates that the grapes come from just one vineyard, rather then being blended from several. Within the Chianti region of Tuscany is Greve, home to Castello di Verrazzano. Perhaps you've heard of the Verrazano bridge in New York City? He's a cousin to the guy they named this castle after. This castle is huge and tons of fun. You'll have as many laughs as sips if you take the tour and wine-tasting class. Stay for a simple snack of meats and cheeses with wine, of course. I was inspired to bring a few bottles home for the family. Make sure to have some biscotti here, too, and dip it in the vin santo, a fortified after-dinner wine. You'll leave here having seen some of the best views in Tuscany and with nice rosy cheeks from all the vino!

● Castello di Verrazzano, Via San Martino in Valle 12, Greve in Chianti, Italy, (011) 39-55-854-243

dinner

This little place is hidden away behind the campo and the tower in Siena. It is cozy and family-owned, as are ninety percent of the restaurants in Italy. Roberto Papei is charming and welcoming and the food, very fairly priced, are perfect examples of Tuscan comfort food. I had a delicious slow-cooked duck. Boar, rabbit, and duck are very popular on menus throughout Tuscany. My meal was simple and delicious, the two words most often used to describe the Tuscan style of cooking.

● Antica Trattoria Papei, Piazza del Mercato 6, Siena, Italy, (011) 39-577-280-894

recipe	SERVES 4	courtesy Antica Osteria da Divo	$40ADAY

APPT - SOUP/SAL - **ENTREE** - VEG/POT - DESSERT - BEV

Lasagnettes au Gratin with Artichokes & Marjoram

3 & 3/4 cups all-purpose flour

4 eggs

1/2 teaspoon salt, plus more to taste

1 tablespoon extra-virgin olive oil, plus more for pan and for serving

1/4 cup lukewarm water

2 lemons

4 whole artichokes

2 garlic cloves, chopped

Freshly ground black pepper

2 cups heavy cream

1 small bundle fresh marjoram, leaves chopped, 3 teaspoons chopped marjoram reserved for garnish

2 fresh tomatoes

7 ounces Parmigiano-Reggiano cheese, grated

● Put flour, eggs, and salt into the bowl of an electric mixer fitted with a dough hook, and mix until a dough is formed. Knead the dough on medium speed for 5 minutes in the mixer. The dough should form a ball and be climbing up the dough hook. Add 1 tablespoon extra-virgin olive oil and water and mix until well combined. Remove the dough from the mixer, cover with plastic wrap and let sit at room temperature for 20 minutes. Roll out into 1/16-inch sheets, or about #4 with a pasta machine.

● Squeeze lemons into a bowl of cold water. Peel, clean, and remove chokes of the artichokes and plunge the hearts in lemon water so they don't brown. One by one, slice artichokes very thinly (you can do this on a mandolin if you prefer), return-ing them to the acidulated water as you finish. Julienne the strips and return to the acidulated water.

● Heat the remaining tablespoon extra-virgin olive oil in a skillet over medium heat and sauté garlic until brown. Drain artichokes and add them to oil with a pinch of salt and pepper. Cook on high heat for 8 minutes, then pour in cream and reduce for about 10 minutes. Add most of the marjoram leaves, reserv-ing garnish.

● Bring a large pot of water to a boil and gently drop in tomatoes; cook for just 10 seconds, remove them with a slotted spoon from the boiling water, and plunge them into an ice-water bath. Keep the water on the stove at a boil. Peel, seed, then dice tomatoes, setting aside a few tablespoons for garnish.

● Preheat oven to 350°F. Grease a 9-inch cake pan with olive oil.

● Add a pinch of salt to the boiling water and gently add 2 sheets of egg pasta; boil them for 2 minutes or until al dente. Remove pasta sheets, let them cool, and cut them into 24 disks with a 4-inch cookie cutter. Arrange 4 individual pasta disks in the prepared cake pan and layer the artichokes, grated Parmigiano-Reggiano, and tomatoes on top. Repeat the procedure 5 times, making 6 layers.

● Bake 8 minutes. Arrange portions of the lasagna in the center of 4 plates and garnish with diced toma-toes and marjoram leaves. Drizzle everything with extra-virgin olive oil. Serve hot.

Sweet

This restaurant is a tomb, literally. The staff is very friendly and the restaurant does a lively business. The osteria itself is housed in ancient catacombs that go down several levels into the earth. It holds many of Siena's secrets in the bones and spirits of former tenants, and the restaurant has an eerie, but surprisingly romantic vibe. The food is spectacular (see recipe on opposite page). If you want to blow your budget in one meal, do it here. Truth be told, I've gone back for several full meals since I taped the preparation of my dessert here for the Siena/Tuscany episode. On the show, I enjoyed a pear dessert set inside a spun-sugar "cage" and it was too artful to eat, almost. Go for as many courses as your waistband and budget allow. PS: If Pino is still the chef, you ladies may want to go to Da Divo just to feast your eyes on him!

● **Antica Osteria da Divo, Via Franciosa 25-29, Siena, Italy, (011) 39-577-284-381**

> **66 Go for as many courses as your waistband and budget allow. PS: If Pino is still the chef, you ladies may want to go to Da Divo just to feast your eyes on him! 99**

Roma! Every since I saw the film Roman Holiday as a child, I wished for two things above all else: to grow up to look like Audrey Hepburn and to be able to wander the streets of Rome one day. Ten years ago, in honor of my mother's birthday, I took a trip with her and half my wish came true. Over the last ten years, I have come to know the streets of Rome like the back of my own hand. I have wandered up and down its hills in every season and through all types of weather. At each day's end, I am left with some blisters on my feet and a huge smile on my face. When in Rome, I do as the Romans. I spend my days outside, moving, laughing, loving life, and of course, eating and drinking. Sometimes, between one and four in the afternoon, I will take a nap. Otherwise, I'm out there, in the streets, all day and night, in one piazza or another. Some of my favorite places are those we visited for the show. If you go, do not be startled to look over your shoulder and find me there, too.

lunch

My friend Ilaria is so gorgeous you can't believe it, until you see her aunt and her sister, too! Apparently, beauty, charm, and smarts run rampant through the women in this family. At their Enoteca Corsi (an enoteca is a wine shop), you can buy many good wines by the bottle. In addition, from eleven to three, Monday to

Spaghetti alla Carbonara

SERVES 4

1 pound spaghetti

4 eggs

1 teaspoon freshly ground black pepper

1/4 cup grated Pecorino Romano cheese, plus extra for serving

2 tablespoons cream (optional)

3 teaspoons extra-virgin olive oil

3 slices pancetta

Spaghetti alla Carbonara

● Cook the spaghetti in boiling salted water until al dente. Drain and set aside.

● Beat eggs in a medium bowl and add pepper and cheese. Add cream, if desired, for a creamier dish.

● Heat the oil in a saucepan, add the pancetta, and sauté for 5 minutes. Add the cooked spaghetti to the pan and sauté for another 3 minutes.

● Remove from heat (this is important, you don't want to scramble the eggs) and add egg and cheese mixture to pasta and mix. Serve with additional Pecorino Romano cheese on top.

❝ From eleven to three, Monday to Saturday afternoons, you can have the best lunch in Rome for a fair price. ❞

Saturday afternoons, you can have the best lunch in Rome for a fair price. The menu changes daily. Raphael the cook knows what he is doing! The place is always packed, mostly with locals, and I eat here most everyday when I'm in town. I have had over a dozen meals here and no two were ever alike, but all were delicious and so reasonably priced. For the show, I had some coal miner's pasta (alla carbonara) with egg and bacon (pancetta) and some roasted chicken, extra spicy with hot pepper "of the devil" (fra diavolo). Wow!

● **Enoteca Corsi, Via del Gesù 87-88, Rome, Italy, (011) 39-66-790-821**

snack

The true cuisine of Rome is in the Jewish tradition. To this day, a visit to the Jewish ghetto is a must for a meal or at the very least, an artichoke. The most famous dish

of Rome is arguably the fried artichoke, Jewish style, in which artichoke hearts are flattened, pressed, and fried in olive oil until very crisp. They are absolutely delicious. Al Pompiere is one of many fine restaurants in the ghetto where you can enjoy this traditional dish.

● **Al Pompiere, Via Santa Maria dei Calderari 38, Rome, Italy, (011) 39-66-868-377**

❝ The true cuisine of Rome is in the Jewish tradition. ❞

recipe	SERVES 4	adapted from Ristorante Spirito Di Vino	$40ADAY

APPT - SOUP/SAL - **ENTREE** - VEG/POT - DESSERT - BEV

Gaio Mazio's Pork
ANCIENT RECIPE FROM JULIUS CAESAR'S TIME

5 tablespoons olive oil

2 pounds pork shoulder meat, cut into 1-inch cubes

1 apple, peeled, cored, and finely chopped

1 leek, finely chopped

2 tablespoons all-purpose flour

Red wine, to cover (about 1 bottle)

1 tablespoon honey

1 tablespoon apple cider vinegar

1 teaspoon freshly ground black pepper

1/4 cup garum (fish sauce, use Thai nuoc mam), for seasoning

1 teaspoon ground coriander seeds

2 tablespoons chopped fresh cilantro leaves

1 teaspoon ground caraway seeds

1 teaspoon powdered lovage seeds (or celery seeds)

2 tablespoons ground mint

Salt and freshly ground black pepper

● Heat the olive oil in a Dutch oven over medium-high heat; add the pork, apple, and leeks. Sprinkle flour over meat and stir. Let it cook for 5 minutes, turning meat often.

● Add enough red wine to cover the pork. Bring to a simmer and reduce heat to low. Cover and cook for 2 hours. After 2 hours, stir in the honey, vinegar, black pepper, garum, and spices. Cover and cook on low until the meat is very tender, another 1 hour to 1 hour and 15 minutes hours, stirring occasionally. Serve over pasta, rice, or mashed potatoes.

dinner

The name Spirito Di Vino is a double entendre meaning divine spirit and spirit of the wine. It is my favorite place for dinner in all of Rome, in my favorite neighborhood Trastevere, which literally means "across the river," in this case, the Tiber. The area and the restaurant are easy to get to; a taxi will have no problem find-

ing it. In fact, the last time I was there, several tables were filled with viewers of our $40 a Day episode. Romeo the owner and his chef wife (a scientist by day) create spectacular and flawless meals. Their son Francesco is a wonderful sommelier and the keeper of one of the finest wine cellars I have ever seen. When Romeo leased this place several years ago, he excavated the site to make a wine cellar. In doing so, he found that his cellar contained the oldest bricks in all of Rome, and that at one time it had been a small, town square. Some of the bricks and a statue dating back before the Pantheon to 80 BC were taken into the col-

lections of the Vatican Museum. Romeo will show you the cellar himself, upon request. If you are smart, you'll let Romeo and Francesco make your food and wine selections for you. I've had countless dishes here, each better than the last.

Some favorites: cacio e pepe or cheese and black pepper pasta, very Roman; another winner, pasta with gorgonzola and poppy seeds; and finally, pork chops with apple and peppers. The pork, prepared as it was in the time of Caesar, is a sometime-special and a masterpiece. (see recipe on opposite page) It's also the dish we filmed for the show.

● **Ristorante Spirito Di Vino, Via dei Genovesi 31 A/B, Rome, Italy, (011) 39-65-896-689**

sweet

There's no such thing as bad gelato in Rome, but there is a difference in quality. San Crispino makes the best, richest, deepest flavors of any gelato I've had. Gelato, a fresh ice milk with intense flavor, is not aerated and has a lower fat content than American ice creams, so it does not become very hard. Choosing your flavor will be twice as hard, however, because there are so many and they are all too delicious! You can get a taste of each before you decide. I'd just try two or three, or you'll be there all night! My favorite last-night-in-Rome ritual is to get a Crispino gelato (pistachio) and take it over to the Trevi fountain. I sit and eat my gelato and while the sweet taste is still in my mouth, I turn my back and throw my three coins into the fountain!

● **Gelateria San Crispino, Via Panetteria 42, Rome, Italy, (011) 39-66-793-924**

To Our Readers

A word to the wise, always call ahead.
As we go to press, we have double-checked all factual material,
but things are guaranteed to change.
Call before heading out for your destination
or take Rachael's advice:
stay flexible and have an adventure!

Photo Credits

All Food Shots in Ovals
courtesy of the Food Network

Mark Daniels

INTRODUCTION
pages 8, 11, 14, 15, 16 17, 18, 19, 20, 21, 22

NORTH
pages 26, 29, 31, 33 (bottom), 34, 36, 37, 40, 41, 44, 45 (bottom), 47,
52, 54, 56 (bottom), 57, 58, 61, 62, 64 (top), 68, 69,

SOUTH
pages 72, 79, 80, 82, 84, 89, 92, 94, 97, 105, 107, 108, 109, 111

MIDWEST
pages 116, 118, 120 (bottom), 123, 124, 125

WEST
pages 128, 138, 139, 141, 142, 143, 145, 146, 148, 150, 151, 152,
154, 156 (bottom), 158, 159, 160, 162, 163, 164, 165, 166, 167 (bottom),
171, 176, 180, 181, 183, 184, 189, 190,191, 192 (bottom), 193, 197,
198, 200, 201, 203, 204, 205, 207 (bottom)

HAWAII
pages 211, 212, 213, 214, 215, 216, 217, 218, 219

EUROPE
pages 224, 225, 227, 228, 229, 230, 232, 233, 236, 239, 240, 242,
243, 244, 245 (top), 247, 248, 249, 250, 251,252, 256

John Cusimano

page 27 (donuts)

All remaining photos from Getty Images